AF712639

Contributions to Management Science

For further volumes:
http://www.springer.com/series/1505

René Rohrbeck

HD 58.8 R64 2011 web

Corporate Foresight

Towards a Maturity Model for the Future Orientation of a Firm

Physica-Verlag

Dr. René Rohrbeck
TU Berlin
Department for Innovation and
Technology Management
Straße des 17. Juni 135
10623 Berlin
Germany
rene.rohrbeck@tim.tu-berlin.de

Dissertation Technische Universität Berlin 2010, D83

ISSN 1431-1941
ISBN 978-3-7908-2625-8 e-ISBN 978-3-7908-2626-5
DOI 10.1007/978-3-7908-2626-5
Springer Heidelberg Dordrecht London New York

© Springer-Verlag Berlin Heidelberg 2011
This work is subject to copyright. All rights are reserved, whether the whole or part of the material is concerned, specifically the rights of translation, reprinting, reuse of illustrations, recitation, broadcasting, reproduction on microfilm or in any other way, and storage in data banks. Duplication of this publication or parts thereof is permitted only under the provisions of the German Copyright Law of September 9, 1965, in its current version, and permission for use must always be obtained from Springer. Violations are liable to prosecution under the German Copyright Law.
The use of general descriptive names, registered names, trademarks, etc. in this publication does not imply, even in the absence of a specific statement, that such names are exempt from the relevant protective laws and regulations and therefore free for general use.

Cover design: WMXDesign GmbH, Heidelberg, Germany

Printed on acid-free paper

Physica-Verlag is a brand of Springer-Verlag Berlin Heidelberg
Springer-Verlag is a part of Springer Science+Business Media (www.springer.com)

Preface

Deutsche Telekom Laboratories' internal organization is designed to stimulate a maximum flow of ideas and develop those that the company deems most relevant. Two main components identify the right topics and deal with them: First, the organizational structure, which is the result of the university–industry partnership, helps bring the best of the academic and business worlds together in a permanent situation of mutual intellectual exchange. Second, a set of non-formal and formal instruments used for corporate foresighting have been adapted to the requirements of practical innovation management. Instruments of corporate foresight now include the Deutsche Telekom Technology Radar, a tool that utilizes a global scouting network, the Product & Service Radar and various other tools for customer behavior and needs.

Deutsche Telekom Laboratories (T-Labs) has thus served both as an environment for the prototypical deployment of new methods and as the object of research providing data and indications for new hypotheses. Rene Rohrbeck's research has been instrumental in developing T-Labs' scouting and foresighting capabilities and exemplifies the value of close cooperation between industry and university.

Information and communication technology is currently radically changing and therefore challenges companies to continuously identify changes in the environment and act accordingly. Technological shifts can exceed the realm of R&D and it is not unusual for them to upset entire industries.

René Rohrbeck cites Kodak as an example to highlight how a globally dominant company can lose its competitive advantage due to technology shift. (In Kodak's case this was the result of the development of digital photography).

Other examples demonstrate how some companies are able to repeatedly reinvent their business. Nokia, for example, has undergone multiple transitions. Though they started as a pulp & paper industry, they successfully shifted to rubber boot and tire production and only later did they become the dominant manufacturer of mobile devices which we know today. Currently Nokia is undergoing another transition as it shifts its emphasis toward Internet-based services.

The work of René Rohrbeck benchmarks innovation techniques. In the second part of this book, René Rohrbeck describes the best practices that he has collected from 19 multinational companies and discusses their connection with corporate foresight ability.

Both the model and practice examples contained within make the book a worthwhile reference for companies seeking to enhance their ability to succeed in a changing environment. We are proud to have supported the effort and successful completion of this work.

Berlin, Germany Peter Möckel, Heinrich Arnold

Foreword 1

In strategic management, it is expected that the competitive advantage of companies is based on distinctive strategic resources. The competitive relevance of these resources is dependent on environmental factors and decreases over time. Teece, therefore, proposes in his "dynamic capabilities" theory that a company needs to develop the ability to transform its portfolio of strategic resources over time and in response to changes in the environment.

Following this line of thought, other scholars have hypothesized about the nature of these "dynamic capabilities". Some argue that they consist of certain routines, such as new product development processes and strategic planning. Teece proposed that dynamic capabilities consist of three process steps: "sensing", "seizing", and "transforming".

In this book, René Rohrbeck uses an extensive set of empirical data to further explore the building blocks of "dynamic capabilities". His concept of the Corporate Foresight ability deals primarily with the first two process steps of Teece's theory. He shows that the overall ability to respond to change in the technological, economical, societal, and political environment can be broken down into 20 building blocks, which he clustered into five capability dimensions.

René Rohrbeck was able to interview 42 users of the foresight information, allowing him to capture an objective account about the real value contribution of the Corporate Foresight ability. He also extended the understanding of Corporate Foresight from being perceived as a process with dedicated methods to being defined as an ability which can be built on processes but can also be achieved without them.

His maturity model and the identified best practices contribute to both strategic management and innovation management theory and will help pave the way toward a better understanding of how companies can build "dynamic capabilities".

Hans Georg Gemünden

Foreword 2

In his thesis, René Rohrbeck analyzes the ways in which companies can develop routines to systematically respond to external change. Through a literature review, he identifies three barriers that need to be overcome: "high rate of change", "ignorance", and "inertia". He then continues to explore the literature on strategic management, innovation management, and future research, from which he draws 12 conclusions that guided his research and which can also serve as a basis for future research.

From his empirical data, René Rohrbeck draws the conclusion that the Corporate Foresight ability can be built on structural (processes, methods, formal communication) and cultural (informal communication, promoting awareness toward the environment) elements. This is an interesting extension of the currently dominant view of Corporate Foresight as a process and a set of methods.

Another contribution of this book is the identification of value contributions or the impact of Corporate Foresight. Previous research has relied primarily on evidence given by the employees who executed the foresight activities, which resulted in an informant bias and a systematic overestimation of the true impact of Corporate Foresight. By interviewing the internal users of the Corporate Foresight results, René Rohrbeck identified 12 distinct value contributions, which he clustered into "reduction of uncertainty", "triggering internal action", "influencing others to act", and "secondary benefits".

The thesis of René Rohrbeck on Corporate Foresight will help managers create an understanding about its breadth and depth; they will learn to know what to expect from their investments and to judge the effectiveness of their Corporate Foresight practices. For academics, the findings in this book will prove useful for defining measurement systems that can be used for theory testing.

Martin G. Moehrle

Foreword 3

In recent years, interest in Corporate Foresight has greatly increased. Companies are searching for strategic orientation in fast-moving environments, and many feel they need to support more future insights to win the innovation race and maintain their competitiveness.

In the current financial crisis, companies need methods to identify emerging change, while at the same time they remain skeptical about the ability of corporate foresight to generate reliable forecasts.

In the light of this ambivalent opinion about Corporate Foresight, René Rohrbeck has engaged in research that is of high relevance to both theory and practice.

For the first time, the author regards Corporate Foresight as an "... *ability* to create and maintain a high-quality, coherent and functional forward view". He identifies needed interfaces between Corporate Foresight and strategic management, corporate development/marketing, innovation management, and strategic controlling. His work contributes to all of these domains and to both theory development and management practice.

This book is a very important contribution to our understanding of foresight in the corporate context. While past research on the topic focused mostly on the enhancement of processes and methods, René Rohrbeck takes corporate foresight research an important step further. He develops a sophisticated Maturity Model of Corporate Foresight and thus creates for the first time a holistic understanding of the future orientation of a firm. In addition, he gives – on the basis of high-quality empirical data – a highly relevant and highly interesting account of best practices in large multinational enterprises.

With this book, the author opens new perspectives, contributes valuable empirical evidence, and generates important new insights, which will take research and management practice in Corporate Foresight to a new level.

I have no doubt that this thesis will earn recognition from both scholars and corporate practitioners, and I would like to thank René Rohrbeck for this excellent research.

Ulrich Krystek

Acknowledgments

There have been a number of organizations and individuals who have made this academic work possible and who have contributed to this book. I am deeply thankful for all the support I have received. In particular, I would like to express my gratitude to . . .

- *The Deutsche Telekom Laboratories*, for not only funding my research but also for sharing their experience and providing access to their methods and tools
- *Prof. Dr. Hans Georg Gemünden*, for his continuous encouragement to increase the depth and breadth of my research and for creating a great environment for research
- *Prof. Dr. Martin Möhrle*, for not only serving as my second adviser but also for giving valuable advice that has broadened my perspective and strengthened my research
- *Prof. Dr. Ulrich Krystek*, for his enthusiasm about my research and for sharing his deep insights into strategic foresight theory and practice
- *Dr. Heinrich Arnold*, for sharing his extensive knowledge of innovation management and for guiding my research to practical and academic relevance
- *My parents*, for opening up so many opportunities and for supporting me in every phase of my education

Above all, I want to dedicate this book to my wife, Josefine, who has carried me through the hard and unrewarding times with her love, her constant encouragement, and her never-failing trust in my ability to successfully complete my research.

Berlin, Germany René Rohrbeck

Contents

List of Tables

List of Figures

Abbreviations

CF	Corporate foresight
CMM	Capability Maturity Model for software development
CO_2	Carbon dioxide
CTO	Chief technology officer
DMS	Document management system
EP	European Parliament
Et al.	Et alli (and others)
EU	European Union
FTE	Full-time equivalents
ICT	Information and telecommunication technology
IM	Instant messaging
IR	Investor relations
IT	Information technology
M and A	Mergers and acquisitions
NPD	New product development
OEM	Original equipment manufacturer
PDMA	Product Development Management Association
PLC	Product life cycle
PR	Public relations
R and D	Research and development
RSS	Really simple syndication
SBU	Strategic business unit
SF	Strategic foresight
SME	Small and medium-size enterprises

Chapter 1
Introduction

1.1 Motivation and Background

The starting point of this thesis is a dynamic view of organizations. The dynamic view assumes that organizations need to constantly adapt to their environment to ensure long-term survival and economic success (Levinthal 1992:427; Teece et al. 1997:509; Helfat and Peteraf 2003:1007; Eisenhardt and Martin 2000:1105). A study solicited by the CEO of Royal Dutch Shell found that even the survival of large, globally operating companies is threatened in times of discontinuous change. The study calculated the average life expectancy of a Fortune 500 company (an index covering the largest private companies in the world) to be less than 40 years (De Geus1997a:2–6).

More research in that area produced evidence that the corporate change is characterized by long periods of slow, incremental change and short periods of rapid discontinuous or radical change (Tushman et al. 1985:299–300; Gersick 1991:10; Brown and Eisenhardt 1997:1). This knowledge leads to the tentative conclusion that the mortality of large companies may be explained in part by their ability to identify, prepare for, and respond to discontinuous change.

It is therefore argued that companies need not only the ability to manage continuous adaptation to incremental change in order to stay ahead of the known competitors, but also the ability to detect discontinuities early and manage radical changes through corporate strategy, innovation management, and changes in internal structures (Hambrick 1982:159; Tushman et al. 1985:299–300; Tushman et al. 1986:29; Romanelli and Tushman 1994:1141; Andriopoulos and Lewis 2009:696).

In this research, I focus on the ability to detect, interpret and respond to discontinuous change. This capability will be referred to as corporate foresight.

To better understand why it is so difficult for large companies to adapt to changes in the environment, the example of Kodak's recent history is helpful:

When in the late 1980s the first digital cameras appeared on the market, it did not come as a surprise to Kodak. Indeed, Steven J. Sasson – an electrical engineer working at Kodak – had already invented a digital camera with the corporate R and D budget in the 1970s (Deutsch 2008:1). But this initial invention at Kodak was not further pursued, because it yielded a highly disruptive and cannibalizing potential

R. Rohrbeck, *Corporate Foresight*, Contributions to Management Science,
DOI 10.1007/978-3-7908-2626-5_1, © Springer-Verlag Berlin Heidelberg 2011

for Kodak's highly profitable film business. Only when other companies started to explore and develop the emerging market for digital photography did Kodak react. A preliminary step was re-examining their research and development (R and D) portfolio, shifting budgets from chemicals research to digital projects (Grant 1998:1–2). A second step was to invest $5 billion to build the digital business from 1990 to 2000 (Upbin 2000:3). A third step was internal restructuring, leading to a cut in the workforce from 145,000 employees in the 1990s to fewer than 27,000 employees in 2007 – making it a very different company (Deutsch 2008:3; Lucas and Goh 2009:5; Macher and Richman 2004:16–18).

From this example, at least three questions arise: Did Kodak respond fast enough? Was the response decisive enough? Could this enormous downsizing of the workforce have been prevented?

While these specific questions about the Kodak case are still subject to public discussion, it is clear that the downsizing of the workforce is a response that Kodak would have been very eager to avoid. And by seeing Kodak in such a dire situation, it is also clear that disruptive change might bring near-death experiences to large, internationally successful companies as well.

Therefore, the question arises:

> Why is it so difficult for companies to adapt to changes in the environment in an effective and timely manner?

Research has pointed to at least three clusters of difficulties faced by large incumbent companies when aiming to adapt to changes in the environment:

First, the high rate of change. In the past three decades, various empirical investigations have been conducted to prove the normative perception that the rate of change is increasing. Some evidence has been identified:

- *Shortening of product lifecycles* (Qualls et al. 1981:79; Kessler and Chakrabarti 1996:1143)
- *Increased technological change* (Sood and Tellis 2005:163)
- *Increased innovation speed* (Kessler and Bierly 2002:7; Langerak and Hultink 2005:35; Parry et al. 2009:627)
- *Increased speed of diffusion of innovations* (Lee et al. 2003:755)

The interest in the rate of change was further spurred by Fines, who claimed – on the basis of historic examples – that companies operating in a *high clockspeed* environment must be able to anticipate and adapt to change, or face rapid extinction (Fine 1998:66). This strategic flexibility along with complex management schemas was found to boost the performance of companies operating in a high clockspeed environment (Nadkarni and Narayanani 2007:264). But any company – regardless of whether it is operating in a high or low clockspeed environment – has to synchronize many temporal cycles to build and maintain a competitive advantage (Rollwagen 2008:217).

Second, ignorance. Even though Kodak had knowledge about the potential – both revenue potential as well as disruptive potential for its film business – it was decided to let others start moving into the disruptive business and follow later.

Previous investigations into why organizations fail to perceive discontinuous change identified five underlying reasons:

- A *time frame that is too short*, so that the corporate strategic planning cycles, which are still coupled with the fiscal-year cycle, fail to produce a timely response (Ansoff 1980:134).
- Announcing signals may stay undetected because they are *outside the reach of corporate sensors*. This failure has been attributed to the nature of corporate sensors, which need to focus on a search area and thus will leave spaces undetected that are at the periphery of the search focus (Day and Schoemaker 2004a:117; Winter 2004:165–166; Pina e Cunha and Chia 2007:559).
- Top management suffers an overflow of information and *lacks the capacity to assess the potential impact* of the issue at hand (Lesca and Caron 1995:59; Eppler and Platts 2009:42).
- *Information does not reach the appropriate management level* that can understand the impact of an issue or that has the hierarchical power to decide on appropriate actions (Krystek 2007:52; Liebl 2005:131).
- *Filtering by middle management*, which may follow its own agenda, aiming, for example, to protect its own business unit (Lucas and Goh 2009:5).

Third, inertia. If a company has perceived a change in the environment with a potentially high impact, it needs to (1) define and plan appropriate actions and (2) implement them. Research has pointed to four underlying reasons for the inertia of large companies:

- *Complexity of internal structures*. Most large companies face two types of complexity: regional reach (forcing firms to build complex multinational sales structures) and product range (forcing firms to build, for example, regionally differentiated product portfolios) (Chandler 1962:2; Christensen and Overdorf 2000:59; Godet et al. 2004:6).
- *Complexity of external structures*. In recent decades, cost pressure has forced companies to outsource parts of their production to other companies and thus forced them to build complex supply-chain networks in which they are bound to many companies (Perona and Miragliotta 2004:102; Kinra and Kotzab 2008:283; Gunasekaran et al. 2008:549). Today, this networking with other companies has reached beyond supply chain and production to include research (Von Zedtwitz and Gassmann 2002:569) and strategic new product development (Kodama 2007:115).
- Large companies have built structures that protect and reinforce successful lines of business. The downside of these protective structures is a *lack of willingness to cannibalize* that prevents the initiation of activities in new business fields (Chandy and Tellis 1998:474; Tellis 2006:4; Nijssen et al. 2005:1400; Schumpeter and Opie 1934; Herrmann et al. 2007:96).
- The current technological capabilities of companies lead to a *cognitive inertia* that inhibits them from perceiving external technological breakthroughs (Vanhaverbeke and Peeters 2005:246).

- There are many *barriers to implementing* organizational change; research has only started to propose effective means of overcoming them (Bridges 1986:24; Vandermerwe and Birley 1997:345; Kaplan and Norton 2006:135; Miller 1997:587–589).

The hypothesis of this research is that *corporate foresight is able not only to detect and interpret weak signals on change, but also to trigger reactions* (Levinthal 1992:430; Krystek 2007:50). Therefore, a particular emphasis of my research is on understanding how these three clusters of difficulties can be surmounted and how appropriate responses can be proposed and triggered. More specifically, corporate foresight is expected to increase the capability of a company to break away from path dependency (Coombs and Hull 1998:252; Åhman and Nilsson 2008:80), enhance its strategic flexibility (De Toni and Tonchia 2005:530–532; Nadkarni and Narayanani 2007:244; Hitt et al. 1998:22), and increase its absorptive capacity (Matthyssens et al. 2005:547; Zahra and George 2002:198).

Given the dire consequences faced by large companies when unprepared or too slow to respond in the face of discontinuous change, and given the inherent challenges, it can be expected that there must exist past research that has dealt with the problem before. And indeed, various scholars have explored mechanisms to help corporate managers manage radical change. The research has been driven from three perspectives: (1) strategic management, (2) innovation management, and (3) managing the future.

The *strategic management perspective* assumes that when faced with external change, organizations can and have to alter their strategy and organization (Jemison 1984:145; Shrivastava and Grant 1985:111). It was shown that environmental scanning is needed to create sound, up-to-date knowledge about direction and magnitude of emerging external change (Jain 1984:117; May et al. 2000:403; Osborn 1998:481). This task is particularly challenging because corporate change is characterized by long periods of slow, incremental change and short periods of rapid discontinuous or radical change (Tushman et al. 1985:299–300; Gersick 1991:10; Brown and Eisenhardt 1997:1; Levinthal 1992:428). Thus, strategic-management research assumes that firms need two types of capabilities:

- The ability to adapt incrementally and exploit current business in times of incremental change
- The ability to adapt radically and explore new markets and business opportunities in times of discontinuous change

The ability to simultaneously exercise both abilities has been referred to as *organizational ambidexterity* (Andriopoulos and Lewis 2009:696; Raisch et al. 2009:685; Tushman and Anderson 1986:439; Tushman and Oreilly 1996:8).

The *innovation management perspective* incorporates research streams that discuss similar concepts. Past research explored and offered advice about the ways in which companies can gain and maintain a competitive advantage in times of discontinuous change by doing the following:

- Acquiring *new technologies* (Lambe and Spekman 1997:102; Nieto and Quevedo 2005:1141; Dushnitsky and Lenox 2005a:947)
- *Linking emerging technologies* to new *customer needs* (Poskela and Martinsuo 2009:671; Herrmann et al. 2007:112)
- Initiating new *R and D projects* to use the window of opportunity created by the discontinuous change (Arnold 2003:171; Rice et al. 2001;406)
- Promoting specific *personal traits in radical innovation teams* (Stevens and Burley 2003:16)
- Finding and binding *promoters and champions of radical innovations* (Gemünden et al. 2007:408)
- Building *separate organizations for developing radical and incremental innovations* (O'Connor and DeMartino 2006:480–486)

In addition, the concept of *absorptive capacity* showed how companies can develop their ability to acquire new capabilities and use them to create a competitive advantage (Cohen and Levinthal 1990:128; Lichtenthaler 2009:822; Zahra and George 2002:192). Similar concepts such as *network competence* explain the development and exploitation of innovation networks from the perspective of a focal firm (Ritter and Gemunden 2003:745; Pittaway et al. 2004:137; Gemünden et al. 1996:449; Gemünden et al. 1992:359). More recently, the network and collaborative innovation perspective were merged within the term *open innovation*. The term has been used to express the ability of an organization to sense change and acquire needed capabilities (Chesbrough 2003:35; Lichtenthaler 2008b:45; Rohrbeck et al. 2009b:427–428; Dodgson et al. 2006:333).

The *managing the future perspective* aimed at identifying methods to systematically explore the future. The primary assumption regarding future studies is that change occurs slowly and in consequence future researchers will be able to detect trends and discontinuous change in time – even though the response can be expected to be slow (Wissema 1981:29; Wilson 1973:39; Krubasik 1982:28). In its early days, future research aimed particularly at forecasting future developments by using s-curves, mathematical modeling, and Delphi studies (Phillips 2007:715; Cuhls 2001:555).

In the 1990s, the limitations of forecasting became apparent, and future research moved away from attempting to predict the future toward identifying *possible*, *probable*, *plausible*, and *preferable* futures (Gerybadze 1990:79; Cuhls 2003:93; McMaster 1996:150). Future research today aims more at discovering undetected currents that will influence the future and at mapping uncertainty by including potential discontinuities (Saffo 2007:124; Ayres 2000:95; Van Nottena et al. 2005:175).

Exceptions to this rule can be found particularly within the national foresight programs. These continue to aim at identifying the technologies that yield the greatest economic and social benefit in order to then provide additional research funding to foster their development (Martin 1995:139; Blind et al. 1999:15; Porter et al. 2004:288). But even in national foresight activities, a gradual move toward more qualitative analysis such as scenarios or visions has been reported (Grupp and Linstone 1999:85; Cuhls 2003:95–101).

Concerning the application of future research in the corporate context, it has been emphasized that it needs to be further integrated into the company's process landscape and organizational structure to create an impact and add value (Gruber et al. 2003:287; Hines 2002:337).

The review of past research has illuminated many recommendations on how to manage discontinuous change. But it also confirmed that the goal of identifying how a stable, integrated, and comprehensive future-oriented management system can be built has not been reached.

One reason is that the three research perspectives have largely failed to build on one another. Little cross-referencing between scholars in strategic management, innovation management, and managing the future attests to the low level of cross-fertilization. Another reason is the cross-functional nature of future orientation. In management practices, the role of scanning for weak signals on emerging change is assumed by different functional units, including strategic management, R and D, corporate development, and controlling. This makes it difficult for scholars to find appropriate informants on a firm's future-oriented management systems.

These three perspectives represent the applied research, which has generated knowledge on how to design corporate foresight systems. In addition, surveys have continuously confirmed that building such systems remains a top priority in corporate boardrooms (Roll and Weber 2006:200; Liebl 2005:123; Schwarz 2007:244), but so far the level of implementation of successful systems remains low (Liebl 2005:123; Herzhoff 2004:189).

1.2 Objectives and Research Questions

In this thesis, I argue that corporate foresight can play the important role that has been proposed by practitioners and scholars alike. To do so, *more knowledge is needed about best practices and the context* in which they are most effective. It can be expected that to further promote the implementation and enhancement of corporate foresight capabilities, a *common maturity model* would help.

Such maturity models have proven to be successful catalysts for promoting good practices. One of the first of the models is the Capability Maturity Model (CMM) for software development (Humphrey 1989). The model consists of the description of recommended practices in key areas and the definition of maturity levels that translate into evolutionary steps – allowing companies to follow these steps to enhance their practices. Overall, the CMM contributed to the enhancement of both quality and efficiency of software development (Paulk 1995:18; Pitterman 2000:196) and increased the satisfaction of developers (Yamamura 1999:84). In the years after its first introduction in 1989, the CMM has been constantly reviewed, enhanced (iCMM 1.1 in 1995), and extended (CMMI in 2002) and has triggered standardization bodies to develop additional maturity models for special purposes (ISO's SPICE in 1998) (Niazi et al. 2005:156).

Following the inspiring example of the CMM, other professions have followed and developed their own maturity models. A recent example is the New Product Development (NPD) best-practice framework (Kahn et al. 2006). This framework has been developed on the basis of a framework of the Product Development Management Association (PDMA), the leading professional association of product development managers in the United States of America (Product Development Management Association 2006). One of the European counterparts of the PDMA, the European Industrial Research Management Association (EIRMA), employs a very similar framework to run their annual benchmarking conference. The maturity model helps identify and suggest successful innovation management practices in a given context.

Such maturity models can be applied for large management disciplines, such as innovation management, or more specific fields, such as the management of radical innovations, where another maturity model is under development (Peters and O'Connor 2002).

From these examples of maturity models, we can conclude that they are successful if they can be used for (1) *assessment* of current proficiency, (2) *identification* of further development steps, and (3) *guidance* on how to implement subsequent steps (Radnor and Noke 2006).

In consequence, this study aims at enhancing corporate foresight practices and is guided by four research questions:

Q1: What are the key *elements* of corporate foresight systems?
Q2: What are *good* and *best* corporate foresight *practices*?
Q3: What are the *levels of proficiency* within the elements?
Q4: How can corporate foresight contribute to *managing discontinuous change*?

1.3 Relevance of Research

The major aim of this study is to contribute to management practice. But some additional theoretical contributions can also be expected.

The expected contributions for management practice are (1) *development of a maturity model*, which can be used for benchmarking and auditing and thus advancing management practices (Camp 2003), (2) *identification of good and best practices* in the different elements of the maturity model to guide the efforts of companies to enhance their own practices, and (3) proposing ways to integrate corporate foresight into existing corporate functions, to enhance firms' abilities to survive discontinuous change in their environment.

The expected contributions to theory are (1) validation of previous findings by using a research design, which addresses the methodological shortcomings of previous research, (2) broadening the understanding of value contribution / benefits generated by foresight activities, (3) identification of additional elements of corporate foresight practices, (4) proposing hypotheses on relationships between capability and value contribution of corporate foresight, (5) recommendation of normative rules for designing corporate foresight systems given a certain context, and (6) extension of the theoretical basis of future research by linking it to strategic management and innovation management literature, by including French literature, and by assessing the applicability of management theories such as contingency theory, the resource-based view, and dynamic capability theory.

1.4 Structure of Thesis

This thesis has been structured into six parts (see Fig. 1.1). In the first part, (introduction) the following are explained: the motivation for the research, relevant research perspectives (strategic management, innovation management, and managing the future), and the research aim. In the second part (literature review), past research is discussed in order to identify past findings on which my research has been built and in order to define the research gap more specifically. In addition, the second part includes the discussion of the theoretical foundations of my research.

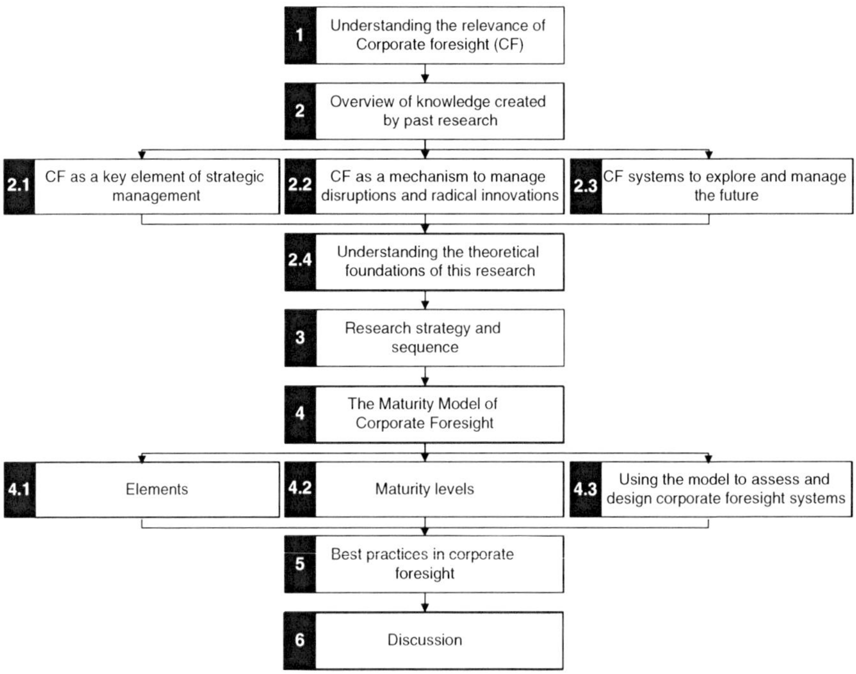

Fig. 1.1 Structure of thesis

In the third part (research strategy and research sequence), the alternative research strategies are identified and my choice is discussed. In addition, the research sequence is explained for both the development of the Maturity Model of Corporate Foresight and for the identification of best practices.

In the fourth (maturity model) and fifth (best practices) parts, research results are presented. In the fourth part, the Maturity Model of Corporate Foresight is explained. In the model description, the dimensions and elements are described first. The maturity levels for each element are then introduced, and in the third part I explain how the model can be used to assess existing corporate foresight systems and how it can be used to design new systems and enhance existing ones.

In the fifth part, individual best practices are described. These best practices are structured along the Maturity Model of Corporate Foresight so that many best practices can be combined into one system. For the reader to be able to choose best practices that are suitable to his or her corporate context, each best-practice description features an assessment of context. In addition, each best-practice description concludes with an evaluation that discusses the strengths and weaknesses of the best practice and gives recommendations for its implementation.

The sixth and last part is the discussion, in which I explain the limitations of my research and highlight contributions for management practice and theory building. In addition, recommendations are given concerning the directions toward which further research on corporate foresight should be directed.

Chapter 2
Literature Review

The research on corporate foresight has its roots in the term *strategic foresight*. The reason for choosing the term *corporate foresight* in this thesis is to emphasize that the research is aimed at understanding foresight applied in private firms as opposed to the application in the public domain.

As is often the case in new research disciplines, the research on foresight in the corporate context has been conducted using different definitions. The major difference is between scholars who define corporate foresight as a process (Becker 2002:12; Horton 1999:5; Müller 2008:25; Müller-Stewens and Müller 2009:9) and scholars who define corporate foresight as an ability (Slaughter 1998:382; Krystek and Müller-Stewens 1999:175; Tsoukas and Shepherd 2004b:10; Nick 2008:21). The ability is the broader definition, which includes in addition to a process any other means by which firms are enabled to detect, anticipate and respond to changes in their environment, including encouraging every employee to be on the lookout for discontinuous change and to take the initiative.

In this research, I follow the understanding of corporate foresight as an ability, without a particular emphasis on processes or other structural elements of a foresight system. More specifically, I assume the following:

> Corporate foresight is an ability that includes any structural or cultural element that enables the company to detect discontinuous change early, interpret the consequences for the company, and formulate effective responses to ensure the long-term survival and success of the company.

Research on corporate foresight has typically been followed by management-science scholars from different research disciplines, including strategic management, technology management, and innovation management. That might be a consequence of the cross-functional character of foresight in the corporate context. Responsibilities for foresighting rest in departments such as strategic management, corporate development, marketing, R and D, innovation management, and controlling (Slaughter 1998:382; Krystek 2007:50; Müller 2008:2). This cross-functionality is also illustrated in Richard Slaughter's definition of *strategic foresight* – a term that he used in a synonymous way to *corporate foresight* – when he lists four outcomes useful to an organization:

DOI 10.1007/978-3-7908-2626-5_2, © Springer-Verlag Berlin Heidelberg 2011

> Strategic Foresight is the ability to create and maintain a high-quality, coherent and functional forward view, and to use the insights arising in useful organizational ways. For example to detect adverse conditions, guide policy, shape strategy, and to explore new markets, products and services. It represents a fusion of futures methods with those of strategic management (Slaughter 1998:382).

To make more explicit the link between corporate departments and corporate foresight outcomes, their linkage is depicted in Fig. 2.1. In the rectangular boxes, the elements of Slaughter's original definition can be found, and the circles show the corporate departments that typically are expected to produce the outcomes.

From Slaughter's definition, we can conclude that strategic management can profit from future insights (i.e., the result of the interpretation of future-related information) to define future strategic directions; that corporate development and marketing can identify and explore new markets; that strategic controlling can identify future risks; and that innovation management can explore new products and services on the basis of these insights.

Research has shown that there is not necessarily a specific corporate foresight department or unit in the corporate landscape (Becker 2002:12–13). Indeed, the strategic management or innovation management often takes over the role of scanning for discontinuous change for the entire company (Daheim and Uerz 2008:325–326).

The same diversity of responsibility in the corporate landscape can be observed in the research landscape of corporate foresight. There are three primary perspectives from which research on corporate foresight has been conducted (see Fig. 2.2).

- The *strategic management perspective*, which includes research on corporate change, ambidexterity (i.e., the ability of companies to excel in both exploitation of current products and markets and exploration of new products and markets), environmental scanning, and decision making.

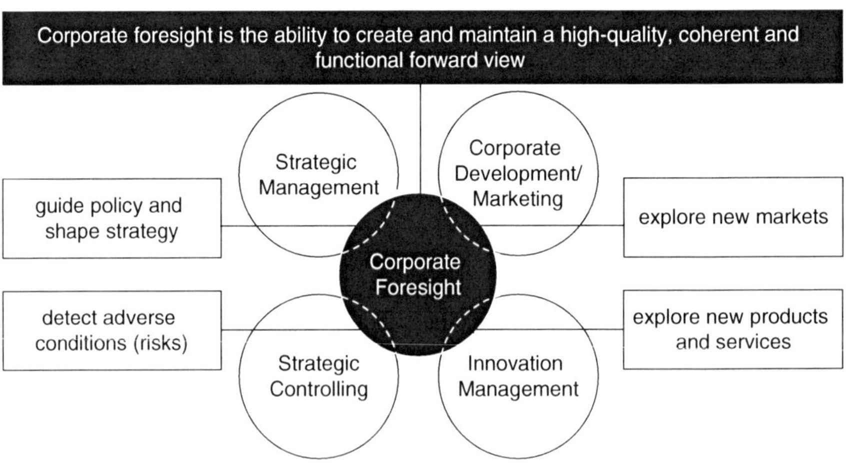

Fig. 2.1 Definition of corporate foresight

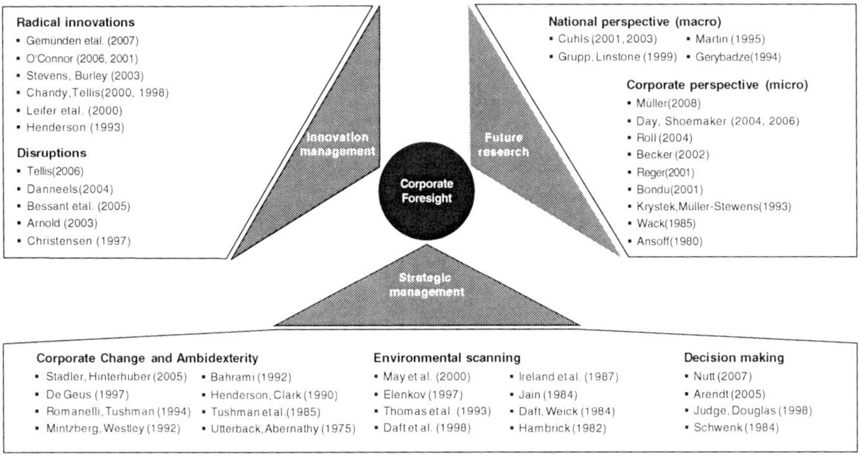

Fig. 2.2 Research perspectives and major authors of works on corporate foresight

- The *innovation management perspective*, in which findings important to corporate foresight have been produced in the research streams on radical innovations and (technological) disruptions.
- And the *future research perspective*, which can be divided into the research stream aiming at studying public foresight activities for national or supranational organizations (macro level) and in the research stream dealing with corporate foresight practices (micro level).

Relevant findings within these three research perspectives will be highlighted and discussed in Sects. 2.1–2.3. In addition, Sect. 2.4 will explain and discuss three major management theories that are relevant to the research on corporate foresight. Section 2.4 will summarize the findings and discuss their implications for the research on corporate foresight.

2.1 Strategic Management Perspective

Research on strategic management aims at understanding how long-term and high-impact changes are planned and implemented in companies. In 1980, Igor Ansoff presented an overview of the historic evolution of (strategic) management systems. Ansoff identified five evolutionary phases and showed that over time there is a correspondence of *dominant assumptions*, *purpose of management system*, and *configuration of the system* (see Table 2.1).

In addition, Ansoff predicts that strategic management systems will move toward real time, emphasizing the need for continuous scanning activities to identify external opportunities and threats and to trigger direct managerial activities. He predicts that the management systems of a company will move toward *strategic*

Table 2.1 Evolution of the strategic management systems

	Control	Long-range planning	Strategic planning	Strategic management	Strategic issue management	Surprise management
Purpose	Control deviations and manage complexity	Anticipate growth and manage complexity	Change strategic thrusts	Change strategic thrusts and change strategic capability	Prevent strategic surprises and respond to threats/ opportunities	Minimize surprise damage
Basic assumption	The past repeats itself	Past trends continue into the future	New trends and discontinuities	Expect resistance. New thrusts demand new capabilities	Discontinuities faster than response	Strategic surprises will occur
Limiting assumption	Change is slower than the response	The future will be like the past	Past strengths apply to future thrusts. Strategic change is welcome	The future is predictable	Future trends are OK	Future trends are OK
	← Periodic			→	← Real time	→

Source: Ansoff (1980:132)

issue management and later to what he calls *management of strategic surprises* (Ansoff 1980:131–132).

The identification of the need to use weak signals for the early detection of changes in the environment (Ansoff 1980:133) is one of the fundamental findings on which my research on corporate foresight is built. Many scholars have used his concept in the field of future research, most of them using the term *issue management* (e.g., Renfro 1987; Dutton and Ottensmeyer 1987; Schwarz 2007).

In addition, three research streams of strategic management have contributed to corporate foresight research: *corporate change and ambidexterity*, *environmental scanning*, and *decision making*. In the following three chapters, the relevant research streams in strategic management will be discussed and the findings on which my research is built will be highlighted.

2.1.1 Environmental Scanning

Environmental scanning has been guided by the primary assumption that detecting changes in the environment is ultimately the responsibility of top management.

The initial proposition of Ansoff, that strategic management should include the continuous scanning of the environment, was attributed by following research to be an obligation of the chief executive officer (CEO) or the executive board (Hambrick 1982:299; Ireland et al. 1987:469; Daft and Weick 1984:284). It was argued that only the top management is capable of triggering the appropriate responses when the discontinuous change affects the whole company or if it is a cross-divisional phenomenon (Daft et al. 1988:123; Thomas and McDaniel 1990:286; Jennings and Lumpkin 1992:791; Thomas et al. 1993:239). It has also been shown that there are significant differences in environmental scanning concerning the scanning frequency (May et al. 2000:403; Sawyerr 1993:287), information source usage (Elenkov 1997:287), aim (Jennings and Lumpkin 1992:791), and scope (Daft et al. 1988:123).

Further research aimed at identifying possibilities to enhance the quality and quantity of information that could be used for detecting changes in the environment. This research identified an additional role in environmental scanning. This role of boundary spanners was defined as an individual who channels the environmental information into the company and feeds it into the appropriate corporate functions or directly to the top management (Jemison 1984:131; Nochur and Allen 1992:265; Floyd and Wooldridge 1997:463).

A recent study by Danneels showed that environmental scanning positively influences the ability of a firm to build new competencies (Danneels 2008:519), thus building the basis for considering environmental scanning vital to managing discontinuous change.

Conclusion 1. *The interpretation of corporate foresight insights should be done at the top management level, and information gathering should be supported by boundary spanners.*

Empirical evidence was collected that indicates that high-performing companies scan more frequently, use a larger variety of information sources, and tailor their scanning systems to fit the context of the company (Daft et al. 1988:123; Sawyerr 1993:287; Yasai-Ardekani and Nystrom 1996:187).

It can be concluded that the research stream on environmental scanning has produced the foundation for corporate foresight by developing the concept of weak signals and identifying the environment as the source of future-oriented information.

An overview of the cited research is given in Table 2.2 on the following two pages. The table shows the author and year, the data, the type of research, and the findings relevant to corporate foresight. The type of research is also an indicator of the maturity of the research stream. Concerning the research type, a comparison can be made of inductive research, i.e., research aimed at identifying new phenomena, and deductive research, i.e., research aimed at testing phenomena. In inductive research, a further differentiation is made into conceptual work and empirical work using case studies or econometrics.

Concerning the maturity of research on environmental scanning, it can be seen that from the late 1980s all research has been deductive, thus aimed at theory testing (see Table 2.2). This leads to the recognition of a high level of maturity of this research stream. Indeed, the research question on how top management scans for changes in the environment has been researched to a point where additional research would not be expected to produce much more knowledge. But at the same time, it needs to be clarified that the broader research topic of how environmental information is channeled and processed in organizations is not fully understood.

Such research, aimed at understanding how organizations integrate and use environmental and future-oriented information, has been conducted within the managing-the-future perspective and will be discussed in Sect. 2.3.

2.1.2 Corporate Change and Ambidexterity

Within the research stream of corporate change and ambidexterity, empirical evidence indicates that corporate change is characterized by long periods of small, incremental change, which are interrupted by brief periods of discontinuous, radical change (Tushman and Anderson 1986:436; Brown and Eisenhardt 1997:1; Romanelli and Tushman 1994:1141; Huy and Mintzberg 2003:79).

How this change affects companies has been the subject of intensive debate among organizational scholars. On one side of the debate are the organizational ecologists, who argue that individual organizations are characterized by a high level of inertia and are thus mostly unable to adapt to external change. On the other side of the argument, the adaptationists assert that organizations can change and that the duty of senior management is to prepare for external change and take measures to make the organization adapt (O'Reilly et al. 2009:76).

Table 2.2 Research on environmental scanning

Authors, year	Data	Type of research				Findings
		Inductive			Deductive	
		Conceptual	Case	Econometric	Econometric	
Danneels (2008)	Data collected at two points in time 2000 (145 firms) and 2004 (77 firms)				n = 145	Willingness to cannibalize, constructive conflict, scanning, and slack have contemporaneous effects, while scanning also has a lagged effect and slack has a U-shaped lagged effect on marketing and R and D competences
May et al. (2000)	96 Russian executives				n = 96	The scanning mode is influenced by the perceived accessibility of sources
Elenkov (1997)	141 Bulgarian SMEs				n = 141	As strategic uncertainty grows, the usage of personal as well as external information sources increases
Yasai-Ardekani and Nystrom (1996)	179 companies from the manufacturing industry				n = 179	Organizations with effective scanning systems tend to align their scanning designs with their environmental, organizational, and strategic context
Sawyerr (1993)	47 CEOs from Nigerian SMEs				n = 47	The greater the perceived uncertainty, the higher the scanning frequency
Thomas et al. (1993)	156 CEOs of hospitals				n = 156	High information use is positively related to the perception of issues as controllable
Jennings and Lumpkin (1992)	44 CEOs from Texan savings and loan associations				n = 44	Companies with a differentiations strategy scan more for opportunities and customer attitudes and less for competitors' threats and political shifts than do companies with cost leadership strategies
Thomas and McDaniel (1990)	151 CEOs of hospitals				n = 151	The contextual factors strategy and information processing structure influence the identification of issues by the management team
Daft et al. (1988)	CEOs and other top level executives of 50 Texan SMEs in the manufacturing business				n = 50	CEOs in high-performing companies scanned more frequently and more broadly than their counterparts in low-performing companies
Ireland et al. (1987)	56 managers from Brazilian and Venezuelan manufacturing companies				n = 56	Perceived environmental uncertainty varied significantly by managerial level as did the perceived relative importance of the issue

(continued)

Table 2.2 (continued)

Authors, year	Data	Type of research				Findings
		Inductive			Deductive	
		Conceptual	Case	Econometric	Econometric	
Dutton and Jackson (1987)	Conceptual/theoretical paper	✓				Identifies the relationship of threat and opportunity to target and magnitude of organizational responses
Jain (1984)	37 personal interviews in 11 companies; 186 questionnaires from Fortune 500 companies		n = 10	n = 186		Identifies four evolutionary phases of scanning activities Descriptive statistics on scope of scanning, organizational forms, information sources, methods and problems currently faced in environmental scanning
Daft and Weick (1984)	Conceptual/theoretical paper	✓				Organizational interpretation happens at the top-management level on the basis of information channeled into the organization by boundary spanners
Hambrick (1982)	165 executives from six private hospitals, and six life insurance companies				n = 165	The company's strategy does not significantly influence the scanning behavior of top management
Ansoff (1980), Ansoff et al. (1976)	Conceptual/theoretical paper	✓				Discontinuous change can be perceived early by scanning for weak signals in the environment

In support of the theory that companies are unable to adapt, empirical research has shown that firms – even large global champions – often do not survive over long periods of time (for an overview of empirical findings, see Stubbart and Knight 2006:79). This led to the conclusion that – faced with discontinuous change – management is unable to accomplish an adequate adaptation in time. Dew, Goldfarb, and Sarasvarthy conclude that "the strategic manager's job is in fact futile in the face of environmental disruptions" (Dew et al. 2006:79). Scholars following this line of argument also believe that firm failure is healthful for the industry and should not be prevented – e.g., by governmental aid – as it would weaken the ability of the economy as a whole to adapt to external change (Bellone et al. 2008:754).

The adaptationists argue that there a number of firms that have survived discontinuous change in their industries. De Geus offers many examples (De Geus 1997a:2) and identifies common traits (or capabilities) that have enabled these companies to survive (De Geus 1997b:53–54). Following this line of argument, change in the economy as a whole occurs when firms are aware of changes in their environment and use different mechanisms to retain strategic flexibility and adapt to their environment (Bahrami 1992:33; Hitt et al. 1998:42). Such firms need to have the ability to (1) *exploit* current products and markets and (2) *explore* new products and markets that emerge when discontinuous change occurs (Levinthal 1992:430; Andriopoulos and Lewis 2009:696).

Conclusion 2. *In order to ensure long-term survival, companies need to ensure strategic flexibility and build capabilities to detect discontinuous change in their environment.*

It can be concluded that the strategic management research stream on corporate change and ambidexterity has produced the theoretical basis to understand *the need for corporate foresight.* Companies aiming at strategic flexibility will need capabilities to detect and interpret changes in the environment. Knowing about the change is a prerequisite to successful responses. Corporate foresight can thus be regarded as a mechanism to counterbalance inertia (Volberda and Lewin 2003:2116) and one that should be useful for managing discontinuous change (Van Den Bosch et al. 1999:551; O'Reilly and Tushman 2004:74; Stadler and Hinterhuber 2005:467).

The research stream on corporate change and ambidexterity appears to still need further inductive research (as in Raisch 2008:483). Only some specific phenomena, such as the characteristics of corporate change, have been studied with deductive, econometric means (Romanelli and Tushman 1994:1141). Therefore, the maturity of the research field can be classified as being at the transition from theory development to theory testing (see also Table 2.3).

Raisch et al. propose four major questions that should guide further research on organizational ambidexterity (Raisch et al. 2009:685):

- Should organizations achieve ambidexterity through differentiation or through integration?
- Does ambidexterity occur at the individual or organizational level?

Table 2.3 Research on corporate change and ambidexterity

Authors, year	Data	Type of research				Findings
		Inductive			Deductive	
		Conceptual	Case	Econometric	Econometric	
Raisch et al. (2009)	Conceptual/theoretical paper	✓				Four tensions within the research field of ambidexterity are identified: (1) differentiation vs. integration, (2) individual vs. organizational level, (3) static vs. dynamic perspective, and (4) internal vs. external ambidexterity
Raisch (2008)	Six case studies in leading Central European companies		n = 6			Proposes normative design recommendations to build ambidextrous organizations
Stubbart and Knight (2006)	Conceptual/theoretical paper	✓				Past empirical findings suggest that the vast majority of firms, even large firms, have a short life expectancy An overview of methodological challenges associated with studying survival rates of firms is given
Stadler and Hinterhuber (2005)	Longitudinal analysis 1980–1990 of Shell, Siemens, DaimlerChrysler		n = 3			The success of corporate change is enhanced by focusing on core corporate values and effectively engaging employees
O'Reilly and Tushman (2004)	35 initiatives for breakthrough innovations, in 15 business units in nine different industries		n = 35			To build ambidextrous organizations firms should establish to separate organizational units (one for exploitation and one for exploration) that are tightly integrated at senior executive level

Huy and Mintzberg (2003)	Conceptual/theoretical paper	✓			Proposes a framework that differentiate corporate change into three modes: dramatic change (revolution), systematic change (reform), organic change (rejuvenation)
Volberda and Lewin (2003)	Conceptual/theoretical paper	✓			Identifies four mechanisms of firms to counterbalance structural inertia: naive selection, managed selection, hierarchical renewal and holistic renewal
Van Den Bosch et al. (1999)	Two longitudinal case studies in traditional publishing companies moving into digital age		n = 2		Organizational form and combinative capabilities influence the ability of a firm to successfully manage discontinuous change
Hitt et al. (1998)	Conceptual/theoretical paper and current economic data	✓			Argues that for developing strategic flexibility firms need to focus on building human capital, develop dynamic core competences and use new organizational structures
De Geus (1997b) and more detail in the book De Geus (1997a)	Historic data on Fortune 500 companies starting in the nineteenth century			n = 700 (approx.)	Average life expectancy of large corporations 40–50 years, but can also reach 700 years Companies that endure are good at "managing for change" and have four common traits: (1) conservatism in financing, (2) sensitivity to the world around them, (3) awareness of their identity, and (4) tolerance of new ideas. Companies that endure need these management skills: (1)

(continued)

Table 2.3 (continued)

Authors, year	Data	Type of research				Findings
		Inductive			Deductive	
		Conceptual	Case	Econometric	Econometric	
						valuing people not assets, (2) loose steering and control, (3) organizing for learning, and (4) shaping the human community
Romanelli and Tushman (1994)	Longitudinal study covering 25 microcomputer producers over 3 years				n = 25	A large majority of organizational transformations were accomplished by rapid and discontinuous change. Small changes in strategies, structures, and power distributions did not produce fundamental transformations Major environmental changes and chief executive officer succession are the major drivers of transformation
Miller (1993)	Conceptual/theoretical paper	✓				Past success is likely to influence firms in such a way that they become simpler over time and focus more narrowly on a single theme, activity, or issue at the expense of all others
Mintzberg and Westley (1992)	Conceptual/theoretical paper	✓				Introduces a framework for explaining corporate change that includes three modes of change: enclaving, cloning, uprooting
Bahrami (1992)	Single case study on the telecommunications company that later was acquired by IBM	✓	n = 1			Argues that companies need to create strategic flexibility by allowing for decentralization and centralization and stability and dynamism as well as uniformity and diversity

Gersick (1991)	Comparison of six change models from different domains: adult, group, organizational development, history of science, biological evolution, physical science	✓				New research questions are proposed for investigations into organizational change: How is it triggered? How do systems function during such periods? How does it conclude?
Henderson and Clark (1990)	Panel data from R and D costs, historic data and interviews on R and D projects at optical photolithographic alignment equipment manufacturer			n = 100		The internal structures of companies tend to be aligned with the architecture (i.e., the combination of components of its products) and are an important source of inertia
Tushman et al. (1986)	Longitudinal case study data of 40 companies in various industries and of various sizes		n = 40			Corporate evolution follows patterns of convergence and upheaval. In the convergence phase, companies exploit their business using their own strengths, and in upheaval phases companies exploit new directions triggered by external discontinuities as well as internal company dynamics
Tushman and Anderson (1986)	Various statistical data sources for the cement, microcomputer, and aeronautics industry				Varying for diff. tests	Technologies evolve through periods of incremental change punctuated by technological breakthroughs that either enhance or destroy the competence of firms in an industry
Tushman et al. (1985)	Longitudinal analysis in the minicomputer industry covering 37 companies and 396 executives				n = 59	Strategic reorientation appears to be an important strategic lever affecting organizational performance over time

- Must organizations adopt a static or dynamic perspective on ambidexterity?
- Can ambidexterity arise internally or do firms have to externalize some processes?

The second question is particularly inspiring for research on corporate foresight. In corporate foresight, it could also be possible that scanning the environment for discontinuous change can be done more effectively by putting every employee on the lookout rather than installing a central scanning unit or system.

The other questions also relate to research on corporate foresight, because corporate foresight can be regarded as an important component of the ambidextrous capabilities of a firm.

2.1.3 *Decision Making*

A third research stream of strategic management relevant to corporate foresight is decision making. For corporate foresight, it is vital to understand how management decisions are taken and how corporate foresight can contribute to the quality and success of a decision.

A first finding of decision making research is that decisions tend not to be the outcome of linear, conscious, rational processes but the outcome of complex, multi-level information processing (Shrivastava and Grant 1985:97; Hitt and Tyler 1991:327; Corner et al. 1994:294; Bulinge 2006:39). In situations in which companies use processes to ensure rational-comprehensive decision making, the success of these decisions is negatively influenced by environmental dynamism (Hough and Ogilvie 2005:417; Hough and White 2003:481). This leads to a tentative conclusion that to ensure value creation of corporate foresight, it should aim to provide the future insights not only to a structured decision making process but also in indirect ways, for example by communicating the insights directly to some of the decision makers.

Research on leadership has also produced a normative model for decision making, which proposes a certain decision making approach given a certain context (Vroom and Yetton 1973). In this contingency model, the participation of stakeholders in the decision making process was found to be critical to the decision making success (Vroom and Jago 1988:32). For corporate foresight, it can be concluded that stakeholder involvement should be ensured not only in the result review but by the project phase of the foresight exercise.

Another finding in this research stream is that a different kind of decision making is needed for hypercompetitive environments. Bogner found that in hypercompetitive environments, decision making should be enhanced by (1) developing cognitive diversity, (2) implementing rapid decision making, and (3) by using experimental actions (Goll and Rasheed 1997:583; Bogner and Barr 2000:224). A previous study by Bourgeois and Eisenhardt found that in high-velocity environments, companies need to balance three paradoxes: (1) make major decisions carefully, but decide quickly, (2) have a powerful, decisive CEO and simultaneously a powerful top-management team, and (3) seek risk and innovation, but execute a safe, incremental implementation (Bourgeois and Eisenhardt 1988:816). For corporate foresight, this translates into the need to allow for experimental actions, which would also help to validate the foresight insights.

Research on decision making also found that decision preparation work has a strong influence on the final decision (Dean and Sharfman 1996:368), thus suggesting that foresight could have an impact. In addition, the role of the adviser, i.e., a person who helps in preparing decisions, is expected to influence the decision outcome (Arendt et al. 2005:680). This leads to the conclusion that if corporate foresight plays the role of an adviser and provides information for decisions, then it can be expected to have an impact on the final decision and thus that it can contribute to the quality and success of a decision.

Another finding is that the integration of environmental information is positively related to organizational performance (Judge and Douglas 1998:241), particularly if this information is used to explore different alternatives (Nutt 2007:604) and if it is introduced into the decision making process with a high level of participation (Zehir and Ozsahin 2008:709). For corporate foresight, it can be concluded that participation should increase the probability of usage of the foresight insights.

Conclusion 3. *To ensure that corporate foresight has an impact, insights should be communicated on many levels simultaneously, and decision makers should participate in the corporate foresight activity.*

More details on the individual research findings can be found in Table 2.4 on the following three pages.

2.2 Innovation Management Perspective

The overall question of innovation management research is how companies should build structures and capabilities to continuously create new products, change internal processes, and develop new markets to ensure long term competitiveness. Within this area, two research streams are of particular importance to corporate foresight: *radical innovation* and *(technological) disruptions*.

Both research streams aim to enlarge the understanding of how fundamental change occurs or can be created. Both mostly take the perspective of large companies. They try to answer this question: How should companies manage endogenous and exogenous fundamental change proactively?

Corporate foresight can be expected to be a mechanism that enables companies to profit from fundamental change. In the following two chapters, the research on radical innovation and on disruptions will be analyzed to confirm the hypothesis that corporate foresight can indeed increase the chances that companies will create value from discontinuous change.

Table 2.4 Research on decision making

Authors, year	Data	Type of research				Findings
		Inductive			Deductive	
		Conceptual	Case	Econometric	Econometric	
Zehir and Ozsahin (2008)	73 large-scale firms operating in the manufacturing industry in Turkey				n = 73	Extensive participation accelerates the pace of strategic decision making
Nutt (2007)	376 strategic decisions (22% from public-sector organizations, 33% from private-sector organizations, and 44% non-profit organizations)				n = 376	The best decision results were achieved when the signal was perceived as a quantitative performance gap and when formal search or negotiation is used to identify alternatives
Hough and Ogilvie (2005)	Sample of managers attending executive trainings seminars				n = 749	Perceptual processes moderate the relationship between judgment processes and decision quality
Arendt et al. (2005)	Conceptual work building on decision theory and the judge adviser role	✓				Development of a CEO-adviser model that emphasizes the influence of decision preparation work on the final decision
Hough and White (2003)	400 decisions in 54 executive teams				n = 400	The relationship between rational-comprehensive, strategic decision making and decision quality is moderated by environmental dynamism
Bogner and Barr (2000)	Conceptual/theoretical paper	✓				A new model for sense making in hypercompetitive environments is presented that follows three rules: (1) develop cognitive diversity, (2) implement rapid decision making, and (3) take experimental actions
Judge and Douglas (1998)	196 companies from various industries				n = 196	Integration of environmental issues into the strategic planning process is

						positively related to organizational performance
Goll and Rasheed (1997)	62 manufacturing firms				n = 62	The relationship between rationality in decision making and performance is moderated by environmental dynamism
Dean and Sharfman (1996)	Longitudinal field study including 54 decisions in 24 companies				n = 54	The success of strategic decisions is influenced by the process used to make the strategic decisions
Corner et al. (1994)	Literature review and initial empirical test of the proposed model	✓				Decisions are outcomes of complex, multilevel information processing. Decisions are not rationally or consciously constructed
Hitt and Tyler (1991)	Random sample of 69 top executives asked to decide on the basis of case descriptions				n = 69	Strategic decision models were found to be more complex than described by previous research
Vroom and Jago (1988)	Conceptual/theoretical paper	✓				Emphasized the participation of subordinates in decision making to ensure their commitment to the task
Bourgeois and Eisenhardt (1988)	Four cases in the microcomputer industry		n = 4			In high-velocity environments, better decisions will be achieved by mastering three paradoxes: (1) deciding carefully and quickly, (2) having powerful CEOs and simultaneously a powerful top management team, and (3) seeking risk and innovation but executing a safe, incremental implementation
Shrivastava and Grant (1985)	Personal interviews with 61 managers in 32 organizations			n = 32		Identification of four models of strategic decision making: Managerial autocracy, systemic bureaucracy,

(*continued*)

Table 2.4 (continued)

Authors, year	Data	Type of research				Findings
		Inductive			Deductive	
		Conceptual	Case	Econometric	Econometric	
						adaptive planning, and political expediency
Schwenk (1984)	Review of literature in the field of cognitive psychology and cognitive simplification processes	✓				Identifies four phases of decision making: (1) goal definition, (2) problem identification, (3) alternatives generation, and (4) evaluation and selection
Vroom and Yetton (1973)	Observations of management decision-making processes in different contexts	✓				Definition of a normative model to propose a certain decision making style, given a certain context. Stakeholder participation is identified as critical to the acceptance of the decision

2.2.1 Radical Innovations

Prior to the interest in radical innovations, research on R and D or new product development (NPD) was mostly focused on understanding how companies can exercise the required rigor that will lead to superior products (e.g., Cooper 1983:2; Rothwell 1992:232; Rothwell 1994:27). Research on radical innovations searches for capabilities that make it possible to generate discontinuous leaps that will bring about a new generation of products (Sorescu et al. 2003:82) that initially outclass those of any current rivals (Ettlie et al. 1984:683; Chandy and Tellis 2000:1; Henderson 1993:248; Bayus et al. 2007:140).

When to classify innovations as being radical is an ongoing discussion in the academic world. Richard Leifer calls innovations radical if they can deliver a fivefold to tenfold increase in product performance, if they introduce entirely new product performance measures, or if they introduce a cost reduction of at least 30% (Leifer 1997:134). More recently, the degree of innovativeness has been understood as a four-dimensional measure, with a market, technological, organizational, and environmental dimension (Gemünden et al. 2007:410; Gemünden and Kock 2009:3).

In the research on radical innovations, at least four major findings are of interest in the context of corporate foresight.

The first finding is that large companies should manage radical and incremental innovation differently Ettlie et al. show that managing radical innovation, as opposed to incremental innovation, requires other strategies and other organizational structures (Ettlie et al. 1984:682), a finding later confirmed by Kelley in a longitudinal multiple case study (Kelley 2009:487). O'Connor and Veryzer agree and specify that radical innovation management systems should have these three competencies: discover, incubate, and accelerate (O'Connor and DeMartino 2006:489–492). Gemünden and Kock show that process formalization, early cross-functional integration, and top-management support negatively influence the success of radical innovation projects (Gemünden and Kock 2009).

A second finding is that the willingness to cannibalize current products for the sake of new products is required to develop radical innovation (Chandy and Tellis 1998:474; Ghemawat 1991:170). This willingness to cannibalize needs to be created in the minds of the top management. In a study in three high-tech industries, Chandy and Tellis identify three factors that drive the company's willingness to cannibalize: (1) product champion influence, (2) future-market focus, and (3) the presence of internal markets for project selection (Chandy and Tellis 1998:483).

Further research has shown that successful radical innovations in large companies are often achieved by committed individuals (Leifer 1997:134; Stevens and Burley 2003:16) that can be described by traits (champions) or by their role and function (promoters) (Gemünden et al. 2007:412; Walter 1999:537). In addition to the champion and promoter role, boundary spanners and gatekeepers were seen as being critical to innovation success (Allen et al. 1971:36; Reid and de Brentani 2004:170). These two roles are also associated with corporate foresight, where (technology) scouts act upon these roles by bringing external knowledge into the company. All key individuals in radical innovations should also be suitable as participants in vision-building activities, which have been shown to be a key capability in both management of radical innovations and corporate foresight (O'Connor and Veryzer 2001:231; Schwair 2001:40).

Another critical factor of success identified by the research is the dominant corporate mindset. It was shown that a corporate mindset which is analytical, proactive, and aggressive positively influences the success of radical innovation projects (Talke 2007:88). Thus, it could be hypothesized that these characteristics could also help companies successfully navigate through times of discontinuous change.

Conclusion 4. *Committed individuals are crucial to radical innovations; they should be used for vision building, and they should be integrated into corporate foresight activities.*

Concerning the maturity of the research stream, Table 2.5 on the following three pages shows that some aspects of managing radical innovations – such as the research on key individuals – has reached the status of tested theory. But other aspects, such as organizational structures for the development of radical innovations, are still being studied with the help of qualitative and inductive means.

2.2.2 Disruptions

Starting from a technological perspective, Christensen built a theory on disruptions that aimed to explain how important performance leaps in technology lead to the failure of large incumbent companies (Christensen 1997). He showed five characteristics of technological disruptions: (1) initial underperformance of emerging technology, (2) new technology generally provides new customer benefit, (3) the emerging technology is first introduced in a niche market, (4) new technology gradually increases performance until it reaches superiority over the established technology and thus is able to capture the mainstream market, and (5) when the new technology reaches superiority the new entrant replaces the incumbent company in the mainstream market.

In the following years, Christensen's theory on disruption has achieved high popularity among managers, but it has also been criticized by scholars for its limited predictive capacity, and thus its limited usefulness in providing managerial guidance (Tellis 2006:34; Danneels 2004:248). Nevertheless Christensen's theses did trigger a research stream that has provided research on corporate foresight with three important findings.

The first finding is that technological disruptions are possibly the most important driver of disruptive change. Christensen illustrated with cases the disruptive potential of emerging technologies (Christensen 1997). By doing so, he followed the line of thought of previous work on technological change that the progress in performance

Table 2.5 Research on radical innovations

Authors, year	Data	Type of research				Findings
		Inductive			Deductive	
		Conceptual	Case	Econometric	Econometric	
Kelley (2009)	Longitudinal case study with 12 leading multinational companies		n = 12			Companies willing to enhance their ability to develop radical innovations created internal programs that (1) have a logical connection to the strategy, (2) use adaptive structures, and (3) have flexible but transparent processes
Gemünden et al. (2007)	146 NPD projects with a high degree of innovativeness				n = 146	Innovator roles have a strong influence on innovation success
Talke (2007)	113 innovation projects				n = 113	For radical innovation, a corporate mindset that is analytical, proactive, and aggressive positively influences new product success
O'Connor and DeMartino (2006)	3-year longitudinal study of 12 large companies		n = 12			Description of different management systems for radical innovations Proposition of a normative framework for building radical innovation capabilities with three steps: discover, incubate, and accelerate
Reid and de Brentani (2004)	Conceptual/theoretical paper	✓				Emphasizes the role of individuals in the radical NPD initiative. Three key roles are discussed: gatekeeper, boundary spanner, and corporate-level decision maker
Sorescu et al. (2003)	380 innovation projects in the pharmaceutical industry				n = 380	The majority of radical innovations come from a minority of firms. The financial rewards of innovation

(*continued*)

Table 2.5 (continued)

Authors, year	Data	Type of research				Findings
		Inductive			Deductive	
		Conceptual	Case	Econometric	Econometric	
						vary dramatically across firms and are tied closely to firms' resource base
Stevens and Burley (2003)	267 NPD projects collected over a 10-year period				n = 267	The personalities of individuals involved in the initial phase of new business development projects influence project success
O'Connor and Veryzer (2001)	11 radical innovation projects in nine large mature organizations		n = 9			Identifies visioning as a key capability for enhancing radical innovation success. Four mechanisms are identified: (1) vision building, (2) evangelizing the vision, (3) availability of tools and methods for vision development, and (4) process of validation and internal acceptance
Chandy and Tellis (2000)	Data on 93 significant innovations, collected over a period of 4 years from 250 articles and 500 books				n = 93	After World War II, the majority of radical innovations have been introduced by incumbent companies. Thus the "incumbent curse" does not appear to be as prevalent as often stated
Chandy and Tellis (1998)	194 respondents from three high-tech industries: (1) computer hardware, (2) photonics, and (3) telecommunications				n = 194	Introduction of the "willingness to cannibalize" as a key factor affecting the success of radical innovations. Three driving sub-factors are identified: (1) product champion influence, (2) future-market focus, and (3) internal markets for project selection

Leifer (1997)	Eight technological innovation projects	n = 8		Innovation project success is positively influenced by (1) strong support of committed champions, (2) accessibility and support by top management, and (3) significant or serendipitous events
Henderson (1993)	Panel data from the photolithographic alignment equipment industry		n = 49	Research efforts of incumbents are less productive than of new market entrants
Ettlie et al. (1984)	147 questionnaires and 69 interviews in the food-processing industry		n = 147	For radical innovation, a unique strategy and organizational structure are needed. Suggested characteristics are (1) centralization of decision making and (2) greater top-management support

of a technology follows an s-curve shape – a concept that has also been associated with many limitations in its application (Abernathy and Townsend 1975:379; Brockhoff 1993:328; Sood and Tellis 2005:152). It was also shown that a technological discontinuity is followed by a phase of technical variations, allowing incumbents and new market entrants to propose new solutions until a dominant design emerges (Anderson and Tushman 1990:604).

More recent research on disruptions has been extended to disruptions with a low level of technological change (Govindarajan and Kopalle 2006:12), product disruptions, and disruptive business models (Markides 2006:19–20). It has also been noted that successful mechanisms with which companies survive disruptions will differ from one firm to another and thus a set of common characteristics should be identified in order that appropriate measures may be proposed (Sandström et al. 2009:14).

A second finding is that large incumbent companies need specific structures to succeed in times of disruptive change (Henderson 1993:248). Through case-study research, many examples have been collected of incumbents failing to catch up to small new companies that have entered the market (Christensen 1997; Markides 2006:20; Arnold 2003:111). Through these observations, a paradigm has been created. According to the paradigm, incumbent companies are too slow and ignorant to compete with smaller, more agile companies (Paap and Katz 2004:20) or produce adequate responses in times of crisis (Weick 1988:305). Although the work of Chandy and Tellis (2000) has provided evidence that the paradigm needs to be approached with care, the general direction of practitioners' and academics' suggestions points to the need to enhance strategic flexibility by building more agile organizational structures.

Another similar concept is absorptive capacity. Zahra and George describe absorptive capacity in this way (Zahra and George 2002:185):

> ...pertaining to knowledge creation and utilization that enhances the firm's ability to gain and sustain a competitive advantage.

It has also been shown that absorptive capacity is positively related to organizational learning and innovation capacity (Garcia-Morales et al. 2007:546; Nieto and Quevedo 2005:1153) and that it is increased by external scanning (Gassmann and Gaso 2005:261; Lichtenthaler 2009:822), alliances (Noke et al. 2008:129), and corporate venturing activities (Dushnitsky and Lenox 2005b:615; Rohrbeck et al. 2009a:50; Day 1994:148).

Conclusion 5. *Large incumbent companies tend to be slow and ignorant and need to build dedicated structures for detecting and proactively managing discontinuous change.*

Research on disruptions has also pointed out two major success factors when attempting to manage discontinuous change. First, the ability to forecast and foresight, i.e., being able to gather information on the potential impact and direction of emerging discontinuities (Arnold 2003:171; Bessant et al. 2005:1374), and second, the ability to create insight, i.e., interpretation of the potential discontinuity in a collaborative fashion, so that the insights become actionable (Burt 2007:747).

From Table 2.6 on the following three pages, it can be seen that the maturity of research on disruptions is still in the inductive theory development stage. Most research is still conducted by means of case studies or is purely conceptual (e.g., Adner and Zemsky 2005:229; Danneels 2004:246; Adner 2002:667).

2.3 Future Research Perspective

2.3.1 A Brief Overview of Definitions and Relevant Terminology

The term *future research* is used here, even though it is not an ideal term. It is used as a term to describe the whole range of research conducted to help organizations, individuals, and governments explore, prepare for, and respond to changes in the environment. Many scholars have aimed to differentiate terms used in this broad field (e.g., Müller 2008:23–30; Nick 2008:31; Müller-Stewens and Müller 2009:6–12). So far, the attempts to develop a common definition have not produced clarity, and many scholars use terms synonymously.

An additional challenge is faced by scholars willing to use findings from different linguistic literature bases. Table 2.7 does not aim to produce clarity on terminology but to provide some guidance for scholars willing to follow up on the literature in German, French, and English that I reference in this research.

One reason for the lack of commonly agreed on and clearly used terminology may be that research is driven by various perspectives. Another reason is the lack of interchange and cross-referencing between the different research streams. For example, scholars taking the strategic management perspective are rarely cited by researchers with an innovation management perspective or a future research perspective.

2.3.2 National Economy Perspective (Macro)

Although this research is aimed at developing a maturity model and identifying best practices on corporate foresight, some valuable results of national foresight research can be used. After the period of economic growth that followed the Second World War, many national governments were looking for ways to boost their national economies. Governments therefore commissioned technological foresight projects (for an overview, see OECD 1996). Their aim was to identify promising emerging technologies and direct national research funding to those technologies that maximized the economic benefit (Martin 1995:139; Blind et al. 1999:15; Durand 2003:161; Van der Meulen and Lohnberg 2001:680) and more generally that enhanced the quality of life (Anderson 1997:676). Today, with many national

Table 2.6 Research on disruptions

Authors, year	Data	Type of research				Findings
		Inductive			Deductive	
		Conceptual	Case	Econometric	Econometric	
Lucas and Goh (2009)	Case study on Kodak, including interviews and much secondary data		n = 1			Kodak did perceive the discontinuous change in the photography industry and invested heavily in digital photography, but middle managers and the organizational culture blocked a transition
Burt (2007)	Action-based intervention in a scenario analysis in the energy industry		n = 1			Top managers were aware of the different factors that have the potential to create major disruptions The scenario analysis provided a structured approach to collaboratively identify and assess the potential disruptions
Govindarajan and Kopalle (2006)	Conceptual/theoretical paper	✓				Broadens the definition of disruptions by including so-called low-end disruptions that are not based on new technologies Argues that ex-post measures of disruptiveness can be used to develop normative management guidance
Markides (2006)	Conceptual/theoretical paper	✓				Introduces the differentiation of the technological, business-model and product disruption for enhancement of theory on disruptions. Shows that they differ in their emergence, have different competitive effects, and require different responses
Adner and Zemsky (2005)	Mathematical modeling and simulation	✓				Identifies four influencing factors on threat level arising from disruptions: (1) rate of technological advance, (2) number of

					firms using the technologies, (3) relative market-segment size, and (4) firm's ability to price discriminate
Tellis (2006)	Conceptual/theoretical paper	✓			Laments the ambiguity of Christensen's definition of a disruptive technology and its usefulness for ex-ante predictions, particularly in the light of problems with the linearity of performance paths of emerging technologies
Bessant et al. (2005)	Conceptual/theoretical paper	✓			Identifies many sources of discontinuous change and suggests that companies need to build new capabilities to manage discontinuous innovations
Sood and Tellis (2005)	14 technologies in four markets			n = 14	Technological evolution does not follow the idealizeds-curve shape but follows a sequence of periods of fast improvement and periods with little improvement
Paap and Katz (2004)	Three case studies		n = 3		Suggest that incumbents in most cases are well aware of the drivers and technologies that will create disruptive change, but for different reasons fail to take them seriously or fail to take appropriate actions
Danneels (2004)	Conceptual/theoretical paper	✓			Questions the predictive capacity of Christensen's (1997) theory of disruptions
Arnold (2003), Danneels (2004)	58 companies from the machine-tool industry				Identifies success factors for managing disruptive change: (1) ability to forecast, (2) management focus, (3) strong financial base, (4) innovating in a modular fashion, (5) first to market, and (6) late market entry

(*continued*)

Table 2.6 (continued)

Authors, year	Data	Type of research				Findings
		Inductive			Deductive	
		Conceptual	Case	Econometric	Econometric	
Adner (2002)	Mathematical modeling and simulation	✓				Introduction of preference overlap and preference symmetry to enhance understanding of disruptive dynamics
Christensen (1997)	Many case studies		Multiple			Identifies technologies as a key driver of disruptive change Defines technological disruptions as (1) initially underperforming established technologies, (2) products based on the new technology satisfy only a niche market, (3) after R and D investments the technology outperforms the existing solutions, and (4) established incumbents fail to catch up to new market entrants that grew through the application of the new technology

Table 2.7 Overview of terminology

Description	English	French	German
Indicators that make it possible to see change early	Weak signals	Signaux faibles	Schwache Signale
Identifying several possible futures	Futures studies	Prospective	Zukunftsforschung
Predicting the future by e.g., extrapolation of a current trend	Forecasting	Prédiction	Prognose, operative Frühaufklärung
Scanning for weak signals in the environment	Environmental scanning, peripheral vision	Veille stratégique	Früherkennung
Scanning for changes in the environment and producing adequate responses	Strategic foresight, strategic issue management	Intelligence économique	Strategische Frühaufklärung
Scanning for changes in the environment and producing adequate responses in the corporate context	Corporate foresight	Intelligence économique en entreprise	Frühaufklärung in Unternehmen

boundaries being blurred by free-trade zones and common markets such as the European Union, foresight exercises are increasingly run on the level of supranational bodies (Loveridge 2001:789–790).

The national foresight projects not only engage in the identification and assessment of emerging technologies, but also trigger research on the methods and practices of exploring the future. From a corporate foresight perspective, two major outcomes are of importance.

The first contribution of past research is a *large toolbox of future research methods* (Heraud and Cuhls 1999:69; Schwarz 2009:291). Many methods, such as the Delphi analysis and trends extrapolation, have been pioneered by national foresight exercises (Bremer et al. 1994:141; Martin 1995:143; Grupp and Linstone 1999:87–89). Various methods have been employed, and recently the Technology Analysis Group, an association of researchers on national foresight practices, has developed a comprehensive overview of different methods (Porter et al. 2004:290–291). Earlier, Gordon and Glenn of the United Nations Millennium Project edited a compact disc that contains detailed descriptions on several foresight methods (Gordon and Glenn 2003).

Another finding important to corporate foresight comes from studying the evolution of national foresight practices (Gerybadze 1994; Martin 1995:139). In the 1970s, the focus was on using mathematical modeling and trend extrapolation to make predictions about the evolution of technology. This changed in the 1980s, when important limitations (particularly a weakness in identifying new technologies and disruptive change) of using past data and extrapolating them into the future became apparent. In the next evolutionary step of national future studies, expert opinions were included, and the Delphi analysis became the method of choice (Grupp and Linstone 1999:90; Cuhls 2001:555; Kameoka et al. 2004:579). Today foresight projects have moved *from prediction to exploration of possible developments* (McMaster1996:150) and include more qualitative methods (Grupp and Linstone 1999:84; Miles 1999:21).

Another element that is being added into current foresight projects is participation. The reason behind the addition is the need to involve stakeholders early in order to ensure that the insight creation is followed by actions. Form the point of view of governments, foresight projects should result in an increase in R and D activities in the identified technological areas (Cuhls 2003:93; Konnola et al. 2007:622–623). That is to say that public research and companies are expected to be more willing to engage in R and D activities when they have participated in the process of defining the R and D priorities (Salo and Cuhls 2003:79–82; Camerona et al. 2008:279). In that respect, online tools are expected to help by making it possible to increase the participation by decreasing the cost and increasing the convenience (Hilbert et al. 2009:892).

Another challenge for national foresight programs is linking the activity to measures of success. Scholars report on the ongoing process of finding appropriate criteria for measuring the impact of foresight exercises (Georghiou and Keenan 2006:775). While some lament the limited prediction accuracy (Eto 2003:231) others see the desired outcome more in the foresight process itself (Blind et al. 1999:33), consequently demanding that success be judged more by the level of social interaction and the resulting R and D collaborations that they have triggered (Sanz-Menendez et al. 2001:661; Meulen et al. 2003:231). Others have developed multi-criteria frameworks that can also serve as a basis for measuring the impact of corporate foresight activities (Amanatidou and Guy 2008:552).

Conclusion 6. *To make corporate foresight actionable, it should move toward qualitative studies and the active participation of the internal stakeholders.*

Concerning the maturity of future research on the national economy perspective, it can be observed in Table 2.8 that past research has been conducted exclusively by means of case studies and conceptual work. It can be concluded that the need for method development and the identification of best practices remains, before research will move toward theory development and subsequently to theory testing.

2.3.3 Corporate Perspective (Micro)

As is the case with national foresight, the examination of the evolution of corporate foresight practices provides some important insights on how foresight is managed today. Van der Duin and Den Harthig compared the evolution of future research in companies with their innovation processes (Table 2.9). In their analysis, they show that the technology focus of corporate innovation management in the 1950s and 1960s was equally present in the way companies were exploring the future. And while the innovation processes changed over time to include the market perspective

Table 2.8 Research from national economy perspective (macro)

Authors, year	Data	Type of research				Findings
		Inductive			Deductive	
		Conceptual	Case	Econometric	Econometric	
Hilbert et al. (2009)	Case study on a three-round Delphi analysis and multiple countries		n = 1			Shows how online tools can be used to increase participation in foresight exercises
Amanatidou and Guy (2008)	Conceptual/theoretical paper	✓				Proposes a set of evaluation criteria to assess the success of national foresight programs
Georghiou and Keenan (2006)	Three case studies and conceptual work		n = 3			Emphasized the need to adapt national foresight programs to their individual context
Porter et al. (2004)	Conceptual/theoretical paper based on a working group of technology futures analysis experts	✓				Overview and classification of futures research methods, applicable both on a micro and macro level
Cuhls (2003)	Case study of the German national foresight activity		n = 1			Description of the German national foresight activity that moved from a Delphi analysis to more participatory study that aims at planning new R and D collaborations
Cuhls (2001)	Case study of the Japanese foresight activity		n = 1			Evaluation of the Japanese foresight activity that is based on Delphi analysis
Blind et al. (1999)	Comparison of the Japanese and German national foresight program		n = 2			In a Delphi analysis, the process is a valuable experience in itself, because experts are forced to think critically about future developments in science and technology

(continued)

Table 2.8 (continued)

Authors, year	Data	Type of research				Findings
		Inductive			Deductive	
		Conceptual	Case	Econometric	Econometric	
Heraud and Cuhls (1999)	Three case studies on the national foresight exercise in France, Spain, and Italy		n = 3			There exists a rich methodological base throughout the European national foresight programs. Many countries have developed their own methods and approaches
Grupp and Linstone (1999)	Comparison of 12 national foresight systems based on literature and expert knowledge		n = 12			National foresight activities move from mathematic modeling toward qualitative, scenario-based approaches, while Delphi analysis prevails as the "backbone" of national foresight activities
Martin (1995)	Seven case studies		n = 7			Comparison of the national foresight activities of Japan, the United States, the Netherlands, Germany, Australia, New Zealand and the United Kingdom
Gerybadze (1994)	Conceptual/theoretical paper	✓				Links evolution of foresight activities to generations of R and D and innovation management

Table 2.9 Generations of innovation management and futures research

	Innovation processes	Future research
1st Generation (1950s–1960s)	Technology push	Technology forecasting
2nd Generation (1960s–1970s)	Market pull	Technology assessment
3rd Generation (1970s–1980s)	Coupled innovation processes	Explorative futures research
4th Generation (1980s–present)	Innovation in systems or networks	Networked or systemic futures research

Source: Van der Duin and Den Hartigh (2007:12)

and later networking as a way to boost the company's own innovation capacity, so did the future research activities. Overall, the assumption of corporate foresight is that earlier detection of external changes will allow the company to create a temporal competitive advantage (Peterson 2002:486; Tsoukas and Shepherd 2004a:137) and increase overall competitiveness (Lackman et al. 2000:17).

For this research on corporate foresight, the analysis of past literature provides three major insights.

First, it can be observed that there is a trend toward *thinking about uncertain and possible futures*. Strategic management was primarily about planning how the company should be changed toward a desired new state and ensuring the transition by controlling the process (Ansoff 1980:132). With the introduction of scenario analysis, companies such as Royal Dutch Shell showed a different understanding of the future. Shell saw the future as something that can not be planned, recognizing that by nature the future is uncertain (Geus 1988:73; Schoemaker and Heijden 1992:41). In consequence, Shell shifted its strategic planning toward scenario analysis, which makes it possible to identify different possible futures in order to be able to judge today's decisions based on their robustness in terms of success in the various possible futures (Wack 1985:73; Van der Heijden 2005:3–5). This has been a shift in the perception of the future as well as a paradigm shift in strategic management. In consequence, corporate foresight has also changed from being focused on predicting change to exploring possible changes (Krystek 2007:52; Mietzner and Reger 2005:220).

It has also been argued that the dominant logic in organizations hinders the acknowledgement of change (Prahalad 2004:171) and hinders acceptance of alternative development paths. The task, therefore, of corporate foresight would be to create doubt about basic assumptions in the firm by running participatory foresight exercises (Blackman and Henderson 2004:265–265).

Additional benefits of using participatory methods to explore possible futures arise from the process itself. It has been shown that the process of scenario planning can play the role of strategic conversation (Chermack et al. 2006:767; Chermack et al. 2007:379) and enhance organizational learning (Cairns et al. 2006:1010; Costanzo 2004:219).

In line with the findings of research on radical innovation, the corporate foresight research also discovered the *high importance of involved actors*. The boundary-spanner – later also called scout – emerged as an important actor to transport external information into the company (Daft and Weick 1984:285). The foresighters are responsible for running foresight activities and facilitating the transition of weak signals to issues to recommendations and finally for triggering actions. A benchmarking study on corporate foresight practices at 24 large and small and medium-size enterprises (SME) blamed the failure of corporate foresight systems largely on the lack of needed skills of foresighters (Bondu 2001:124).

In line with the findings in decision making, corporate foresight research has also adopted the paradigm that *participation is crucial to* the usage of the foresight insights (Barker and Smith 1995:27; Scapolo 2005:1059). It has been shown that in order to ensure the success of foresight activities, experts and decision makers need to be integrated into the process (Schwarz 2005:22; Van der Helm 2007:4; Oner and Gol 2007:451; Harroussi 2004:4). To do so, motivation mechanisms need to be put in place and adapted to meet the expectations of each stakeholder and be aligned to the corporate context (Salo 2001:694; Stuckenschneider and Schwair 2005:776).

Conclusion 7. *Successful corporate foresight is built on its actors. Ensure the usage of foresighters with desirable characteristics and traits and the participation of major stakeholders.*

Although there exists a sound body of knowledge about technological foresighting (e.g., Ashton and Klavans 1997; Lichtenthaler 2002; Savioz 2002; Carlson 2004; Reger 2006), the way in which an integrated corporate foresight practice should be organized – including scanning the political, technological, competitive, consumer, and socio-cultural environment – remains an open question. Past research has been either conceptual (Krystek and Müller-Stewens 1993; Liebl 1996; Day and Schoemaker 2004b; Pillkahn 2007) or inductive (see Table 2.10). In the inductive research, Josse 2004 and Daheim and Uerz 2006 used surveys to explore the implementation of corporate foresight practices. Schwarz (2007) used a Delphi analysis to capture experts' opinions on future directions in corporate foresight, and many other authors used case studies to broaden the knowledge about the configuration of corporate foresight systems. These case studies have been conducted in the insurance industry (Käslin 2008) and the airline industry (Roll 2004) and with cross-industry samples (Bondu 2001; Nick 2008; Müller 2008).

One major methodological shortcoming of past research has been the exclusive usage of the foresight manager as sole informant. Of the 14 empirical studies mentioned in Table 2.10, only two have used internal customers (i.e., the internal stakeholder, who uses the foresight insights for decision making or triggering managerial actions).

Conclusion 8. *There is a need for a common framework for corporate foresight research and coverage of both the foresight manager's and the foresight customer's perspective.*

It can be concluded that corporate foresight research – like foresight on the macro perspective – is still driven by the aim to identify successful methods and processes. To enhance the maturity of corporate foresight research and to move closer to theory development, a common framework with its constituting elements

Table 2.10 Research from corporate perspective (micro)

Authors, year	Data	Type of research				Findings
		Inductive			Deductive	
		Conceptual	Case	Econometric	Econometric	
Müller (2008)	Five case studies (DaimlerChryster, TUI, BASF, Deutsche Bank Research, Hilti)		n = 5			Description of how companies adapted their foresight processes in response to a change in contextual factors
Davis (2008)	Interviews of experts at 20 large companies			n = 20		Identification of barriers to the implementation of corporate foresight systems in large companies and some findings on the impact of corporate foresight
Käslin (2008)	Four case studies in insurance industry (Swiss Re, Münchner Rück, Allianz, Zurich)		n = 4			Important success factors of corporate foresight activities are (1) culture that supports openness toward the environment, (2) usage of many information sources, and (3) central interpretation and processing unit
Nick (2008)	Ten multinational companies with headquarter in Europe and one longitudinal action based case study		n = 10 + 1			Development of a typology for roles of corporate foresight in respect to strategic and innovation management
Rollwagen et al. (2008)	Action-based case study at Deutsche Bank research		n = 1			Proposition of a set of assessment criteria for corporate foresight practices and success criteria for implementation
Hergert (2007)	Action-based case study at Volkswagen		n = 1			Descriptive analysis of internal cognition processes in corporate foresight
Schwarz (2007)	Delphi study with 64 foresight experts from industry, academia and consultancy			n = 64		Growing importance of future studies in corporate context
Chermack et al. (2007), Chermack et al. (2006)	Survey data from participants in a scenario planning exercise		n = 1			Some evidence suggests that scenario planning might improve strategic conversation and enhance organizational learning

(continued)

Table 2.10 (continued)

Authors, year	Data	Type of research				Findings
		Inductive			Deductive	
		Conceptual	Case	Econometric	Econometric	
Daheim and Uerz (2006)	40 foresight professionals from multiple industries			n = 40		Overview of configurations of foresight practices. Introduction of a historic evolution of corporate foresight
Roll (2004)	Four case studies in the aviation industry (two network carriers, one regional carrier, and one low-cost carrier)		n = 4			Perception of a high need for corporate foresight, but limited capabilities
Josse (2004)	24 respondents from travel agencies and 30 experts from tourism industry			n = 24		Comparison of survey results with past findings from the literature
Day and Schoemaker (2004b), Day and Schoemaker (2006)	Conceptual/theoretical paper	✓				Introduction of a peripheral vision (largely synonymous with corporate foresight) process framework Using flashlight metaphor to emphasize that any scanning mode will inherently neglect peripheral information, after being directed at a specific target area
Becker (2002)	18 case studies at multinational companies known to have strong foresight capabilities		n = 18			Introduction of a typology of corporate foresight practices ranging from "think tank" (large scope and high degree of specialization), through "observatory" to "collecting post" (small scope and low degree of specialization)
Burmeister et al. (2002)	Four case studies and survey data with 26 respondents		n = 4	n = 26		Data on motivation, goals, information sources, methods, organization setting, impact, and future challenges of corporate foresight
Reger (2001a)	74 interviews in 26 multinational companies		n = 26			Technology foresight in companies is increasingly conducted from a broader perspective to include also economical, social, environmental, and legal aspects

Bondu (2001)	24 mostly large companies		n = 24	The failure of implementing stable foresight systems is blamed on the absence of measures of success and a lack of focus on foresighters' skills and traits
Liebl (1996)	Conceptual/theoretical paper	✓		Development of a model for perception of discontinuities and integration with inside-out and outside-in perspective of strategic management
Krystek and Müller-Stewens (1993)	Conceptual/theoretical paper	✓		Conceptualization of discontinuities and practical advice on how to implement foresight methods and systems
Wack (1985)	Case study on Shell's scenario-based foresight activity		n = 1	Emphasizing the need for and benefit of foresight to educate managers to think about an uncertain future
Krubasik (1982)	Conceptual/theoretical paper	✓		Framework to link technology forecasting based on s-curves with portfolio management for R and D priority setting

is needed. Such a framework can be an important step for developing testable constructs and hypotheses and thus can lead the transition to deductive research.

2.4 Management Theories

When engaging in scientific research, scholars aim to advance the existing knowledge base. The philosopher Thomas Kuhn defines science as "research firmly based upon on or more past scientific achievements, achievements that some particular scientific community acknowledges for a time as supplying the foundation for its future practice" (Kuhn 1970:10). When scientific research meets the two characteristics of being (1) sufficiently new and (2) sufficiently open-ended to attract additional research, it creates a paradigm that is followed by other researchers (Kuhn 1970:10). Such paradigms help researchers build on previous knowledge and serve as theoretical frames. Such theoretical frames are also often referred to as theories, and they help guide and position the research. For this study, the theoretical frames are (1) the contingency theory, (2) the resource-based view, and (3) dynamic capabilities.

2.4.1 Contingency Theory

The core idea of the *contingency theory* is that there is not one best way to organize a company, but that managers need to aim to match their management actions to contingency factors. The idea originated with the work of Woodward, who argued that technologies directly determine differences in organizational attributes such as span of control, centralization of authority, and the formalization of rules and procedures (Woodward 1958). This finding was revolutionary at a time when general management theory was dominated by the idea that given a certain goal there is one best way to organize a company.

This initial work triggered a whole school of thought in which scholars defined technology as the contingency factor and studied its impact on organizational factors (e.g., Harvey 1968; Pennings 1975). Other researchers applied the theoretical frame to other contingency factors and thus showed its applicability to other domains. In this line of research, the books of Lawrence and Lorsch and Khandwalla are possibly the most prominent works (Lawrence and Lorsch 1967; Khandwalla 1977). Their research led to the increasing popularity of the contingency theory and motivated its application in additional domains.

Today, the contingency theory is one of the most prominent management theories and has been applied to many research domains (Donaldson 1999:51). The major criticism concerning the contingency theory is about its deterministic nature (Schreyögg 1978). Particularly Lawrence and Lorsch expected the optimal organizational structure to be determined entirely through the contingency factors (Lawrence and Lorsch 1967), excluding the possibility that the organization itself could change the contingency factors or that there is more than one optimal way. The organization was thus expected to have only the option of adapting itself to the external contingency factors, success being determined by the ability of a firm to adapt effectively and in a timely manner (Child 1972:17–19; Child 1997:43).

For research on corporate foresight, the contingency theory can be applied to observe the relationship between contextual factors (the contingency factors) and the corporate foresight capabilities (configuration, which is dependent on the contingency factors). In addition, it would be interesting to investigate whether certain combinations of contextual factors and corporate foresight capability have more impact (effectiveness measure of the contingency-structure-fit) than others. For the development of the maturity model and the description of best practices, this leads to two conclusions.

Conclusion 9. *The ideal corporate foresight capability mix depends on contextual factors.*

Conclusion 10. *The success of best practices depends on contextual factors.*

2.4.2 Resource-Based View

The *resource-based view* builds on the central concept that the ability of a company to compete successfully against rivals depends on certain (strategic) resources (Barney 1991:99; Wernerfelt 1984:171). This means that in contrast to the contingency theory it is not the ideal fit between contingency factors and organizational structure that determines the competitive advantage, but certain resources (Moore 1993:75). The first to introduce this concept was Penrose, who explicitly stated the importance of certain resources for value creation (Penrose 1959:31):

> The business firm [. . .] is both an administrative organization and a collection of productive resources; its general purpose is to organize the use of its 'own' resources together with other resources acquired from outside the firm for the production and sale of foods and services at a profit.

In order to provide a competitive advantage, the resource needs to have certain characteristics. The resource should be (1) valuable, i.e., yield a competitive advantage, (2) rare or scarce, (3) inimitable and (4) non-substitutable (Collis and Montgomery 1995:120; Barney 1991:105; Eisenhardt and Martin 2000:1105). Using such resources, firms can achieve sustainable competitive advantage by implementing value-creating strategies that cannot be easily duplicated by competing firms (Barney 1991:105; Eisenhardt and Martin 2000:1105).

In this research, I have argued that corporate foresight capabilities are a resource in their own right. An implemented corporate foresight system allows a company to discover and exploit arising business opportunities ahead of rivals that lack similar systems. This would qualify corporate foresight as being valuable. In addition, corporate foresight systems are rare, given the lack of successful implementation of corporate foresight systems (Liebl 2005:123; Herzhoff 2004:189). The criterion "inimitable" is not so easy to confirm, but it could be argued that it resides in the difficulty to implement corporate foresight in different corporate contexts. And the criterion "non-substitutable" could also be affirmed, because the function of corporate foresight is put in place because other mechanisms fail to produce responsiveness and fail to reduce inertia.

Conclusion 11. *Corporate foresight capabilities qualify as a resource with competitive relevance.*

2.4.3 Dynamic Capabilities

Based on the criticism that the resource-based view fails to explain how companies gain a competitive advantage in dynamic markets, Teece, Pisano, and Shuen have extended the concept and created the concept of dynamic capabilities. They define dynamic capabilities as:

> The firm's ability to integrate, build, and reconfigure internal and external competences to address rapidly changing environments (Teece et al. 1997:516).

Eisenhardt and Martin have taken the concept further, integrating the notion of organizational and strategic routines which the firm uses to reconfigure its resource portfolio. They define dynamic capabilities as:

> The firm's processes that use resources – specifically the processes to integrate, reconfigure, gain and release resources – to match and even create market change. Dynamic capabilities thus are the organizational and strategic routines by which firms achieve new resource configurations as markets emerge, collide, split, evolve, and die.

Dynamic capabilities thus reflect the ability of an organization to achieve new and innovative forms of competitive advantage. A discontinuous change – the core of the interest of this study – will challenge a company to exercise its dynamic capabilities in order to change and acquire new resources that enhance its ability to compete (Danneels 2008:519). In addition, dynamic capabilities will enable firms to replace capabilities that have become invaluable over time (Helfat and Peteraf 2003:1004; Afuah and Utterback 1997:183; Helfat 2007a; Ambrosini and Bowman 2009:29).

Conclusion 12. *Corporate foresight systems can be regarded as a dynamic capability that enables a firm to detect a need to renew its portfolio of resources.*

2.5 Implications from Past Research for Corporate Foresight

From the literature review on strategic management, innovation management and future research, and relevant management theories, 12 major conclusions have been drawn (see Table 2.11). These conclusions can be used to define the current body of knowledge, identify the research gap, and guide the research design.

Table 2.11 Overview of conclusions from the literature review

Research stream (conclusion no.)	Conclusion for research on corporate foresight
Strategic management perspective	
Environmental scanning (Conclusion 1)	The interpretation of corporate foresight insights should be done at the top management level, and information gathering should be supported by boundary spanners
Corporate change and ambidexterity (Conclusion 2)	In order to ensure long-term survival, companies need to ensure strategic flexibility and build capabilities to detect discontinuous change in their environment
Decision making (Conclusion 3)	To ensure that corporate foresight has an impact, insights should be communicated on many levels simultaneously, and decision makers should participate in the corporate foresight activity
Innovation management perspective	
Radical innovations (Conclusion 4)	Committed individuals are crucial to radical innovations; they should be used for vision building, and they should be integrated into corporate foresight activities
Disruptions (Conclusion 5)	Large incumbent companies tend to be slow and ignorant and need to build dedicated structures for detecting and proactively managing discontinuous change
Future research perspective	
Macro perspective (Conclusion 6)	To make corporate foresight actionable, it should move toward qualitative studies and the active participation of the internal stakeholders
Micro perspective (Conclusion 7)	Successful corporate foresight is built on its actors. Ensure the usage of foresighters with desirable characteristics and traits and the participation of major stakeholders
Micro perspective (Conclusion 8)	There is a need for a common framework for corporate foresight research and coverage of both the foresight manager's and the foresight customer's perspective
Management theories	
Contingency theory (Conclusion 9)	The ideal corporate foresight capability mix depends on contextual factors
Contingency theory (Conclusion 10)	The success of best practices depends on contextual factors
Resource-based view (Conclusion 11)	Corporate foresight capabilities qualify as a resource with competitive relevance
Dynamic capabilities (Conclusion 12)	Corporate foresight systems can be regarded as a dynamic capability that enables a firm to detect a need to renew its portfolio of resources

These 12 conclusions can be translated into two basic motivations for building corporate foresight systems, six guidelines for building corporate foresight systems, and the definition of the research gap.

The primary motivation for building corporate foresight systems is derived from the findings on corporate change and on disruptions. The two primary arguments for the need of corporate foresight systems are:

- Large incumbent companies tend to be ignorant and slow to respond to discontinuous change (Conclusion 5).
- Companies need specific systems to detect and manage discontinuous change (Conclusion 2).

In addition, the conclusions can also be used to define guidelines for the design and successful implementation of corporate foresight systems. Six such guidelines can be identified from the conclusions:

- Interpretation of future-related information by top management (Conclusion 1).
- Information gathering by boundary spanners (Conclusion 1).
- Dissemination of foresight insights by participation and multi-level communications (Conclusion 3).
- Use of qualitative data to make participation easier and ensure use and impact of foresight insights (Conclusion 6).
- Focus on choosing the right people as foresighters (Conclusion 7).
- The ideal design of corporate foresight systems depends on contextual factors (Conclusion 9, Conclusion 10).

Conclusion 8 hints at the research gap in the research on corporate foresight. This research gap has two aspects, one methodological and one concerning the content of the research.

The methodological shortcoming is the lack of usage of informants with a customer perspective. Without questioning the internal stakeholder, data on value creation of corporate foresight is subject to a *single informant bias*. This could results in (1) overestimating the impact of corporate foresight and (2) limiting the ability to identify the whole range of benefits created by corporate foresight. Particularly troubling is that in the only research on corporate foresight in which top management and the persons reporting directly to top management were questioned, the top management reported a limited use of foresight insights, and thus a limited impact of corporate foresight (Roll 2004:260). It is therefore important for future research to put the internal customers (or stakeholder) of corporate foresight insights at the center of the empirical investigation.

The content aspect of the research gap is *too narrow a view* of corporate foresight. Research has described corporate foresight either as a set of methods and tools (Porter et al. 2004:287; Schwarz 2009:291; Salo et al. 2003:235; Specht et al. 2003:71) or as a process (Amanatidou and Guy 2008:539; Becker 2002:12; Horton 1999:5; Müller 2008:25; Müller-Stewens and Müller 2009:9). In consequence, it neglected other elements such as actors (foresighters and their internal customers), information sources, and the cultural characteristics of a firm, which may have an important impact on the overall corporate foresight ability of a firm.

Where inductive research has already provided descriptive results, it is generally expected that research should move toward deductive research or toward theory testing. In the case of corporate foresight, the most obvious – and possibly also the most interesting – question for deductive investigation is this: Does corporate foresight contribute to the ability of a firm to survive discontinuous change? As the survival of a company relies on many factors and actions outside corporate foresight systems, empirical investigation would need to control most other variables to obtain sufficient effect strengths.

Another question: Does corporate foresight contribute significantly to the success of an organization? As discussed in more detail in the section on impact and value contribution (see Sect. 4.1.3), researchers interested in this question would need to further investigate these questions: What are the potential positive impacts of corporate foresight? How can the impact be made operational? What are the elements of corporate foresight capabilities? And how can these elements be made operational?

In addition, there is also the more practical interest in understanding more of the elements of corporate foresight practice for being able to develop them and enhance the ability of an organization to respond to discontinuous change. If the individual element were identified, then it would be vital to obtain a common framework that could be used for both benchmarking and planning the enhancement of corporate foresight abilities.

Chapter 3
Research Design

3.1 Research Aims

Building on the literature review, the research aims can be further specified. These aims can be divided into aspects whose purpose is to advance theory and aspects whose purpose is to advance management practice.

To contribute to *advancing theory*, this research pursues three aims:

- *Identifying the elements of corporate foresight systems*, by building on previous research, testing the relevance of previously identified elements, and extending the number of elements in which practitioners have found gaps.
- *Define elements of corporate foresight systems*, by identifying items within the elements and combining them.
- *Build a common framework*, by creating hypotheses on the relationship between the elements.

Management practices should be advanced by three additional aims:

- *Identifying proficiency levels* within the elements of the corporate foresight system.
- *Defining a maturity model*, to guide the designing and improving of corporate foresight systems.
- *Identifying best practices* and identifying the contextual factors that are essential to implementing the best practice. In addition, the best practices should be matched with the maturity model to allow the systematic selection and adoption of best practices.

In addition to the aims for advancing theory and management practice, this research aims to overcome methodological shortcomings of past research by

- *Using a sample with multiple industries*, to enhance the generalizability of the findings.
- *Using multiple data collection instruments*, to ensure sufficient triangulation of data.

R. Rohrbeck, *Corporate Foresight*, Contributions to Management Science,
DOI 10.1007/978-3-7908-2626-5_3, © Springer-Verlag Berlin Heidelberg 2011

- *Using informants with the foresighter's and internal customer's perspective*, to limit the single-informant bias (Yin 2003:86), which could lead to overestimating the impact of corporate foresight.

3.2 Research Strategy

In order to explore a field that is relatively new and about which knowledge is limited, exploratory methods are recommended as the research method (Yin 2003:12; Eisenhardt 1989:532; Voss et al. 2002:195). Case studies are particularly suitable for ensuring a strong qualitative base upon which to produce useful and correct theory (Helfat 2007b:185; Langley 1999:691) and reduce the risk of oversimplification associated particularly with quantitative research, which uses statistical modeling (Lamnek 2005:4).

Although case studies are recognized as a valid research method in the social sciences, some traditional prejudices remain. Yin points out that many researchers tend to believe that cases studies lack a systematic procedure, leading to concerns about subjectivity (Yin 2003:3). Eisenhardt and Graber argue that, on the contrary, "well-done theory building from cases is surprisingly 'objective', because its close adherence to the data keeps researchers 'honest'" (Eisenhardt and Graebner 2007:25) and thus is an important tool for empirical investigation and theory building (Shavelson and Towne 2002:3).

Single case studies are particularly powerful in exploring a phenomenon in its context while maintaining the richness of the phenomenon and its context (Eisenhardt and Graebner 2007:27). Multiple case studies sacrifice some richness but will typically be able to develop theory that is more robust, more generalizable, and better testable. (Eisenhardt and Graebner 2007:27). For this study, a multiple case study design was selected, because past research has already created knowledge about how corporate foresight systems are implemented in companies. Some richness, therefore, could be sacrificed. In addition, it was important to use different perspectives in order to ensure the identification of the widest possible scope of aspects.

For the development of the Maturity Model of Corporate Foresight, I follow inductive research logic. Eisenhardt advises to engage in such research without assumptions or predefined hypotheses but potentially with defined constructs that may be tested within the research (Eisenhardt 1989:536). Others argue that some theoretical background should help focus and direct the research as well as ensure that all the data relevant to answering the research question are collected (Yin 2003:28).

As shown in the literature review, corporate foresight has different research streams on which it can build and which can be used to guide new research. In consequence, it was aimed in this research to build upon prior knowledge, use constructs that are available, and use original empirical data to fill in the gaps and enhance the understanding where needed.

3.2.1 Sample and Case Selection

In case study research, each case should be selected for a special purpose and contribute to answering the research question in a different way (Yin 2003). Case study research follows a theoretical sampling logic. The sampling is unlike large scale statistical research in that it is not driven by achieving a representation of the whole population (Eisenhardt 1989:537; Eisenhardt and Graebner 2007:27). Cases are chosen and added to the sample for replication, extension, contrary replication, and elimination of alternative explanations of a phenomenon (Eisenhardt and Graebner 2007:25).

Because we aim to define a maturity model that can be applied to any organization, we aimed for a high level of generalizability. For that reason, this study uses companies that differ from each other in *industry, position in the value chain*, and their primary *business driver*, which could be either *technology* or the *market*. This made it possible to identify new phenomena (extension), to search for the same phenomenon in different companies (replication), and check the limits of application by finding cases in which the particular element of a corporate foresight system is not being used (contrary replication).

The focus of the study was on five case study clusters (see Table 3.1). In these clusters, the identified phenomena have been described and compared using replication and contrary replication logic. After the cases in the five clusters were studied and interpreted, two more cases were conducted to extend the data on particular phenomena.

In the case of Deutsche Bank Research (the research unit of the financial institution), the focus was on observing a specific way of using scenario analysis.

Table 3.1 Case study sample

Company	Industry	Country
Deutsche Telekom	ICT (Operator)	Germany
Telekom Austria	ICT (Operator)	Austria
British Telecom	ICT (Operator)	UK
Telefonica	ICT (Operator)	Spain
Volkswagen	Automotive (OEM)	Germany
Continental	Automotive (Tier-1)	Germany
ThyssenKrupp Automotive	Automotive (Tier-2)	Germany
Philips	Electronics (Manufacturer)	The Netherlands
Osram	Electronics (Manufacturer)	Germany
Bosch Siemens Hausgeräte	Electronics (Manufacturer)	Germany
Infineon	Electronics (Manufacturer)	Germany
Vattenfall Europe	Energy (Producer)	Sweden
Endesa	Energy (Producer)	Spain
Iberola	Energy (Producer)	Spain
EDP	Energy (Producer)	Portugal
General Electric Energy	Energy (Manufacturer)	USA
MAN Turbo	Energy (Manufacturer)	Germany
Deutsche Bank Research	Finance (Service)	Germany
Hugo Boss	Fashion (Manufacturer, Retailer)	Germany

At Hugo Boss, the aim was to study a specific approach to customer foresight, which has been identified in the Volkswagen case.

3.2.2 Data Collection Instruments

Regarding data collection, it is important to use many sources of evidence to ensure the sufficient triangulation of data (Yin 2003:97; Rubin and Rubin 2005:64). Many instruments are available for data collection, among them documents, archival records, interviews, direct observation, participant observation, and physical artifacts (Yin 2003:86). The use of multiple instruments is recommended to allow for sufficient triangulation (Flick 2007:12).

Interviews are particularly useful when the aim is to investigate strategic phenomena, in which informants need to reflect on their everyday practices (Eisenhardt and Graebner 2007:28). In comparison to other instruments, interviews are also more flexible, allowing researchers to adapt to the interviewee's and company's context (Trinczek 2005:211).

Multiple interview types can be differentiated and are associated with specific strengths and weaknesses (Mayring 2002:66). For this study, the "guided interview" has been chosen. With its set of standardized questions, the guided interview provides a structure that ensures that all relevant aspects are being addressed while leaving enough room to investigate particular topics that emerge through the interview. The structure also provides the foundation for cross-case comparisons (Mayer 2006:36–40; Mayring 2002:69).

The study uses four *data collection instruments*. The three major instruments are interviews, internal documents, and external academic publications by the foresight manager. In addition to these classical instruments, interview templates have been used to allow for direct validation of my interpretation of the responses in the interviews.

- The *interviews* were guided semi-structured and supported by templates that were filled in along with the informant (the interview guideline can be found in Sect. 7.1). This made it possible to structure the interview but provided enough flexibility to follow up on new topics that came up during the interview. In total, 107 interviews were conducted. At the start of each interview, the informant was asked for permission to record the conversation to prevent data loss and increase validity (Gillham 2000:69–72; Schofield 2002:171). This made it possible to record 80% of the interviews, all of which have been transcribed. Interviews that were not recorded were documented with the interview templates and by minutes of memory, which were cross-checked by a second researcher. The interviews lasted 1–2 h. In each interview, the research objective, research framework, and key concepts were described in order to avoid misunderstanding. To improve objectivity on the context, a standardized questionnaire was used. The questionnaire consisted of four sections: (1) company profile, (2) nature of strategy, (3) complexity of environment, and (4) industry clockspeed (the context questionnaire can be found in Sect. 7.2).

- The *templates* were used to visualize the answers of the informant during the interviews. They are standardized figures that provide a framework into which the informant fills in his or her data. The templates were refined and enhanced throughout the case study phase. The latest version consisted of seven templates on (1) goals, (2) actors, (3) process, (4) methods, (5) organizational structure, (6) information sources, and (7) value contribution. The templates were used to draw organizational charts, processes, and actor networks. Methods were collected in the template as either technology-oriented or market-oriented methods. The templates for goals and value contribution were used for an initial clustering of the answers. The use of the template made it possible to validate the answers and their implications during the interview itself. This decreased the risk of misunderstanding and misinterpreting and increased the validity (the interview templates can be found in Sect. 7.3).
- The *internal documents* consisted mostly of presentations on CF processes, CF results, and working documents from CF projects. In addition, organizational charts, annual report presentations, and general company presentations were collected for analysis of the company's context. An overview of the internal documents is given in Sects. 7.5 and 7.6.
- In some cases, the companies provided academic *publications* on their CF or innovation management practices. These were primarily used for clarification of CF processes and for understanding the logic behind their CF practices. An overview of the academic publications of informants is given in Sect. 7.7.

The amount of data collected in the case studies varied, as the research aim was not to compare the case studies but to ensure the identification of as many aspects as possible. In Table 3.2, an overview of the number of *data sets per case study* is given.

It can be seen that a particular emphasis in the amount of collected data was put on the cases Deutsche Telekom, Telekom Austria, Volkswagen, and Vattenfall Europe. This is because they were the first cases and thus were used for defining and improving the initial version of the maturity model. The following cases were then used for validation and for identification of additional elements of corporate foresight systems. Fewer data, therefore, were required.

3.2.3 Key Informants

As discussed previously in the literature review, the major methodological shortcoming of previous case studies was the exclusive use of foresighters as informants. This prevents the researcher from giving an unbiased account of the impact of corporate foresight. To be able to observe the entire range of corporate foresight elements, this researcher used three types of informant: the internal customer, the corporate foresight activity manager, and the corporate foresight activity team.

Table 3.2 Data structured by case and collection instrument

Cases	Data collection instruments			
	Interviews	Internal documents	Publications	Templates
Deutsche Telekom	26	8	4	19
Telekom Austria	12	1	0	11
British Telecom	3	3	2	0
Telefonica	2	1	0	1
Volkswagen	9	3	2	0
Continental	3	2	3	2
TK Automotive	5	2	0	1
Philips	3	7	4	3
Osram	4	2	0	3
BSH	5	1	1	1
Infineon	2	1	0	0
Vattenfall Europe	10	4	0	10
Endesa	5	1	0	0
Iberola	2	0	0	0
EDP	3	0	0	0
GE Energy	6	0	0	0
MAN Turbo	2	1	0	0
Deutsche Bank Research	3	1	2	0
Hugo Boss	2	0	0	1
Total	107	38	18	51

- The *internal customer* is the person who stands to profit from the corporate foresight activity. He is the key informant for value creation and context aspects. In addition, he can report on the capabilities from a more objective perspective, i.e., he will most likely have a reduced fake-good bias, as he is not reporting on the results of his own work.
- The *activity manager* is the person in charge of the corporate foresight activity. He is not necessarily the person who executes the activity. The activity manager is the key informant for explaining the motivation, goals, and logic of the corporate foresight activity as well as the organizational setting and characteristics of the foresighters (i.e., the activity team) on his team or the company in general. He may also be a good informant for the capabilities if he has enough knowledge of the actual execution of the activity.
- On the *activity team*, informants were questioned who are executing corporate foresight activities. They are the key informants on information usage, methods, and networks. Their reporting on value creation may be subject to the fake-good bias and was considered with care.

A particular emphasis was put on recruiting a high number of informants with the internal customer's perspective. The number of informants per case and perspective is given in Table 3.3. A list of all informants for each case is given in Sect. 7.4.

It can be seen that different emphases were made in different cases. For example, the Deutsche Telekom case was used primarily to explore the usage of foresight

Table 3.3 Interviews structured by case and informant position

Cases	Informant position		
	Internal customer	Activity manager	Activity team
Deutsche Telekom	19	5	2
Telekom Austria	3	4	5
British Telecom	0	1	2
Telefonica	1	1	0
Volkswagen	1	3	5
Continental	1	1	1
TK Automotive	2	3	0
Philips	1	1	1
Osram	2	1	1
BSH	1	2	2
Infineon	1	1	0
Vattenfall Europe	4	4	2
Endesa	1	0	4
Iberola	0	1	1
EDP	2	1	0
GE Energy	1	5	0
MAN Turbo	1	1	0
Deutsche Bank Research	0	1	2
Hugo Boss	1	1	0
Total	42	37	28

results and their value creation, while GE Energy, Telekom Austria, and Vattenfall Europe were used to thoroughly investigate corporate foresight activities and to identify elements of corporate foresight capabilities.

3.3 Research Sequence

The research sequence can be divided into four steps, with two practitioner conferences after the second and third step. Figure 3.1 shows the sequence that has been followed.

In *the first phase*, the literature review and a pilot case study were used to explore the research gap and the need for corporate foresight from a practitioner's point of view and to identify an initial set of relevant aspects among corporate foresight practices. In the *second phase*, five complete case studies, including 41 interviews and an additional five benchmark talks,[1] were conducted. The result was the first-draft version of the maturity model.

[1]The benchmarking talks are meetings with corporate foresight managers in companies in which practices have been discussed but from which no evidence was used directly. The benchmark talks were used to broaden the understanding of CF in various contexts and helped direct the observations in the case studies.

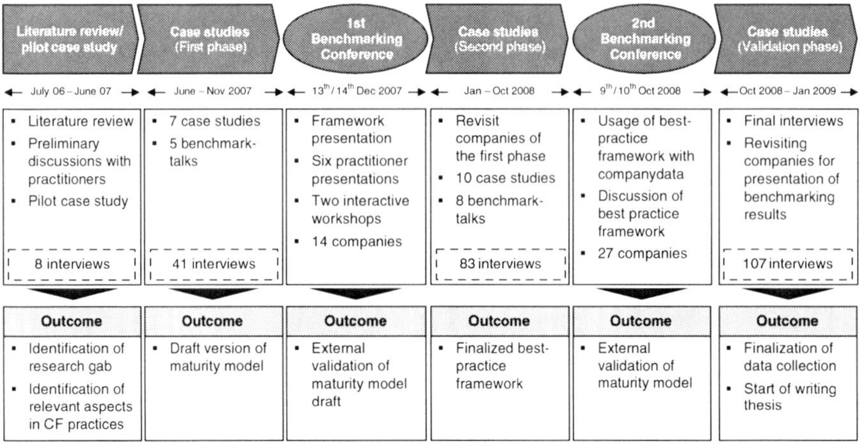

Fig. 3.1 Research sequence

In December 2007, the first benchmarking conference was organized to validate the preliminary version of the maturity model and obtain recommendations from practitioners regarding the research aims. During the conference, the maturity model was used to position and classify the best-practice examples. The maturity model was also presented and discussed. The feedback was used to optimize and extend the interview guideline and identify additional aspects.

With the feedback of the benchmarking conference, the *third phase* – or second phase of case studies – was used to revisit the companies from the first case study phase and to conduct an additional ten case studies and eight benchmarking talks. The additional 42 interviews brought the number of interviews to 83 and made it possible to improve and complete the maturity model.

To validate the final version of the maturity model, a second benchmarking conference was organized. The conference attracted companies that had not participated in the case studies or in benchmarking talks. In total, 27 companies were present, a number that allowed for an intensive discussion on best practices as well as on the maturity model. The feedback from the conference let to increased confidence that the presented maturity model was ready to use for the scoring of the case study participants.

In the final phase, 24 validation interviews were conducted, bringing the number of interviews to 107. In addition, the six companies were visited to present their score on the maturity model and discuss the findings. All six judged the analysis to be an accurate assessment of their corporate foresight abilities, and they were pleased with the recommendations for further improvement of their practices. Three companies used the results to plan and start projects to improve their corporate foresight capabilities ability.

3.4 Data Reduction and Coding

The large amount of data gathered in a case study poses a particular challenge to researchers. The data need to be reduced in order to be crisp and to make it possible to derive focused conclusions (Lee 1998:34). But the data need to be rich and extensive enough to allow for an adequate account of contextual information (Richards 2005:52). In this study, the transcripts alone run to more than 1,600 pages, and additional data from internal presentations, publications, and templates adds another 500 pages. To handle so much data, electronic text-analysis software is recommended (Bortz and Döring 2006:329).

To be able to store and manage this amount of data, the computer-based qualitative research tool NVIVO 8 was used. This software made it possible to store any kind of document and organize it by information source and content.

To make sense of the data, it is recommended to use a category system for coding the data – a process that involves attaching keywords (the codes) to words, sentences, or diagrams in the documents (Saunders et al. 2007:482). In this study, the system of codes was created, both deductively from literature and inductively from collected data (defining new codes for interesting aspects that are identified while reading the documents). The final category system is given in Table 3.4. It consists of seven categories and 31 codes.

Table 3.4 also shows the number of *informants* and the number of *sentences* (or *words*) that have been assigned a particular code. The number of informants can be used as a measure of relevance of an element, and the number of sentences represents the breadth of the element, i.e., how many aspects were mentioned within an element.

Overall, the high number of informants and coded sentences provides confidence that the elements can be regarded as relevant across cases and thus can be generalized across industries and position in the value chain and for companies in both market-driven and technology-driven markets. The complete coding tree can be found in Sect. 7.8.

3.5 Drawing Conclusions and Verifying Data

In case study research, there are three options for drawing conclusions. First, follow a theoretical framework; second, identify and test rival explanations; and third, make a case description (Saunders et al. 2007:488; Yin 2003:111). This research uses a theoretical proposition and aims to test and further develop it. The two guiding propositions are that (1) a company can develop certain capabilities that will enable it to survive and succeed when encountering discontinuous change and (2) that the ideal set of capabilities will depend on certain contextual factors. As described in the research strategy, this proposition builds on the theories of the resource-based view, dynamic capabilities and used the contingency theory as theoretical frames.

Table 3.4 Category system and coding

Category	Codes	Informants	Sentences
Context	Size of company	6	7
	Nature of strategy	9	10
	Corporate culture	5	5
	Source of competitive advantage	4	4
	Complexity of environment	8	9
	Industry clockspeed	9	10
Information usage	Reach	22	77
	Scope	33	149
	Sources	38	148
	Time horizon	28	62
Methods	Communication capacity	25	52
	Integrative capacity	29	59
	Match with context	8	15
	Match with problem	10	17
People and Networks	Characteristics of foresighters	28	63
	Internal communication	39	98
	Network scope	39	136
Organization	Mode	29	60
	Integration with other processes	43	105
	Formal diffusion of insights	14	31
	Accountability	9	40
	Incentives and rewards	8	17
Culture	Organization's attitude toward periphery	3	8
	Readiness to listen to external sources	7	10
	Informal diffusion of insights	3	3
	Willingness to share across functions	9	28
	Willingness to challenge assumptions	6	16
Impact	Reduction of uncertainty	56	188
	Triggering actions	63	315
	Influencing others to act	24	82
	Secondary benefits (marketing and sales; organizational learning)	23	50
		Average: 21	Total: 1,874

3.5.1 Developing the Maturity Model of Corporate Foresight

For *developing the maturity model*, the coded data – which were structured into context, capabilities, and impact – were further analyzed to identify relevant aspects among the codes. This aspect identification and regrouping of categories was an iterative process. In this process, each iteration consisted of (1) identification of aspects, (2) comparison of them to the literature, (3) clustering them, and (4) revisiting the data in light of the new category system. To reduce the researcher bias and increase reliability, changes to the maturity model were discussed in the monthly meetings of the research group. On average, six to ten diploma thesis students were present at these meetings. To be included in the model, the categories had to meet three criteria:

- *Detectable*. The aspect can be observed in any kind of company, independent of industry, size, and organizational structure.
- *Explanatory power*. The aspect was linked by an informant or literature to the impact of foresight.
- *Measurable*. The aspect can be made operational and thus allows for an objective judgment on the capability level.

After the finalization of the category system, the data were searched for differences between the companies that could serve as maturity levels. In addition, literature was used to reflect on the capabilities. The result is qualitative descriptions of the intensity with which and the extent to which a company can implement a corporate foresight system.

3.5.2 Identification and Discussion of Best Practices

For the *identification of best practices*, it is important to choose an appropriate unit of analysis. In this study, two possibilities exist. First, the level of an integrated case study, in which all components of a corporate foresight system are discussed, and second, the level of components of a corporate foresight system. Such a component could be a dimension or an element of the Maturity Model of Corporate Foresight.

The advantage of analyzing *integrated cases* is the richness of the description, which gives the reader, for example, a good understanding of why certain approaches have been used in favor of others. Another advantage is the understanding of interdependencies between different components of the foresight system. The downside is the limited generalizability, a result of the uniqueness of each case (Eisenhardt and Graebner 2007:30).

Analyzing *individual components or approaches* sacrifices some of the richness in the description of the cases but boosts the generalizability of best practices (Eisenhardt 1989:537). Another argument for using components as units of analysis is the sample of this study, which is particularly well-suited to attaining a high level of generalizability. The analysis of 19 companies from different industries, different countries of origin, different positions in the value chain, and different corporate cultures has produced rich knowledge about the context and configuration of the corporate foresight systems. Thus the comparison of different approaches within the sample would lead to the identification of generic best-practice approaches and the identification of the context in which the best practice can be applied successfully.

Another advantage of presenting components comes from the interplay with the Maturity Model of Corporate Foresight. Managers who have assessed their corporate foresight capabilities with the Maturity Model are interested in receiving suggestions about which practices they can use to improve their corporate foresight ability. The description of integrated corporate foresight systems would most likely not help them, as the case has a different context from that of their own company.

In contrast, if best practices are presented on the level of components, then the manager is able to select the individual best-practice approaches and integrate them into his or her corporate foresight system. The description of the context for each approach allows the manager to select only the components that have proven successful in corporate environments similar to his own.

For these reasons, it was decided to *identify and analyze best practices on the level of components* of the corporate foresight system.

The identification of best practices among the components was guided by the capability dimension of the maturity model (i.e., the capability dimensions: information usage, method sophistication, people and networks, organization, culture). In the first step, the maturity model was used to score the participating companies in order to make them comparable. In the second step, the companies with the highest scores in a certain area of the maturity model were further analyzed to investigate (1) the context in which the activity was implemented, (2) the activity itself, and (3) if possible, some indications on the impact and value creation of the activity. The cross-case analysis made it possible to discern the contextual factors in which the best practices have proven successful against contextual factors that would endanger its success.

3.6 Measures Taken to Ensure Research Quality

When attempting to use scientific methods to reveal relationships between management actions and desired outcomes, the most important question is "How do I ensure that my evidence will truly support my conclusions and that I have not deceived myself?" (Saunders et al. 2007:149) One answer is that a researcher can never be 100% sure. Another answer is that scientific methods can be used to reduce the risk of finding false relationships. For case study research, Yin identifies three relevant tests with which to judge the quality of the research design and the quality of its execution (Yin 2003:34):

- *Reliability* demonstrates that the operations of the study can be repeated with the same results.
- *Construct validity* establishes that the operational measures are suitable for representing the phenomenon being studied.
- *External validity* defines the domains to which the findings of a study can be generalized.

In order to pass these quality tests, researchers need to develop tactics to deal with possible threats to their research (Yin 2003:34).

Regarding the test for *reliability*, the researcher needs to ensure that another researcher following the same steps will come to the same conclusion. This test poses a particular challenge for case study research, as the process relies heavily on the interpretation of the collected data. Yin points out that the first step in ensuring the ability to reproduce research results is to document the research process

(Yin 2003:38). In this research, the documentation includes the research sequence, the preliminary results at different stages and the documentation of the workshops of the research group, and the coding of the transcripts.

To further improve reliability, a systematic approach to limit research errors and biases should be employed (Eisenhardt and Graebner 2007:28). An overview of the tactics employed is given in Table 3.5. The prime tactic that is used to limit the respondent bias is the emphasis on using several highly knowledgeable informants. The 107 interviews in 19 case studies made it possible to question informants from three perspectives: (1) the activity team, (2) activity manager, and (3) internal customer. Particular emphasis was put on recruiting top management respondents for the internal customer perspective, including in two case studies the CEO of the companies. In addition, respondents were asked to provide examples, when they reported on successful practices – another tactic to limit the respondent bias.

To limit observer errors and bias, the interviews were conducted by two researchers with the support of semi-structured interview guidelines. In addition, interview templates were used to improve the comparability between cases as well as boost the validity by collecting instant feedback by the respondent on the interpretation by the researchers.

Table 3.5 Tactics to ensure reliability

Threat	Definition	Tactic
Procedure unclear	Reproducing research results depends on the knowledge of how the research was conducted in the first place	• Documentation of research sequence • Documentation of preliminary results at various stages • Documentation of workshops within research group • Coding of transcripts with a software tool
Respondent error	The respondent may judge activities differently in different circumstances. E.g., during phases of strategic review, he may judge the use of corporate foresight activities stronger because they are more present	• No interviews were conducted during periods of annual financial or strategic review
Respondent bias	The respondent gives desired answers to present his company or his work in a better light	• Using several highly knowledgeable informants • Triangulation by asking informants from different perspectives • Asking for examples
Observer error	Interviews by different researchers may have limited comparability	• Semi-structured interviews • Use of templates to guide the description of the respondents
Observer bias	Different researchers may interpret answers differently	• 80% of the interviews were conducted by a team of two researchers

When testing *construct validity*, the researcher answers the question of whether the models used to describe observations are appropriate to describe certain phenomena (Yin 2003:34). In research based on quantitative data, this test is a straightforward statistical analysis. In research based on qualitative data, this major question is, "How did the researcher limit his own subjectivity, and how did he operationalize the phenomenon he describes?" The tactics employed to ensure construct validity in this research are given in Table 3.6. An early tactic employed in the data collection phase was to define each code – thus clarifying the phenomenon that was being observed. In addition, the many informants and many data collection instruments made it possible to validate the phenomenon identified and redefine it on the basis of data from different perspectives. A final measure to reduce subjectivity was the review by the informants of transcripts – ensuring the accuracy and allowing them to clarify certain comments – and later review of case study results – which made it possible to validate the importance and correct definition of the aspects of corporate foresight activities.

Another tactic was discussing the aspects or elements of corporate foresight with a wider group of researchers. This was done in a group of six to ten diploma thesis students and took place monthly. In addition, constructs previously used by other researchers were used when suitable. Two such examples were the constructs on "environmental complexity" and "environmental volatility," introduced by Day and Schoemaker (2005:157).

The test for *external validity* is particularly important for research that aims at building theory and research that is aims for making recommendations to management practice in different kinds of industries or organizational settings. In consequence, this test is also called by some authors the test of generalizability (Saunders et al. 2007:151).

Table 3.6 Tactics to ensure construct validity

Threat	Definition	Tactic
Subjectivity	The observations, particularly in case studies, are subject to the subjective interpretation of the researcher	• Identification of phenomenon by coding • Use of several informants and various data collection instruments • Review of transcripts by participants • Review of case study results with respondent workshops
No operationalization	The limited definition of a phenomenon prevents its observation and interpretation	• Where possible, previously used constructs were employed • Frequent discussion on interpretation and categorization in research group

Table 3.7 Tactics to ensure external validity (generalizability)

Threat	Definition	Tactic
No generalizability	The observations may be interpretable only within the case setting	• Replication logic by using at least two cases for each difference in industry, positions in the value chain, and primary business driver • Two practitioner conferences to validate the relevance of the identified factors and discuss their generalizability
No robustness to other settings	Limited knowledge about the contingency factors prevents the transferability of conclusions to other companies	• Identification and definition of six contingency factors that influence the design of corporate foresight systems

The first tactic to enhance generalizability in case study research is to chose a multi-case study in favor of a single case study research approach – which is the case for this research (see the overview of the tactics in Table 3.7). In addition, the choice of cases (i.e., the sample) is important to ensure high external validity. Eisenhardt and Graebner's advice is to use theoretical sampling, which unlike sampling in quantitative research is not designed to achieve a representation but to ensure that all relevant phenomena and constructs can be observed (Eisenhardt and Graebner 2007:27).

To further enhance generalizability, replication logic can be applied, in which two cases are compared and the second case is expected to replicate the results of the first. This study used clusters with at least two cases. These clusters differed by industry, primary business driver, and position in the value chain. In addition, the extensive discussion during the two benchmarking conferences generated many insights into the generalizability of the findings.

To increase the external validity by highlighting the robustness of the findings in various industries and organizational settings, it is also advisable to identify and define the major contingency factors. This has been done for each best-practice example, in which six contingency factors were used to describe the corporate context in which the practice has been found to be successful. The same factors were also used to discuss the limitation of the application of the practice in other contexts.

When judging the tactics employed in this research, some concerns remain in the reliability domain. But as noted above, these are inherent to case study research and have been limited by careful documentation and specific measures in research design. The particular strengths of this research are the high external validity, which was achieved by the high number and quality of respondents as well as the intensive interaction with practitioners through the benchmarking conferences and the benchmarking talks.

Chapter 4
The Maturity Model of Corporate Foresight

4.1 The Elements

Companies wishing to improve their management practices often take the approach of comparing themselves to others, particularly companies that are known to be good at certain practices. This approach – known as benchmarking – has been applied to almost all areas of management, including procurement, research and development (R and D) (Dutta et al. 2005:277), production, marketing, and sales (Mittelstaedt 1992:310). The usefulness of benchmarking arises from the possibility of (1) gaining knowledge about how good one's own management practices are in comparison to others, and (2) being able to learn from others and improve one's management practices. To use a definition from Camp (Camp 2003:12):

> Benchmarking is finding and implementing best practices.

For benchmarking and advancing management practice, it has proven useful to develop common frameworks. Successful uses of such frameworks range from the Capability Maturity Model (CMM) for software development (Humphrey 1989) to benchmarking of R and D processes (Kahn et al. 2006). Maturity models make it possible to measure the company's level of proficiency and suggest steps for improvement. In addition, they support the detection of best practices.

In order to benchmark effectively, there is a need to establish criteria on which to compare companies and their practices. The more detailed the set of criteria, the more specific the recommendations for improvement can be. The downside of very detailed criteria sets is the limited ability to balance the whole system. To be able to control the relevant levers for optimization of corporate foresight capabilities and be able to control the balance of the whole system, this study aims to build a framework with between three and seven benchmarking dimensions with three to five criteria in each.

The development of the framework has followed two paths. First, the study used previous research to identify an initial set of criteria, and second, the case studies were used to filter and complement the criteria set. The result is the Maturity Model of Corporate Foresight. It is structured into three major parts (see Fig. 4.1):

DOI 10.1007/978-3-7908-2626-5_4, © Springer-Verlag Berlin Heidelberg 2011

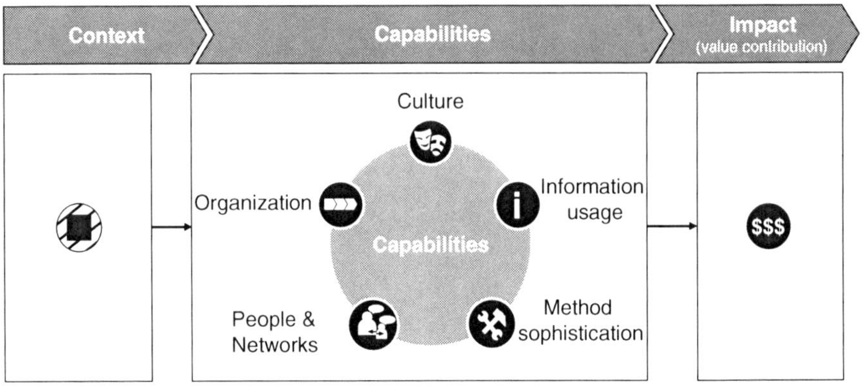

Fig. 4.1 Maturity model – framework

The *context* (or the contingency factors) is used to judge the companies' needs for corporate foresight and to derive normative recommendations on designing corporate foresight systems. The context is described by six criteria: (1) *size of company*, (2) *nature of strategy*, (3) *corporate culture*, (4) *source of competitive advantage*, (5) *complexity of environment*, and (6) *industry clockspeed*.

The *capabilities* are used to assess the corporate foresight system concerning its strength in identifying, interpreting, and responding to discontinuous change. In addition, the maturity level in each capability dimension can be used to guide improvement projects. The capabilities are structured into five dimensions: (1) *information usage*, to describe the kind of information that enters the corporate foresight system, (2) *method sophistication*, to describe the methods used to interpret the information, (3) *people and networks*, to describe the characteristics of individual employees and the networks the company uses to communicate information and foresight insights, (4) *organization*, to describe how information is gathered, interpreted, and used in the organization, and (5) *culture*, to describe the extent to which the corporate culture supports or hinders the foresight effort. In each dimension, there are between three and five criteria on which to assess the maturity of the foresight system. In total, the capabilities are measured with 21 criteria.

The *impact* is used to assess the kind of outcome or value contribution created by the corporate foresight activities. The impact is structured into four categories: (1) reduction of uncertainty, (2) triggering actions, (3) influencing others to act, and (4) secondary benefits. In these four categories, impact is assessed according to 12 criteria.

In Sects. 4.1.1–4.1.3, the context, capability, and impact criteria will be introduced and defined. In addition, it will be shown which elements have been identified by previous research and which elements have been identified by this case study research. In Sect. 4.2, the maturity levels for the individual elements in the capability dimensions will be described. Section 4.3 gives recommendations on how to use the model.

4.1.1 Context

When describing and assessing management systems, the contingency theory emphasizes that it is important to take into account the context in which the management practices are applied (Donaldson 1999:66). In this study, contingent factors are referred to as the *context* of the company. In total, six context factors relevant to corporate foresight have been identified. It is assumed that (1) differences in the context of a company will change the need for specific corporate foresight capabilities and (2) that assessing the context can help guide the design of the corporate foresight systems.

Table 4.1 shows the six context elements identified in this study. To describe the elements, five criteria are used:

Table 4.1 Elements of context

Element	New	Description	Authors, year: page	Original name of element
Company size	✓	Describes the company size by revenue and number of employees		
Nature of strategy		Describes which generic strategy is followed: (1) differentiation strategy, (2) cost leadership, (3) focus strategy	Day and Schoemaker (2005:144)	Nature of strategy
Corporate culture	✓	Describes the corporate culture in terms of empowering the individual initiative and reaching the attention of top management quickly	Tripsas and Gavetti (2000:1157)	Cognition
			Nick (2008:133–134)	Kontextfaktor
		Unternehmenskultur	Source of	✓
Describes the primary driver of success (e.g., technology or customer orientation)		Burmeister et al. (2002)	competitive advantage	Motivation
		Jain (1984)	Objectives of enterprises engaged in foresight	
Complexity of environment		Describes the number of interdependencies in the market that need to be monitored and taken into account	Day and Schoemaker (2005:144)	Complexity of environment
Industry clockspeed		Describes the rate of introduction of new products, processes and organizational structures	Fine (1998)	Volatility of environment

- *Element*. The name of the element
- *New*. Shows whether the element has been newly identified by this research or whether it has been derived from previous research
- *Description*. A brief definition
- *Author, year, and page*. If the element has been identified in earlier research, the short reference is given to point to the research in question
- *Original name of element*. Gives the name given to the element by the original author

In Table 4.1, it can be seen that three of the six elements have been identified through previous work. The element *corporate culture* is not entirely new, as it builds on previous research from Tripsas/Gevitt and Nick, but this research introduces empowering the individual as the primary driver. The other element, which is not entirely new, is the *source of competitive advantage*. It builds to some extent on the measures *motivation* and *objectives of enterprises engaged in foresight*, which have been proposed by Burmeister et al. and Jain. However, the new element describes the primary driver of success in the company's market. This driver is an important indicator for the scanning areas a company should use.

Other typical contextual elements (such as *industry*) are not explicitly part of the framework, but are implicitly considered among the six elements. For example, variance in *industry* is often derived from differences in *source of competitive advantage* (technological leadership vs. customer orientation) or *industry clock-speed*, which describes the rate of introduction of new products, processes, and organizational structures.

4.1.2 Capabilities

4.1.2.1 Information Usage

In the proposed maturity model, the capabilities are structured into five dimensions. Information usage is the dimension that has been studied most frequently. It describes the kind of information that is gathered and fed into the corporate foresight process. From the four elements of information usage, three have already been studied. Becker has described and assessed the elements *scope*, *time horizon*, and *sources* with personal interviews in a sample of 18 multinational European companies. Eighteen years earlier, Jain assessed the *scope* and the usage of sources of information with a survey of 186 Fortune 500 companies.

Table 4.2 gives an overview of the four elements of *information usage*. This research adds the element *reach*, which describes the depth to which companies scan their environment. The depth can be described by differentiating into current business, adjacent business, and white spaces.

The relationship of reach and scope is illustrated in Fig. 4.2. The scope is represented by four segments: *political*, *technological*, *consumer*, and *competitive*

Table 4.2 Elements of the capability information usage

Element	New	Description	Authors, year: page	Original name of element
Reach	✓	Describes how deeply a company scans; current business, adjacent business, and white spaces	Reger (2001b:539)	Introduces white spaces
Scope		Describes how broadly a company scans (technology, socio-cultural, customer, competitors, and political environment)	Becker (2002:15) Jain (1984:120)	Thematic areas Scope of scanning
Time horizon		Describes the time horizons of foresight activities (ranging from the near future to 30 years into the future)	Becker (2002:14–15)	Time horizon
Sources		Describes the sources of information; differentiated into internal vs. external, formal vs. informal	Jain (1984:124) Becker (2002:15)	Information sources Selection of sources of information

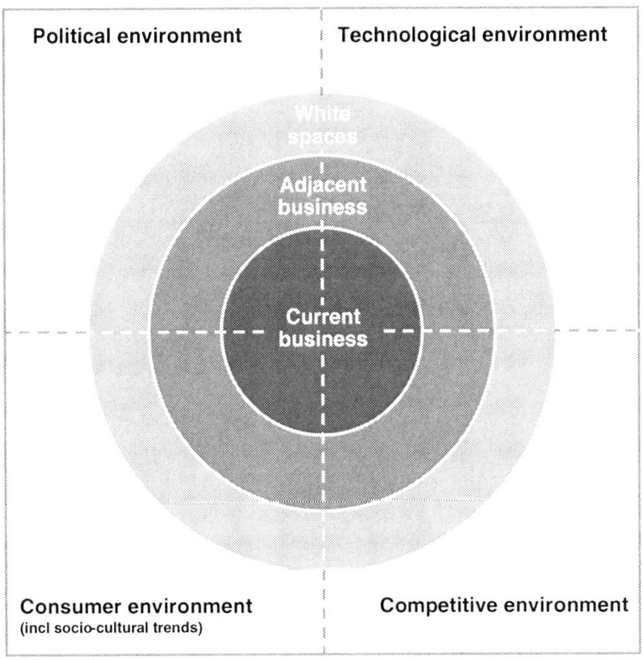

Fig. 4.2 Reach and scope of information usage

environment. For the reach, the concentric circles indicate the depth of scanning, reaching from *current business* and *adjacent business* to *white space*. White spaces are areas that currently seem to have no relevance to the company but which could breed disruptive changes that are difficult to perceive and to prepare for. The illustration can also help companies assess the current information usage of a company and visualize the improvement potential.

In addition to *reach* and *scope*, companies need to consciously choose an appropriate time horizon and appropriate sources of information. For example, companies operating in high clockspeed environments cannot rely entirely on the usual sources of information on technological change, such as patent data, because of the time lag of approximately 18 months between the initial discovery and the publication of the patent (Lichtenthaler 2002:386). Companies in high clockspeed industries should therefore rely more on information gathering through personal networks or research collaborations with industry partners and research institutes.

4.1.2.2 Method Sophistication

Whereas the capability area *information usage* describes the ability of a company to gather future-oriented information, the capability area *method sophistication* describes its ability to systematically interpret information.

Future research is focused primarily on establishing knowledge about method usage (Jain 1984:125; Burmeister et al. 2002:78) and giving recommendations to managers on which method to choose and in which context (Lichtenthaler 2005:388; Porter et al. 2004:287). Other scholars work on enhancing individual methods, such as:

- The scenario technique (Chermack 2005; Mietzner and Reger 2005; Van der Heijden 2005; Visser and Chermack 2009)
- Delphi technique (Ament 1970; Ono and Wedemeyer 1994; Rowe and Wright 1999; Rowe et al. 2005)
- Cross-impact analysis (Gordon and Hayward 1968; Weimer-Jehle 2006)
- Backcasting (Höjer and Mattsson 2000; Quist and Vergragt 2006)
- Gaming (Helmer 1972; Watman 2003; Oriesek and Friedrich 2003; Schwarz 2009).

For the maturity model, the aim is to find measures that capture the capability of the overall method portfolio rather than individual methods. Table 4.3 gives an overview of the four measures that have been chosen.

The first two elements (*match with context* and *match with problem*) assess how deliberately the methods are being chosen given a certain context (as discussed in Sect. 4.1.1) or a certain problem (e.g., an investment decision or the use of a certain technology for a future project). These elements have been included because several companies in our sample indicated that no deliberate choosing is in place and that methods are primarily employed because they have been used in the past and/or because the available skills make it possible to use them.

The other two newly proposed elements measure certain strengths of the method portfolio. The element *integration capacity* describes the capacity of integrating different types of information. Given the amount of data gathered and the timely and causal interdependencies of data gathered from different time horizons, different environmental areas (political, technological, consumer, and competitor environment), and different depths of the environment (current business, adjacent business,

Table 4.3 Elements of the capability method sophistication

Element	New	Description	Authors, year: page	Original name of element
(Overall)		Past research has primarily focused on identifying methods and establishing knowledge about frequency of usage	Becker (2002:16)	Data processing and analytical approaches
			Jain (1984:125), Burmeister et al. (2002:78)	Techniques used
Match with context	✓	Describes how deliberately the method is chosen, given a certain context		
Match with problem	✓	Describes how deliberately the method is chosen, given a certain problem		
Integration capacity	✓	Describes the usefulness of a method portfolio for integrating various types of information		
Communicative capacity	✓	Describes the usefulness of a method portfolio for communicating insights internally and externally		

and white spaces), this capacity can be expected to play an important role in the overall interpretation capacity of the company.

The element *communication capacity* describes the usefulness of the method portfolio for communicating information and interpretations internally and externally. This can be achieved with participation in the method, as is the case for example in roadmapping (Phaal et al. 2004a:45; Lichtenthaler 2008a:47; Petrick and Echols 2004:81; Lischka and Gemünden 2008:201), and by producing results that can easily be communicated, as is the case with methods such as the scenario technique, which produced an alternative future that is transparent and easy to understand by outsiders and thus easy to communicate (Schoemaker 1993:193; Chermack et al. 2007:379; Mietzner and Reger 2005:220; Van der Heijden 2005). In addition, some companies use specific mechanisms to communicate insights, such as making videos of lead customer interviews, which are presented to board-level decision makers (Jasner 2006:49).

4.1.2.3 People and Networks

Considering the great need for effective and efficient communication in a corporate foresight system, it can be expected that there is a need for strong internal and external networks. In addition, the informants observed that involving the right people is also essential to ensuring a high impact from the foresight activity. These capabilities of corporate foresight are captured in the dimension *people and networks*. Its elements are described in Table 4.4.

Table 4.4 Elements of the capability people and networks

Element	New	Description	Authors, year: page	Original name of element
Characteristics of foresighters	✓	Describes the degree to which characteristics of the foresighters meet the ideal characteristics	Wolff (1992:11) (identifies internal network, broad knowledge, and team player as key characteristics)	Characteristics of scouts
External network	✓	Describes the extent and intensity of external ties		
Internal network	✓	Describes the extent and intensity of internal ties		

The first element of people and networks measures the degree to which the *characteristics of foresighters* satisfy the desired characteristics. In the case studies, the informants pointed to five characteristics that they considered essential for successful foresighters:

- *Deep knowledge* in one domain, in order to understand how far a topic needs to be understood to come to conclusions
- *Broad knowledge*, to quickly access new information domains and relate them to one another
- *Curiosity and receptiveness*, to ensure the eagerness to capture external information
- *Open-mindedness and passion*, to ensure that issues outside the dominant worldview of the company are considered and disseminated
- *Strong external networks*, for ensuring access to high-quality information
- *Strong internal networks*, for ensuring the efficient diffusion of information throughout the company

In addition, the elements *external network* and *internal network* describe the extent and intensity of the external and internal ties of the company as a whole. In contrast to the internal and external network of the foresighters, these ties are built and maintained by the organization as a whole and/or by other employees individually. Whereas the external primary function of the network is to source and channel external information into the company, the internal network are crucial to bringing the foresight insights to the internal stakeholders and enabling the stakeholders to use the insights in ways useful to the company.

4.1.2.4 Organization

In the capability dimension *organization*, past research has focused on identifying organizational units that are responsible for corporate foresight and differentiated into various organizational settings, such as the corporate level, divisional level, and virtual structures (Becker 2002:11; Reger 2006:255–256). It has been hypothesized that to respond to discontinuous change it is important to foster linkages between units responsible for developing new products and units with complementary assets needed to commercialize the innovation (Taylor and Helfat 2009:718).

For the maturity model, the aim is to capture the ability of a company to systematically identify, interpret, and diffuse future insights, independent of the nature of the foresight units and the place where they are operating. To capture this ability, five elements are proposed, of which three build on previous research (see Table 4.5).

The first element, *mode*, describes the ways in which companies engage in foresight activities. Becker has differentiated it into top-down (i.e., top management requests an investigation) and bottom-up (i.e., foresight units scan the environment undirected and report emerging issues to the decision makers). One informant, who is the head of the strategic foresight unit reporting directly to the chief technology officer (CTO), explained that

> My boss requests that any time I identify a really disruptive technology I should go directly into his office and jump up and down on his desk until he listens to me.

In addition to the top-down and bottom-up differentiation, the *mode* says whether corporate foresight is carried out as a continuous exercise or is run as projects for investigating certain issues.

The element *integration with other processes* describes the number of processes that are linked to the foresight activity. The expected links are to R and D, innovation management, corporate development, marketing, controlling, and strategic management.

The last two elements have been proposed by Day and Schoemaker and have been only slightly redefined. *Accountability* describes the extent to which employees are responsible for detecting and acting on weak signals. *Incentives* describes whether rewards or bonuses are awarded to encourage future orientation and a wider vision (Day and Schoemaker 2005:147).

4.1.2.5 Culture

In the capability dimension *culture*, four of the five elements have been adopted from Day and Schoemaker (Day and Schoemaker 2005:147). An overview is given in Table 4.6. It should be noted that for culture only, elements have been chosen that are expected to have a direct influence on the corporate foresight capability of a firm. Elements relating to the corporate culture or the innovation culture have been excluded. The four elements derived from Day and Schoemaker are (1) *willingness to share across function*, (2) *readiness to listen to scouts and external sources*, (3) the *attitude of the organization toward the periphery*, and (4) the *willingness to test and challenge basic assumptions* (Day and Schoemaker 2005:147).

This research adds to the cultural dimension the element *informal communication*, which describes the role and effectiveness of informal communication in the diffusion of future-oriented information and future insights. This element was

Table 4.5 Elements of the capability organization

Element	New	Description	Authors, year: page	Original name of element
(Not used)		Which and what kind of unit is responsible for environmental scanning	Jain (1984:123)	Organizational responsibility of environmental scanning
(Not used)		Organizational setting in which foresight work takes place (corporate level, divisional level, and "lateral" or "virtual" structures)	Becker (2002:11), Reger (2006:255–256)	Organizational characteristics of foresight process
			Wolff (1992:11) (recommends positioning the scouting activity on the corporate level)	Characteristics of scouts
Mode	✓	Describes how companies engage in foresight activities. Differentiated into top-down vs. bottom-up continuous and issue-driven	Becker (2002:14) (differentiates only by bottom-up vs. top-down)	Determining information needs and core questions
			Krystek (2007:54) (recommends continuous undirected scanning)	Konstruktions-elemente Strategischer Frühaufklärung
Integration with other processes	✓	Describes the follow-up processes to which the foresight activity is linked		
Formal diffusion of insights	✓	Describes the role and effectiveness of formal communication to transfer future insights	Rollwagen et al. (2008:338) (provides a list of recommendations to enhance the impact of foresight work)	Criteria for improving impact of foresight studies
Accountability		Describes the extent to which employees are responsible for detecting and acting on weak signals	Day and Schoemaker (2005:147)	Accountability for detecting and acting on weak signals
Incentives		Describes whether rewards or bonuses are awarded to encourage future orientation and a wider vision	Day and Schoemaker (2005:147)	Incentives to encourage and reward wider vision

Table 4.6 Elements of the capability culture

Element	New	Description	Authors, year: page	Original name of element
Willingness to share across functions		Describes the degree of openness and inclination to share information across functions	Day and Schoemaker (2005:147)	Willingness of customer-contact people to forward market information Sharing information about periphery across functions
Readiness to listen to scouts and external sources		Describes the openness and inclination to listen to external sources of information	Day and Schoemaker (2005:147)	Readiness to listen to scouts on the periphery
Informal diffusion of insights	✓	Describes the role and effectiveness of informal communication for the diffusion of future insights		
Attitude of the organization toward the periphery		Describes the level of curiosity of the top management toward the periphery	Day and Schoemaker (2005:146)	The attitude of the organization toward the periphery
Willingness to test and challenge basic assumptions		Describes the degree of willingness of executives to challenge underlying assumptions	Day and Schoemaker (2005:146)	Willingness to test and challenge basic assumptions

highlighted particularly by companies with weaknesses in formalized processes but with a good track record of surviving and succeeding in times of discontinuous change.

Overall, the dimension "culture" can be seen as an important enabler for corporate foresight systems as well as to some extent a substitute for formal processes. For example, it can be argued that if a company manages to encourage (through cultural means) its employees to be open to external information and to diffuse it effectively throughout the company, then it can be expected that this will support strongly its ability to retain a competitive advantage in times of discontinuous change.

4.1.3 Impact/Value Creation

The research on corporate foresight lacks insights on impact and value creation. It has been shown that there may be several internal stakeholders that can be expected to profit from corporate foresight, particularly as regards the improvement in strategic decision making (Nick 2008:190), or by exploring new markets (Slaughter 1997:1) and new products and services (Becker 2002:18; Andriopoulos and Gotsi 2006:50). Many authors remain vague, expecting the impact of foresight to be an improvement in the ability of a company to respond to opportunities and threats (Krystek 2007:50) or allowing companies to respond to strategic change in a timely manner (Schwarz 2005).

More recently, Davis established a set of impacts on the basis of expert interviews. These impacts are still on different levels and thus difficult to relate to the activities in corporate foresight, but they help show that corporate has the potential to provide a wide range of benefits. The impacts identified by Davis are (1) broadening the horizon of top management, (2) identifying influencing factors on current and future business, (3) enhancing market understanding, (4) enhancing strategic focus and guidance, and (5) intensifying internal networks (Davis 2008:202–203).

Through the case studies, four categories of impact or value creation have been identified: (1) the *reduction of uncertainty*, (2) *triggering actions*, (3) *influencing others to act*, and (4) *secondary benefits*. This last category was created to describe evidence of value creation that has not been the initial aim of the foresight activity but that had a positive impact on the company. An overview of the categories is given in Table 4.7.

In the following Sects. (4.1.3.1–4.1.3.4), the impact category will be described in more detail. In each category, a table shows

- *Element*. The individual elements of the cluster
- *Description*. The description of the element
- *No. of references*. The number of quotes that have referenced the element
- *Quotes*. One or two sample quotes that led to the creation of the element

4.1.3.1 Reduction of Uncertainty

The first impact/value creation category is the *reduction of uncertainty*. In the category, four individual elements have been identified. The common attribute that led to the creation of the category is that none of the elements directly triggers a response. They are all designed to capture certain information and to make it available inside the company, without having a predefined process that would lead to actions being taken. The four elements of reduction of uncertainty are given in Table 4.8.

The first value creation element is *early warning*. Informants claimed that having the information of potential disruptions and communicating is itself valuable. One company regularly produces two reports that identify and discuss emerging technologies and new business models with disruptive potential. These reports are distributed throughout the company.

Producing a list of disruptive issues is seen as a value contribution even if this list is not directly linked to a follow-up process. Equally, identifying possible futures

Table 4.7 Impact/value creation categories

Element	New	Description	Authors, year: page	Original name of element
(Not used)		Describes who the "internal customer" of the foresight activity is: top management, middle management divisional units, or individuals such as researchers	Becker (2002:13)	Addressees of foresight
(Not used)		Describes the value from corporate foresight in enhancing the ability to respond to threats and opportunities and the enhancement of strategic decision making	Krystek (2007:50), Nick (2008:190)	Wirksamkeit der Strategischen Frühaufklärung
Reduction of uncertainty	✓	Measures the extent to which uncertainty in the environment has been made controllable		
Triggering internal actions	✓	Measures the number and value of actions that have been triggered in the company		
Influencing others to act	✓	Measures the number and value of actions that have been triggered outside the company (e.g., other companies, policy makers)		
Secondary benefits	✓	Describes impacts that are not initial aims of the activity but create additional value for the company		

Table 4.8 Impact category "reduction of uncertainty"

Element	Description	No. of references	Quotes
Early warning	Identification of weak signals on disruptive change	24	Naturally we don't want to experience such dire surprises as those faced by Grundig and Agfa [both companies filed for bankruptcy following discontinuous change]. It is important to learn from others to keep yourself from making the same mistakes[a]
Challenge basic assumptions and dominant business logic	Monitor the prerequisites for the success of the company	57	I need to continuously monitor my basic assumptions. For instance, I recognize that (1) the oil might be gone forever and (2) we are doing nothing else; and then I can deduct that (3) I should extend my business along the value chain or move into totally new business fields[b]
Trend identification, interpretation, and prediction	Identify emerging change that will remain stable for a certain time	54	[One task of foresight is] the identification of relevant trends. For example, the issue LOHAS (lifestyle of health and sustainability) and to start not with a concrete question, such as "How do we change our products?" But rather, "How big is the trend? How long will it last? How will it evolve? How do other industries respond? How do culture, politics, architecture, or the gaming industry respond to the trend?"[c]
Improve decision making	Provide information that allows decision makers to make better-informed and high-quality decisions	28	We operate in a market with a high level of uncertainty. If you provide information that can reduce this uncertainty, then this has value. By doing so, we can build our investment decisions on firmer ground

[a]Translated from German by the author. Original quote: "Wir wollen natürlich nicht, wie Grundig oder Agfa (Kommentar: Zwei Unternehmen, die durch externe Umbrüche insolvent geworden sind) solche bösen Überraschungen erleben. Man lernt ja von dem anderen, was man falsch gemacht hat, damit man das halt nicht widerholt"
[b]Translated from German by the author. Original quote: "Ich muss immer meine Grundannahmen prüfen. Also zum Beispiel wenn, 1. Das Öl vielleicht irgendwann ganz weg ist und 2. Wir im Moment nichts anderes machen, dann folgt natürlich 3. Ich muss mal sehen, dass ich mich entweder entlang meiner Wertschöpfungskette weiterentwickle oder in komplett andere Geschäftsfelder reingehe"
[c]Tranalsated from German by the author. Original quote: "Dann Scouting als Einsatz zur generellen Aufnahme von relevanten Trends in der Zukunft. Zum Bespiel das Thema Loha-Trend (Anmerkung LOHAS is an acronym for Lifestyles of Health and Sustainability). Und erst einmal gar nicht mit einer konkreten Fragestellung, wie die Übersetzung ins Produkt, sondern erst einmal, wie groß ist der Trend? Wie lange wird der anhalten? Wie prägt er sich aus? Wie gehen andere Industrien damit um? Wie geht die Kunst, die Politik, die Architektur, wie geht die Gaming-Industrie damit um?"

with the help of scenario analysis is expected to enhance the ability of the company to prepare for change. Such scenario-building projects are not necessarily linked to decision-making processes, but they are expected to help make future uncertainty controllable.

> An issue is that as a large tanker [tanker being a metaphor emphasizing the size and reaction speed of large companies], you offer a large surface for attacks. [Therefore,] generating knowledge about threats is an objective. What you do with this knowledge is a different issue[1]

To emphasize the logic behind implementing continuous scanning for potential disruptions, informants pointed frequently to examples of other companies that had to file for bankruptcy. Regarding the question of whether the scanning activities need to be linked to a follow-up process – which for instance reports the disruption to the executive board and proposes management actions – the informants expressed divergent opinions.

Some argued that given the limited time available on the executive board to think about the future, there is little chance that a regular meeting to discuss disruptions can be introduced. They claim that dealing with discontinuous change can never be a straightforward process. The recognition that a change indeed has disruptive potential involves challenging basic assumptions and opening up mind-sets, which are neither fast nor manageable in a process fashion. Therefore, trying to build such a process is doomed to failure. Consequently, foresight should only provide information, and it should not be linked to a follow-up process.

Others argue that without direct links to other processes, the insights generated by foresight will be ignored in the same way that the original weak signals on discontinuous change are ignored. Discussions of weak signals that may announce discontinuous change are both unpleasant and difficult to deal with, and thus are often pushed to the back of workshop agendas. These respondents conclude that either internal stakeholders are forced to deal with foresight insights or there is no chance that foresight works will produce any value.

The second element, *challenge basic assumptions and business logic*, was explained as creating value by showing the organization the limited robustness against future changes. The informants gave examples of foresight exercises being allowed to challenge the world view of top management by confronting them with future insights and alternative futures. Particularly for new product development projects or activities directed at the development of new business fields, it was judged important to frequently determine whether the basic assumptions on which the success of the development work depends are still valid.

The third element, *trend identification and interpretation*, has been quoted mostly on the level of macro trends such as an aging society, which predicts the growth of the part of the population beyond the retirement age. But some

---

[1]*Translated from German by the author. Original quote: query"Zum einen ist natürlich so das man als großer Tanker auch große Angriffsfläche bietet an möglichen Sachen. Wissen um mögliche Gefahren ist grundsätzlich, eine Aufgabe. Was man mit dem Wissen macht ist was anderes".*

informants pointed also to micro trends, such as the trend toward a lifestyle built around health and sustainability – so-called LOHAS (lifestyle of health and sustainability). Both macro and micro trends were used in the companies to challenge and extend current world views and possibly more importantly to trigger idea generation for new product development.

The fourth and last element of reduction of uncertainty, *improve decision making*, was explained in most cases as being based on the additional information being supplied by corporate foresight. The informants argued that by bringing additional information to the decision makers, the decision quality should increase, particularly by extending the time horizon of the impact of the decision.

4.1.3.2 Triggering Internal Actions

When talking of foresight, *triggering actions* is identified by most informants as the major value that they expect from a corporate foresight system. Companies that have experienced discontinuous change in their industry are looking for ways to enhance their ability to trigger responses early, avoid threats, and seize opportunities. The four elements of triggering actions have been identified by clustering impacts that have been generated for the same functional units. These functional units can be seen as the internal customer of the foresight activity and at the same time as the units responsible for acting on the basis of the foresight insights. The value will be created only if both the insight generation by corporate foresight and the insight usage by the functional unit are effective. An overview of the elements is given in Table 4.9.

The first element, *triggering R and D projects*, is linked to the innovation management or R and D department. For example, innovation management could use future exploration projects to identify needed capabilities and identify market opportunities. The internal customer of such a project explained that

> We have worked extremely hard to identify white spaces. We have not identified disruptions, but we have started many [R and D projects] where we have identified gaps.

The gaps are then the basis for planning R and D activities. In one example, a scenario analysis was used to identify the future of a certain product range in the year 2020. One of the consistent scenarios was then used to identify the needed technological capabilities, and roadmapping was used to plan the development path toward building the needed capabilities.

On the basis of the answers given in Table 4.9, a further differentiation can be made between impacts that have been triggered directly by a process link or indirectly by inspiring the initiation of innovation or R and D activities.

The second element, *change of current product portfolio*, is either linked to the marketing department or the innovation management, depending on the organizational structure and the definition of the functions in the company in question. In the quoted example given in the table, the informant explained that the output of two foresight projects has the introduction of new car models in two important markets.

Table 4.9 Impact category "triggering actions"

Element (department)	Description	No. of references	Quotes
Change product portfolio (marketing or innovation management)	Foresight activity sheds light on customers' needs and preferences and makes it possible to reorganize the product portfolio	73	[As a result of the foresight project] we have changed the product portfolios in China and the United States. In China we introduced four new cars and in the United States three[a]
Trigger R and D projects (innovation management)	Foresight activity leads to the creation of new R and D projects (a) directly by a process or indirectly by (b) inspiring project managers to start new products	97	(a) Process: We first did an extrapolation to the year 2015. We then planned backwards and concluded: Dear operational unit, in that [technological] field you have nothing. And this led to the initiation of new R and D projects to bridge this gap[b] (b) Inspiring: It is important to create images in the mind of the participants [the participants of the foresight project, who are from the divisional innovation management units]. Not a clear, predefined picture, but an image with intended fuzziness to inspire them to create new innovation activities[c]
Trigger new business development (corporate development)	Foresight activity helps to identify new business fields and triggers their exploration and development, including the acquisition of companies	76	We hired a foresighting company.... They showed us that in 20 to 30 years there will be wars over water supply. So water shortage is a big issue. And this was for us the initial trigger to say, OK, we will enter the market of water processing technologies and water treatment[d] In projects – in which we look at specific topics and the start-ups and companies in that field – we are closely collaborating with the foresight unit[e]
Support strategic decision making	Foresight provides information for strategic	65	[Our foresight report has created value by providing issues and insights for] the

(*continued*)

Table 4.9 (continued)

Element (department)	Description	No. of references	Quotes
(strategic management)	decisions and identifies new strategic issues		strategic discussion with the executive board[f] Roadmapping is used to push strategic recommendations into the divisions[g]

[a]Translated from German by the author. Original quote: "Wir haben [...als Ergebnis des Frühaufklärungsprojekts...] in China und in USA das Produktportfolio geändert. In China vier neue Fahrzeuge, in den USA drei neue Fahrzeuge"
[b]Translated from German by the author. Original quote: "Wir haben erst von heute bis in das Jahr 2015 extrapoliert. Und dann habe wir von der Zukunft zurück geplant und festgestellt: Aha, lieber Fachbereich, da [technologisches Feld] habt ihr ja gar nichts. Und das hat dazu geführt, dass wir neue F&E Projekte aufgesetzt haben um diese Lücken zu füllen"
[c]Translated from German by the author. Original quote: "Wichtig ist dass die unterschiedlichen Teilnehmer (Anmerkung: Teilnehmer des Frühaufklärungsprojekts, die internen Stakeholdern) ein Bild im Kopf haben. Aber nicht ein klar definiertes, vorgegebenes Zukunftsbild, sondern absichtliche Unschärfe um zur Initiierung von neuen Innovationsaktivitäten zu ermuntern"
[d]Translated from German by the author. Original quote: "Wir hatten da so eine Foresighing Company, (...) die haben uns aufgezeigt, dass es in 20 bis 30 Jahren Kriege um Wasserversorgung geben wird. Also Wasserverknappung ist ein riesen Thema. Und das war für uns die Initialzündung, dass wir sagten: Ok, dann gehen wir mal in den Bereich Wasserprozesstechnologie und Wasseraufbereitung rein"
[e]Translated from German by the author. Original quote: "In Projekten, wo wir gezielt irgendwelche Themen anschauen, welche Start-Ups, welche Firmen gibt es da auf der Welt, da sind wir eben eng mit der Frühaufklärung verwoben"
[f]Translated from German by the author. Original quote: "[Unsere Frühaufklärungsstudie hat als Wertbeitrag...] einen strategischen Dialog mit der Führung der Bank"
[g]Translated from German by the author. Original quote: "Die Roadmaps werden benutzt um strategische Empfehlungen in die Divisionen zu schieben"

The introduction followed a consumer and competitor foresight project that was conducted locally in the United States and China. With the help of the foresight insights, the company identified the need to change the customer segmentation and in consequence realized that the current product portfolio was misaligned to customers' needs.

The third element, *triggering new business development*, is linked to corporate development. In the given example, a company entered a completely new market. To do so, it had to invest heavily in R and D as well as buy external technologies and acquire other companies. Several informants emphasized the need to steer the foresight and business development activity at the top management level, preferably by one person. This was explained to be particularly important in large companies, because they tend to be focused extensively in their current business and on divisional structure, resulting in a systemic blindness toward business opportunities outside this structure. One head of a business unit explained how new markets outside the current structure – which is organized by market segments – may go unnoticed:

> Because of our structure along market segments, emerging new markets may be overlooked. Because for me it [the market for CO_2 capture and storage] is not an oil and gas upstream topic, but it is also not a downstream topic, it is also not a midstream topic, and it is also not a topic of industrial gas. And these are all our business segments. Therefore, some markets may be overlooked, and in consequence an organizational unit is needed that can take care of markets that are not dealt with today.[2]

The relationship of foresight, new business development, and mergers and acquisition is also highlighted in the second quote. The quote was taken from an example in which the corporate development unit used the foresight unit to help identify start-up companies that can be partnered with. The eventual goals were to acquire new technologies and new customer groups and to explore and develop new markets.

The fourth element, *support strategic decision making*, was identified through responses in which foresight insights were used to help strategic management. The first of the two explains the usage of the insights of a large scenario-based future exploration project. In this example, the company ran a 6-month project involving three people full-time and 30 as experts. The result was a set of four scenarios that described how the economy could evolve until 2020. The detailed result and implications were used to trigger a strategic discussion in the executive board and for presentations to key customers.

The second quote highlights how roadmaps have been used to plan the future and how they enabled the management to influence the activities of a business unit. The detailed planning and implementation tracking has been done collaboratively with innovation and strategic management of the business unit.

4.1.3.3 Influencing Others to Act

Influencing others to act has been identified as a third category of impacts. Previous research has emphasized that the future is uncertain and not predetermined; this means that it is constructed by individual actions (Blass 2003:1045; Gáspár and Nováky 2002:372–373). Multiple informants shared examples in which they were able to influence *other companies* or *policy making* by developing compelling visions or publishing future scenarios. More details can be found in Table 4.10.

The impact element *influencing other companies* was derived from an example of an automotive supplier. The informants reported that foresight activities had typically been carried out on the level of products and had mostly been aimed at identifying new technologies to enhance their products. The informant worked for a

[2]*Translated from German by the author. Original quote: "Durch unsere Strukturierung nach Marktsegmenten, wird dann so ein neuer Markt vergessen. Weil für mich ist das kein Öl und Gas Upstream Thema, es ist aber auch kein Downstream Thema, es ist auch kein Midstream Thema und das sind alle unsere Geschäftsfelder. Es ist auch kein Thema der industriellen Gase. Also dann vergisst man vielleicht mal einen Markt und deshalb braucht man auch Organisationen, die sich mit Märkten beschäftigen kann, die heute noch gar nicht behandelt werden".*

Table 4.10 Impact category "influencing others to act"

Element	Description	No. of references	Quotes
Influence other companies	Foresight activity makes it possible to influence other companies (often the customers and suppliers of the company running the foresight activity)	11	We don't want to be slow or a fast-follower, but a trend-setter![a] It [the foresight activity] has helped us a great deal, with the OEM (original equipment manufacturer), our customer, to open the door to strategic discussions. We talk with them about projects in the time frame 2010–2012 [4 to 10 years in the future at the time of the interview] before, but being included in their strategic planning was new [and was made possible by the foresight project][b]
Influence policy making	Foresight activity makes it possible to influence public opinion as well as legislation	29	We have the task of the executive board to get involved in the economic-policy and social-policy discussions[c] We have a corporate function that we call governmental relations, and there are various reasons why they are there. But first of all it is really to explain to the outside world what we are doing: to tell our story I would call it politician consulting. We frequently explain the impact [of new laws] on the individual company or the overall industry[d]

[a]Translated from German by the author. Original quote: "Wir wollen nicht Slow- oder Fast-follower sein, sondern Trendsetter!"

[b]Translated from German by the author. Original quote: "Es hat uns schon sehr geholfen, bei OEMs, bei unseren Kunden, die Tür für weitere Gespräche zu öffnen. Wir sind zwar im Gespräch für Projekte im Zeitrahmen 2010–2012, aber dass man uns in die strategischen Überlegungen des OEMs mit einbezieht, dass ist neu [...und wurde durch das Frühaufklärungsprojekt ermöglicht]"

[c]Translated from German by the author. Original quote: "Wir haben den Auftrag vom Vorstand, uns aktiv in die gesellschaftliche und wirtschaftspolitische Diskussion Deutschlands einzumischen"

[d]Translated from German by the author. Original quote: "Ich würde das Politikberatung nennen. Wir können die unternehmensindividuelle oder die branchenindividuelle Betroffenheit darstellen [die sich durch das diskutierte neue Gesetz ergeben würden]"

component manufacturer. The products included automobile parts such as axles and shock absorbers and parts of the car body.

In the new approach, they aimed at developing scenarios on the level of an entire car, taking the perspective of their customer, the original equipment manufacturer (OEM, the car company). This new approach was a 6-month foresight project with a budget of approximately 4 years of full-time equivalents. The goal was to develop scenario or future mobility concepts with a particular emphasis on driver assistance systems.

The outcome was a set of scenarios that were used to challenge and update the R and D roadmaps of both the OEM and the supplier. The scenarios and their implications were presented to the OEM using short movies and visualizations of R and D roadmaps. In the roadmaps, the supplier showed its ability to deliver the future products and demonstrated how these new products could be integrated into the future car concepts of the OEM.

As quoted in Table 4.10, the project allowed the supplier to initiate its first strategic discussion about future products with the OEM. The possibility of entering into such an intensive discussion about future roadmaps was judged an important value contribution for the supplier. It allowed it to collect early feedback from the OEM and thus decrease uncertainty. Getting early planning on product concepts translates into real cost savings, by preventing costly changes in product development and production planning. The internal customers, therefore, judged the large-scale project to have been a worthy investment, even though neither the internal customer nor the foresight manager made an effort to quantify the value creation from the foresight activity.

Another impact of corporate foresight is the ability to *influence policy making*. Companies operating in highly regulated industries have reported success here. For example, the head of a political foresight unit said this about the expected outcome of his work:

> We try to make the regulatory, social, industrial framework friendly or friendlier to our interest.

One informant from an energy company explained that since politicians deal with a large variety of issues, they have generally little knowledge about the domain or issue they are dealing with. As a result, they rely on staff units that gather and analyze information and on personal talks with involved stakeholders. As such a stakeholder, companies are also involved in what he calls "*politician consulting*," referring to personal talks in which the company can present background information on the new law and highlight its implications for their company as well as for the industry.

One concrete example that was mentioned is from the time when the European legislative bodies were still discussing the details of the emission trading scheme. This law was designed to allow governments to regulate emission levels by giving out permits or certificates. These emission certificates are then traded on stock-exchange-like markets and thus have a price that discourages companies from emitting and motivates them to cut their emission levels.

During the preparation phase of the emission trading scheme and the drafting of the laws, one important discussion was on how the initial amount of emission permits will be distributed to the emitting companies. The first value contribution of the corporate foresight was that it identified two major issues that would be of relevance:

- The consideration of so-called "early actions," which emitting companies have taken to reduce emissions prior to the introduction of the emission trading scheme
- The distribution of permits on the basis of two or three production benchmarks including either gas and coal and in case of three benchmarks also brown coal

The second value contribution of corporate foresight was to create an internal discussion to identify the impact of the issues. After having consolidated the internal discussion, the information was provided to policy makers through multiple personal talks and roundtable workshops. The first outcome was that the new law considered early actions, which reduced the cost of buying additional permits and thus allowed the company to save a substantial amount of money. The manager noted that

> It was a lengthy discussion and on some occasions also one that was rather unpleasant, but one that led the consideration of early actions to a satisfactory degree.[3]

On the second issue, the company also provided information about the impact of using only two benchmarks in contrast to using three:

> We told the political decision makers that the failure to use a [third] brown coal benchmark will cost our company around 200 million to 300 million euros.[4]

But on this issue, the political decision making process finally opposed the use of a third benchmark, and thus the outcome of the corporate foresight activity was unfavorable to the company. But the example illustrates the potential impact and offers a quantified value creation potential from political foresight activities.

4.1.3.4 Secondary Benefits

This fourth category, *secondary benefits*, contains impacts that can be characterized as by-products of corporate foresight activities. They yield some additional value, and in some cases, a value which is perceived to be higher than the value from the intended outcome. The head of a corporate foresight unit explained:

---

[3]*Translated from German by the author. Original quote: "Das war eine lange Diskussion und auch von der einen oder anderen Stelle auch keine spaßig Diskussion, aber sie hat zumindest [...] dazu geführt, dass die Early Actions in einem akzeptablen Umfang tatsächlich anerkannt wurden".*

[4]*Translated from German by the author. Original quote: "Die Nichteinführung, eines Braunkohlebenchmarks, haben wir der Politik auch gesagt, belastet die Braunkohlestromerzeugung unseres Unternehmens in der Größenordnung zwischen 200 und 300 Millionen Euro".*

> One value contribution is also helping our PR (public relations) and IR (investor relations) teams. If asked for the most important value contributions for us, I would probably say that it is the contribution for PR and IR, because it is our [the corporate strategic foresight unit's] life insurance, but challenging the innovation management guys is probably generating the most value for our company.

In his explanation, he raises the issue of corporate foresight insights being used to promote and enhance the external image of the company. Using foresight reports for communication purposes is a use that has been pointed out on 17 occasions and has been integrated into the value creation element *marketing and sales* in Table 4.11. Direct value creation has also been reported to be opening sales channels or allowing sales to portray the company as prepared for the future. For example, the internal customer of a future exploration project explains that the exercise has

> Helped us open doors for further talks with the OEM [original equipment manufacturer in the automobile industry, the customer of the company].

These initial talks have then been used to increase sales to this OEM and give their business relationship a long-term perspective.

The impact element *organizational learning* captures the extent to which foresight projects and reports channel knowledge into the company and promote common views and terminologies. From the quotes in Table 4.11, it can be observed that foresight reports are used as glossaries that make it possible to consolidate terminologies in a firm. Particularly in fast-moving industries and in large companies, divergent terms are used to describe the same emerging phenomenon. This has been said to slow down processes and increase the likelihood of redundant activities. Therefore, promoting common terminology can be regarded as an added value.

In addition, foresight reports are also used by employees as encyclopedias or glossaries to get informed about emerging issues. Particularly in the technological foresight field, multiple informants reported having the foresight report on their desks at all times. When confronted with new information, they use it to look up the keywords and the corresponding information on the emerging technologies.

Another value added is organizational learning, which occurs when a foresight activity forces internal experts and internal stakeholders to think about future trends and confronts them with insights from other foresight activities. Through intensive discussions, this confrontation – or provocation – triggers the creation of consolidated opinions and reduces the risk of double or unaligned work.

4.2 Maturity Levels

In addition to establishing a set of elements, building a maturity model involves defining maturity levels that make it possible to judge the level of proficiency among the different elements.

For our framework, we have used (in analogy to Kahn et al.) a four-maturity-level logic, in which the proficiency for each characteristic is described as poor or

Table 4.11 impact category "secondary benefits"

Element	Description	No. of references	Quotes
Public relations, marketing and sales	Foresight insights are used to enhance the image of the company for customers and investors	17	One value contribution is also helping our PR (public relations) and IR (investor relations) teams. If asked for central value contributions, I would probably say: It is the contribution for PR and IR which is our [the corporate foresight unit] life insurance, but challenging the innovation management guys is the most important
Organizational learning	Foresight projects and reports channel knowledge into the company and promote common views and terminologies	34	I (and I know many of my colleagues as well) am using the foresight report as a glossary to understand the terminology in our company The foresight report is used as an encyclopedia [throughout our company][a] At the end of the day, what we do is provoke. By doing so, we trigger a valuable discussion in the company, a discussion that is not directly linked to product development or to starting a new business field, but a contribution to the overall discussion in the company which produces a common mindset[b]

[a]Translated from German by the author. Original quote: "Der Führaufklärungsreport wird [in unserem Unternehmen] als 'Lexikon' genutzt"
[b]Translated from German by the author. Original quote: "Was wir machen, ist im Endeffekt ein Stück Provokation. Aber es kommt jetzt zu einer Diskussion, einer sehr guten Diskussion im Unternehmen, die nicht nur der direkte Produktentwicklung dient oder einer direkten Gründung eines Geschäftsbereichs, sondern es ein Beitrag zur Unternehmensdiskussion zur Entwicklung eines gemeinsamen Gedankenguts"

rudimentary (Level 1), better practice (Level 2), good practice (Level 3), and best practice (Level 4) (Kahn et al. 2006:108). Using the qualitative data from the case studies, each level and maturity level is described. Companies can then use these descriptions to rate their own proficiency in corporate foresight. In that way, a company that did not score a best practice can directly identify room for improvement by using the description of the next maturity level. The fourth maturity level can be seen as the maximum effort within the element and dimension (see Fig. 4.3).

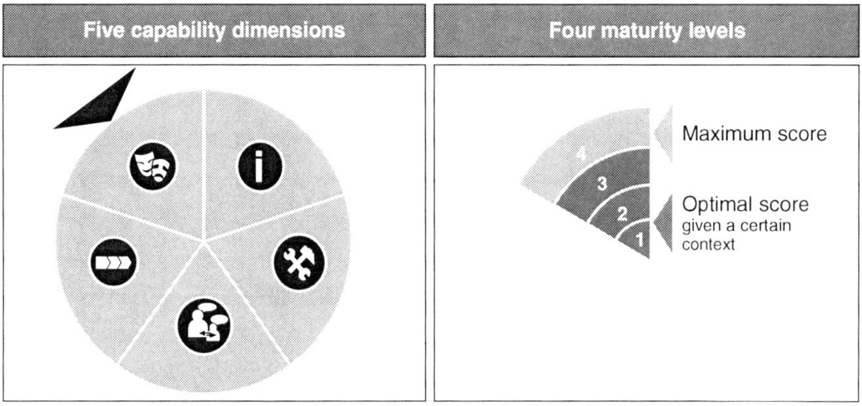

Fig. 4.3 Maturity model – levels

The maturity levels for each element have been defined using qualitative descriptions. In the following five paragraphs, these maturity levels are described and discussed, using the structure of the capability dimensions: information usage (Sect. 4.1.2.1), method sophistication (Sect. 4.1.2.2), people and networks (Sect. 4.1.2.3), organization (Sect. 4.1.2.4), and culture (Sect. 4.1.2.5).

4.2.1 Information Usage

In 2004, a special issue of the journal *Long Range Planning* investigated the ability of companies to detect and act upon weak signals. Based on a large variety of incidents in which large companies missed important changes in their environment, Day and Schoemaker conclude that companies typically focus on certain types of information and neglect other types in neighboring areas (Day and Schoemaker 2004b:140)

Winter explains this phenomenon as being a logical consequence of the success of companies:

> As organizations become more successful they tend to reinforce the sensing system that made them successful.

Winter concludes that the sensing systems are more adept at detecting changes in the current business environment than outside it (Winter 2004:165). Sensors, therefore, for adjacent business and toward white spaces will be underdeveloped, and the aim for any corporate foresight system should be to broaden the *reach* of *information use*.

Companies, therefore, need to build units whose aim is to continuously scan for weak signals in their environment. These units often report directly to the CEO, because he is ultimately responsible if an issue is completely outside current corporate structures:

Table 4.12 Maturity levels of the capability dimension information usage

Aspects	Level 1	Level 2	Level 3	Level 4
Reach	Scanning only in current business	Scanning in current business and areas of interest	Scanning in current and adjacent business	Scanning in current business, adjacent business, and white spaces
Scope	Focus on technology scanning	Scanning technologies and some other areas poorly	Scanning the areas of the environment to a different extent	Scanning in all areas (technology, political, competitor, customer, and socio-cultural environment)
Time horizon	Emphasis on short term	Short and medium term are taken into account (1–2 product life cycles)	Long, medium and short term are taken into account	Pro-active scanning in long, medium and short term in place
Sources	Use of few and easily accessible sources	Use of multiple easily accessible sources	Use of some restricted sources that provide a competitive advantage	Use of many sources that provide a competitive advantage

> There are people on the corporate level who identify what can be combined cross-divisionally and bring people together on cross-divisional projects and also identify what we call white spaces; they report directly to the CEO office.[5]

For proposing a maturity level, I therefore defined that only companies that scan at all depths (current business, adjacent business, and white spaces) attain the fourth maturity level. An overview of all elements and maturity levels in information usage is given in Table 4.12.

Concerning the scanning areas or the *scope* of scanning, various deficiencies have been reported. Jain showed – with a sample of 188 Fortune 500 companies – that of the economic, technological, political, and sociological environment, the economic environment is the most thoroughly scanned (Jain 1984:129) and the others need to be further developed. Others are more concerned with weaknesses in the consumer and political environment while reporting on strengths in the technological and competitor area (Becker 2002:15).

---

[5] *Translated from German by the author. Original quote: "Und in Ergänzung dazu gibt es Leute im Konzern, die sich damit befassen, was man geschäftsbereichsübergreifend voranatreiben kann, also sprich die Zusammenführung von Geschäftsbereichen für einzelne Projekte, oder auch zur Identifikation dessen, was wir" white spaces "nennen, und das ist in erster Linie auch aufgehängt bei unserer CEO Organisation".*

Among the case studies, many foresight activities have been identified that are directed exclusively at one specific field of the environment, such as the political environment:

> One thing that we also do, and we actually do it quite well, is, in some countries, depending on the changes in the government, we try to predict what the behavior of the government is going to be in the coming years.

Or exclusively at the competitive environment:

> The competitor analysis is an ongoing process.... We have a number of competitors, so we need to actually monitor the most recent developments of our competitors.... They [the competitive analysis unit] will analyze them [the competitors] as a company, and as part of that, they will identify what type of products these companies will actually bring out.

Many companies reported that the customer and socio-cultural environment are the biggest challenge of corporate foresight:

> And on the customer side it becomes even worse [trying to forecast and predict], because this adds the emotional factors, and these can only be integrated into the scanning with much difficulty, which does not mean that they should be neglected – quite the contrary. They need, in my opinion, to be pursued with even more intensity.[6]

The technological environmental scanning has been reported to be the best developed and was done in all companies, but to different degrees. One respondent explained how technology foresight is combined with corporate strategy:

> Normally, they are first doing a technology map, where they are watching what may be the main technology topics around the world. They are already highlighting the hot topics at a very general level. After that, they do as a second step a strategic mapping or a strategic feed to feed the foresight results into the general strategy.

Best-practice companies are expected to have scanning activities in all environmental areas, including technological, political, competitor, customer, and socio-cultural environment. Other authors also include areas such as environmental issues (Ruff 2006:281). But for our framework, these environmental issues are included either on the side of the competitor (if they affect the competitor's situation) or in the consumer foresight (if they affect demand).

A study conducted for the European Commission has shown that the *time horizon* of SF activities differs greatly, ranging from 2 to 30 years (Becker 2002:14–15). Some of that spread can be attributed to differences in the industry clockspeed and can be made more comparable by using the number of product life-cycles rather than years as an operationalization of time horizon.

Most participating companies conduct foresight work simultaneously on different time horizons but invest the greatest effort in the short term. There are only a

---

[6]*Translated from German by the author. Original quote: "Und auf der Kundenseite wird es noch viel schlimmer, weil da dann auch noch Emotionsfaktoren dazu kommen und die kann man natürlich ganz, ganz schwer überhaupt ins Beobachtungsfeld mit einbeziehen, was keineswegs heißt, dass man das deswegen nicht machen muss, im Gegenteil, man muss es glaube ich umso intensiver verfolgen".*

few examples of long-term foresight activities being conducted and succeeding – such as this case:

> We hired a foresighting company. . .they showed us that in 20 to 30 years there will be wars about water supply. So water shortage is a big issue. And this was for us the initial trigger to say, 'OK, we will enter the market of water processing technologies and water treatment'.[7]

The best practice is expected to be one that includes different time horizons, possibly assigning operational units to explore the short term, while the mid- and long-term future is explored by staff, strategy and innovation management units.

The cross-case analysis revealed a large variety of *sources of information*. An overview of sources is given in Table 4.13. Overall, companies operating in highly competitive environments have reported more often that they use sources that are not easily accessible and that are expected to yield a competitive advantage. Although it is difficult to say which source yields a competitive advantage, it can be recommended to regularly assess and enhance the portfolio of sources being used.

Best-practice companies use various means to tap into information which is inaccessible to their competitors. Deutsche Telekom, for example, created a worldwide network of technology and competitor scouts. These scouts are often hired exclusively, ensuring that access to crucial information is available to Deutsche Telekom alone.

4.2.2 Method Sophistication

After having gathered data, methods are used to process it and extract meaning. This is particularly important if large amounts of data have been gathered and if interdependencies are expected with information from different sources.

In the past, the most effort in advancing foresight methodology was invested by policy makers and associated research institutes. Larger initiatives include the Technology Futures Analysis Group (Porter et al. 2004:287) and the Millennium Project of the American Council of the United Nations (Gordon and Glenn 2003).

In recent years, new methods have emerged that are based on advances in information technology. For new and relatively unstructured business areas, methods have been developed that make it possible to create meaning in a collaborative fashion. Such a method or tool is a wiki – a software application that allows registered users to create, change, and organize content on Web sites in real time. Two companies in the sample indicated that they regularly use wikis to identify and

[7] *Translated from German by the author. Original quote: "Wir hatten da so eine Foresighing Company, (...) die haben uns aufgezeigt, dass es in 20 bis 30 Jahren Kriege um Wasserversorgung geben wird. Also Wasserverknappung ist ein riesen Thema. Und das war für uns die Initialzündung, dass wir sagten: Ok, dann gehen wir mal in den Bereich Wasserprozesstechnologie und Wasseraufbereitung rein".*

Table 4.13 Information sources and application areas

Source		Environmental area			
Name	Description	Competitor	Customer	Political	Technological
Analyst reports	For trends analysis and financial data	✓	✓	✓	✓
Blogs	Online journals written by individuals	✓	✓	✓	✓
External experts	External people with specific knowledge	✓	✓	✓	✓
Internal experts	Employees with specific knowledge	✓	✓	✓	✓
Internet	Searched with standard search engines	✓	✓	✓	✓
Journalists	Specific group of experts who have domain knowledge and are well-connected	✓	✓	✓	✓
Newspapers and magazines	Particularly industry-specific magazines	✓	✓	✓	✓
Personal contacts	To gather informal information	✓	✓	✓	✓
Regional representatives	Product, marketing, and sales managers in regions	✓	✓	✓	✓
Statistical databases	OECD, World Bank, International Monetary Fund and from governments	✓	✓	✓	✓
Benchmark talks	Talks with direct competitors on non-competitive issues			✓	✓
Conferences and fairs	Trade fairs and for example technology conferences	✓			✓
Patents, publications	Accessed by databases and analyzed with specific software	✓			✓
Research reports	From public research projects such as EU- or nationally funded projects		✓		✓
Risk capital market	Tracking start-ups and private equity companies	✓	✓		✓
Scouts	Dedicated internal or external people hired to gather and disseminate information		✓		✓
Supplier and customer talks	Contacts to companies directly linked in the value chain		✓	✓	✓

interpret weak signals on emerging issues. Such an issue was for example the phenomenon that has become known as Web 2.0 – a term used to show that information on the Internet is increasingly generated by users and no longer exclusively by the established news and media companies.

When such a phenomenon emerges, there are often rival terms to describe it. In the case of Web 2.0, similar terms include *crowd sourcing* and *user-generated content*. In such a case, the usual methods such as data mining – which makes it possible to search large databases by using keywords – will not be adequate, because they will identify only information related to one of the terms. Wikis can help by allowing multiple foresighters to simultaneously work on descriptions of the phenomenon and relate the phenomenon in an efficient way and thus create knowledge.

With the large amount of data available today on the Internet and other open-source databases (i.e., databases without usage restrictions, open to everyone), foresight has gone from having a problem gathering information to a problem interpreting information. A particular challenge is to identify the interrelation of information from different perspectives. When asked about the most important area of foresight (consumer, competitor, political, and technological), one respondent pointed out:

> I believe the most important thing is to be able to understand and handle the interdependencies between the different areas.... You can only get better at this [corporate foresight] by promoting the interplay of the different areas.[8]

Similar opinions were expressed by other companies and led to use *integration capacity* of the overall method portfolio as one of the key elements within the dimension method sophistication (see Table 4.14).

Methods characterized as being particularly effective for integrating from different perspectives are the scenario technique (Chermack et al. 2001; Godet and Roubelat 1996; Schoemaker and Heijden 1992; Schwenk 1984) and roadmapping (EIRMA 1998; Groenveld 1997; Möhrle 2004; Möhrle and Isenmann 2005; Phaal et al. 2004b).

Roadmapping is reported by many companies to be a key element for integrating multiple perspectives and facilitating future exploration among different units. One respondent who was asked to describe a typical roadmapping exercise responded:

> Product marketing, product management, development and industrial engineering gather and bring together all relevant aspects: financial, technical, "Which technology is mature?" and "What are the market expectations?[9]

---

[8]*Translated from German by the author. Original quote: "Ich glaube das Entscheidende ist, dass Sie das Wechselspiel zwischen diesen verschiedenen Feldern beherrschen. (...) Man kann hier nur besser werden, indem man das Zusammenspiel zwischen diesen vier verschiedenen Feldern fördert".*

[9]*Translated from German by the author. Original quote: Produktmarketing, Produktmanagement, Entwicklung, Industrial Engineering, die sitzen dann alle zusammen, gehen dann durch die Roadmap und bringen da alle Gesichtspunkte zusammen, die hier eine Rolle spielen, die betriebswirtschaftlichen, die technischen, "Welche Technologie ist reif?" und "Was sind die Anforderungen vom Markt?"*

Table 4.14 Maturity levels of the capability dimension method sophistication

Aspects	Level 1	Level 2	Level 3	Level 4
Integration capacity	No integration	Some integration methods are used	Integration methods are used but do not integrate all three dimensions	Methods integrate, scope, reach and time horizon of foresight
Communicative capacity	Methods don't support communication	Some methods are known that facilitate internal communication	Some methods are used that help internal communication	Methods help internal and external communication
Match with problem	No deliberate method selection	Some parts of the company choose methods deliberately	Most parts of the company choose methods deliberately	Methods are deliberately selected to match the business issue
Match with context	No deliberate method selection	Some parts of the company choose methods deliberately	Most parts of the company choose methods deliberately	Type of method and effort is consistent with context of company

These roadmapping exercises make it possible to identify future directions and consolidate opinions about how to align demand and customer needs with technology and product development. The outcome is a plan that shows critical milestones of products, services, and technology development. In comparison to traditional planning workshops, roadmapping workshops enhance the capacity of identifying and managing multiple interdependencies between the market and technology perspective.

Some companies have developed their own methods to be able to integrate weak signals from a wide scope, reach, and time horizon. One company in the sample uses an approach that combines the scenario technique with roadmapping (see best practice 5.3). The process integrates various internal stakeholders and external experts. In order to facilitate the dissemination and use of the results, different visualizations are used, among them pictures and videos.

Methods that use visualizations create the additional benefit of enabling effective communication. Pictures and videos help explain future visions much more effectively than reports and presentations. The additional benefit of methods with high communication potential is that they make it possible to validate future insights with a high number of internal and external experts and integrate many internal stakeholders into the foresight process.

The importance of integrating the stakeholders and allowing time for discussion was also highlighted by a foresight manager:

> There is always the question, how fast can you make such a foresight exercise? I believe that you could do it in 14 days. But this would not bring the desired result. The people responsible for bringing about the change in the company need to get familiar with

> alternative points of view. They need to talk with others. You will always need the buy-in of the management.[10]

In another company, insights from customer scouting in the United States needed to be transferred back to the corporate headquarters and R and D. This was done in two ways: First, by showing interviews with lead customers who have been filmed by customer foresight scouts, and second, displaying racks 2 m wide, which are filled with approximately 200 items that represent newly defined customer segments. These items include goods, clothes, personal belongings, and magazines typically associated with the customer segment. These racks were positioned in the R and D department so that the engineers would have a better idea about their target customers.

Given the importance of transfer of information and insights within a foresight process, the *communicative capacity* of the overall method portfolio has been judged crucial and is included as an element in the methods sophistication dimension.

The last two elements have been included as a consequence of the lack of deliberate choosing of methods. Almost all companies reported that the choice of methods was more a result of familiarity with the methods or habitual use. Only one informant reported on the deliberate choosing of a method:

> Concerning this method, we have thought how it would be possible to allow for more structure in the cognition process. In consequence, we have modified and adapted the methods to solve the problem at hand.[11]

Other companies reported clear mismatches between the problem – i.e., the foresight task – and the chosen method. For instance, one company was using SWOT (strengths, weaknesses, opportunities, and threats) analysis – a method usually in strategic management – for exploring a new business field, even though little knowledge about the future competitive environment and little knowledge about the company's own strengths and weaknesses existed. The informant himself said that using a method that takes into account the high level of uncertainty such as a scenario analysis would have been much more advisable.

For our benchmark, we expect best-practice companies to choose methods deliberately ensuring a *match with the problem* and a *match with the context* of the company.

---

[10]*Translated from German by the author. Original quote: "Es gibt immer Diskussion, wie schnell kann man so ein Frühaufklärungsprojekt machen? Ich meine, ich könnte Ihnen eines innerhalb von 14 Tagen machen. Aber das wäre nicht zielführend. Die Leute die Veränderungen im Konzern herbeiführen, müssen sich an die alternative Denke gewöhnen. Sie müssen Dinge durchdiskutieren, mit anderen Leuten reden. Sie brauchen immer den Buy-in vom Management".*

[11]*Translated from German by the author. Original quote: "Wir haben bei dieser Methodik überlegt, wie es möglich ist noch strukturierter denken zu können. Wir haben sie modifiziert und so adaptiert, dass wir diese Aufgabenstellung bewältigen konnten".*

4.2.3 People and Networks

When studying companies that have been affected by an external disruption, many researchers have found that the information about the disruption had been available. This was the case when Kodak was hit by the introduction of digital photography (Deutsch 2008:1). In the case study of Lucas and Goh, they attribute the inability of Kodak to respond to the disruptive change to bureaucratic organization and risk-averse middle managers (Lucas and Goh 2009:9). From their case study, it can be concluded that ensuring future insights – the product of interpretation of data – depends on two abilities of an organization: first, to channel information effectively through the organization to the managers who can make the appropriate decisions and take action, and second, to inform relevant internal stakeholders, ensuring their support in the process of changing the organization. To emphasize the importance of involving internal stakeholders, the informant explained:

> They [the foresight projects] are successful if they make it possible to integrate the future stakeholders into the development process.[12]

The capability dimension *people and networks* describes the ability to capture and channel information. It consists of three elements: *external network*, *internal network*, and *characteristics of foresighters*. An overview of the maturity levels is given in Table 4.15.

When asked to comment on the effectiveness of channeling information by means of IT-based systems or by networks, informants pointed clearly to the networks. One informant from an information and telecommunication technology company insisted that

> 80% of all information is channelled through people.

Another informant said

> Exploring the future is a dialogue.[13]

In consequence, the maturity model uses internal networks and external networks to measure the ability of the firm to channel information through people. More specifically, the informants pointed to the *external networks* for the ability to capture external data, while the *internal networks* were associated with the ability to effectively disseminate information and insights into the organization.

[12]*Translated from German by the author. Original quote: "Sie [die Frühaufklärungsprojekte] sind dann für uns erfolgreich, wenn sie es schaffen die späteren Stakeholder im Entwicklungsprozess mit einzubinden".*

[13]*Translated from German by the author. Original quote: "Die Zukunft zu explorieren ist ein Dialog. So sehen wir es!"*

Table 4.15 Maturity levels of the capability dimension people and networks

Aspects	Level 1	Level 2	Level 3	Level 4
External network	Some employees have formal and informal external contacts	Formal contacts are encouraged and in addition informal contacts are maintained by some employees	Formal and informal external contacts are encouraged	Building and maintaining a network of external partners is encouraged and perceived as important for every employee
Internal network	Some employees have formal and informal contacts to other units in the company	Cross-functional formal contacts are encouraged	Cross-functional formal and informal contacts are encouraged	Every employee is expected to build and maintain formal and informal networks to other units and functions
Characteristics of foresighters	Foresighters have deep knowledge in their domain	Foresighters have both deep and broad knowledge	Foresighters have deep and broad knowledge and are selected for being curious and open-minded	Foresighters have a strong internal and external network and deep and broad knowledge and are passionate, curious, and open-minded

Many informants also pointed out the importance of selecting the right people for the foresight activity. Overall, informants identified six desired *characteristics for foresighters*. An overview is given in Table 4.16.

The findings from the case studies are in line with the characteristics for technology scouts that have been collected by Wolff. He proposed the following as desired traits for technology scouts: to be a lateral thinker (curious and receptive), knowledgeable in the scouting field (deep knowledge), respected inside the company (strong internal network), cross-disciplinary orientated (broad knowledge), and imaginative (Wolff 1992:11). The suggestion that being curious and receptive is more important than understanding the company is also supported by Prahalad, who emphasized the role of foresight in challenging the dominant logic of the organizations (Prahalad 2004:176).

4.2.4 *Organization*

Within the maturity model, the dimension "organization" captures the ability of a company to translate information into future insights and insights into action in a structured way. To measure this ability, five elements are used:

Table 4.16 Desired characteristics of foresighters

Characteristic	No. of references	Quotes
Curious and receptive	15	"People who continuously read, people who look out the window" "You have to be curious. I mean, you have to be actively searching for things, not just waiting for information to come to you"
Open minded and passionate	11	"I mean people who are trying to do things in a very different way, who have a vision of the future, who are interested in looking for new things." "Passion is also important!" "Inventive of mindset"
Broad knowledge	13	"People who are very open, who have a broad knowledge of many things" "First of all, a good background in this industry, good engineers with some years of expertise, basically" "Strong industrial domain knowledge"
Deep knowledge	3	"You need to be certain at least on topics in order to be attractive to others. I believe that it will be difficult for you if you are able to only skim the surface on all the topics"[a]
Strong external network	13	"[Being] well connected, having a good contact network, being able to access information easily, being respected. It is always a give and take"[b]
Strong internal network	6	"The internal network is something that we have learned to value and certainly had not judged to be so important previously. The people [scouts] need to understand the need of the company they report to. They need to understand the language, and I do not mean English or German, I mean the terminology: How to describe and articulate issues?"[c]

[a]Translated from German by the author. Original quote: "Man muss schon, zumindest in einem Thema, Sattelfest sein, um auch selber wieder für andere als Netzknotenpunkt interessant zu sein. Wenn man bei allen Themen nur an der Oberfläche kratzt, dann habe ich das Gefühl, dass es eher schwer ist"
[b]Translated from German by the author. Original quote: "Gut verdrahtet, hat ein gutes Kontaktnetzwerk, kommt leicht an Informationen ran, wird auch respektiert, das ist ja immer ein Geben und Nehmen"
[c]Translated from German by the author. Original quote: "Internes Netzwerk, ist etwas was wir wirklich gelernt haben zu schätzen und sicherlich vorher nicht so hoch bewertet hätten, wie wir es jetzt tun. Die Leute müssen die Bedarfslage in dem Unternehmen, an das sie berichten verstehen. Sie müssen die Sprache dort verstehen, wobei ich nicht Deutsch oder Englisch meine, sondern In welchen Begrifflichkeiten drückt man sich da aus? Wie bringt man Sachlagen rüber?"

- *Mode* differentiates activities into how foresight activities are triggered (top-down or bottom-up) and how they are executed (issue-driven or continuous).
- *Integration with other processes* captures formal links between the foresight activity and follow-up processes.
- *Formal diffusion of insights* describes the extent to which formalized communication is used to channel information and insights.
- *Accountability* captures defined responsibilities for detecting and acting on weak signals.

- *Incentives* describes how employees are encouraged to scan the environment and plan for the future and how they are rewarded for their efforts.

An overview of the maturity levels is given in Table 4.17.

In our sample, not all companies follow a structured process. They differed in the *mode* of organizing their corporate foresight system. Some are primarily issue driven, conducting foresight work only when asked to by top management. Others have established a continuous scanning process that is designed to provide early warning as well as trigger innovation activities, but which is not directly linked to follow-up processes.

Many companies have reported that issue-driven or project-based foresight activities are the only way to ensure an impact. The primary reason is that only by joint projects with the internal stakeholders (the one's that after the insights have been developed are the ones that need to take the appropriate actions) it will be possible to trigger appropriate management actions. One of the informants who runs large foresight projects pointed out:

> You need the classic project dynamic. If you make a project [on your own] and you say we have found something with high potential and you – the strategic business unit (SBU) – need to do it now. Then you have first to deal with "not-invented-here" syndrome. Then you have to train missionaries, and then you have to convince these people.[14]

A similar problem is faced by continuous foresight activities. Many scholars have suggested that the ideal foresight system would have a permanent environmental scanning process and integrate the executive board into the process of interpreting strategic issues and translating them into insights that can be acted upon (Krystek 2007:52; Daft et al. 1988:123; Sawyerr 1993:287; Yasai-Ardekani and Nystrom 1996:187). Alas, this ideal setup was judged by all informants as unrealistic because of the limited time that is reserved for such kind of strategic discussion on the executive board. And if the members of the executive board are not integrated into the process, then the risk of also facing a "not-invented-here" syndrome has been judged to be very high.

In all cases the need for a close link to top management was emphasized. Particularly large foresight projects reported to be steered by the executive board or by strategic business units heads:

> The leading sponsor of the project was the executive board. In addition, the steering board included all the division heads.[15]

---

[14]*Translated from German by the author. Original quote: "Was Sie brauchen ist eine ganz klassische Projektdynamik. Wenn Sie ein Projekt machen und sagen, jetzt haben wir eine ganz tolle Sache und du bist die SBU, also mach das', dann haben Sie als erstes das 'Not-invented-here'-Syndrom. Dann müssen sie Missionare ausbilden, dann müssen sie die Leute massieren, das ist schlecht".*

[15]*Translated from German by the author. Original quote: "The leading sponsor of the project was the executive board. In addition the steering board included all the division heads".*

Table 4.17 Maturity levels of the capability dimension organization

Aspects	Level 1	Level 2	Level 3	Level 4
Mode	Foresight activities are top-management triggered and issue specific	Most foresight activities are issue driven	Continuous foresight complements project-based, issue-driven foresight	Both continuous and project-based foresight is triggered bottom-up and top-down
Integration with other processes	Technology foresight gives input to the technology strategy	Foresight triggers innovation management activities	Insights from foresight are used for strategic and innovation management	Foresight is linked to corporate development, strategic controlling, and strategic and innovation management
Formal diffusion of insights	Future insights are discussed on cross-functional board	Future insights are discussed as one element in functional boards	Future insights are discussed in functional and divisional boards	Future insights are integrated into most decision making processes and can be brought onto boards by the foresight unit
Accountability	No defined responsibility to detect weak signals	Responsibility is defined within technology domain	Responsibility falls to specific units	Every employee is responsible for detecting weak signals; foresight unit serves as information hub
Incentives	No incentives to reward wider vision	Rewards are available only if a financial impact can be identified	Incentives are primarily financial and are handed out within annual review	Incentives are recognition from senior management and financial rewards

For transferring insights and triggering management actions, the most logical way would be to integrate the foresight processes to other follow-up processes. In the sample the predominant *integration with other processes* was a link to *innovation management*, which leads to the initiation of new initiatives, such as starting a new R and D project.

The second most quoted link was to *corporate development*, in which corporate foresight helps to identify and explore new business fields and gives early warnings about threats to the current business.

The link of corporate foresight to *strategic management* was often quoted to be either weak or nonexistent. The reason was that the corporate strategy units are primarily issue driven and often need to respond fast. In consequence, the response of corporate foresight units may be too slow, and an issue transferred in a bottom-up mode toward strategic management is crowded out by issues requested by for example the board of directors:

> Issue-driven, good point! That's how it is. The strategy department has strong staff unit characteristics, i.e., they take on the hot issues, work on them, and then off to the next.[16]

In Level 4 companies, it would be expected that the integration with other processes would be extensive in order to use the full potential of the future insights. The major functions and processes to which a linkage has been reported are innovation management, corporate development, strategic management, and strategic controlling.

In addition, foresight activities are also linked to the market-driven division to validate their current business and suggest future directions. These links are generally not by means of a process but by a *formal communication channel for the diffusion of insights*. Such channels include regular participation on boards, such as monthly technology circles and/or foresight reports on request. For a best-practice company, it is expected that formal communication would include push-and-pull mechanisms and the integration of foresight into decision making processes.

Further organizational characteristics are *accountability for sensing weak signals* and *incentives to reward a wider vision*. In best-practice companies, the accountability and incentives are expected to include not only the SF unit, but all employees. In such a company, the foresight unit would serve as a hub for future insights and would facilitate and conduct large-scale foresight projects. Making all employees accountable and providing incentive schemes to reward the detection of weak signals are particularly important for complex and high clockspeed environments:

> Considering the high number of issues and products and the size of the region which I am responsible for, it is impossible to do it [scanning for emerging issues] alone. In my opinion, it would be impudent to say that you can do that all here from Brussels. On the contrary, this is a process that needs to involve the whole company.[17]

4.2.5 Culture

Whereas the advancing proficiency in the first four dimensions will enhance both the identification of insights and their use, culture will enhance mostly their use and help trigger appropriate actions. The five elements of the capability dimension culture are shown in Table 4.18.

---

[16] *Translated from German by the author. Original quote: "Guter Punkt! Genau so ist es! Die Strategieabteilung hat stark einen Stabscharakter, d.h. die nehmen halt die heißesten Eisen und versuchen die dann zu schmieden und dann ab zum nächsten".*

[17] *Translated from German by the author. Original quote: "Bei der Vielzahl der Themen, und der Vielzahl der Produkte und auch der Größe der Region die ich zu verantworten habe kann man das alleine gar nicht. Das wäre, glaube ich, vermessen zu sagen, das könnten wir hier alles von Brüssel aus mache. Also ganz im Gegenteil, das ist ein Prozess, der letztendlich das ganze Unternehmen mitnimmt".*

Table 4.18 Maturity levels of the capability dimension culture

Aspects	Level 1	Level 2	Level 3	Level 4
Willingness to share across functions	Poor: Information is ignored and hoarded	Exchange of information is rare and happens only in predefined formal channels	Exchange of information occurs on various levels but mostly in formalized channels	Excellent: Ongoing information sharing on many levels
Readiness to listen to scouts and external sources	The organization is closed. Contacts with the outside are discouraged	Some external personal contacts are called upon, but gathered insights are disguised as coming from the inside	Personal contacts are regarded as valuable. Few have a variety of external contacts	The organization is open. Building and maintaining an external network are encouraged
Informal communication	Poor: No informal communication	Limited informal information across functions	Informal communication is encouraged	Future insights are diffused effectively and reach the relevant decision makers through informal communication
Organization's attitude toward the periphery	Limited and myopic: few people care	Some people are looking into the periphery, but they are not known and called upon	Some people are looking into the periphery, they are known but not called upon regularly	Active and curious: Scanning the periphery is commonplace
Willingness to test and challenge basic assumptions	The basic assumptions are neither known nor made transparent	Some basic assumptions are known but not challenged	There is a good understanding of basic assumptions and they are tested	Basic assumptions are explicit, much talked about, and frequently challenged

The lack of *willingness to share across functions* is often the most important obstacle blocking the dissemination of foresight insights. As was argued earlier, the successful interpretation of weak signals can often be achieved only by a collaborative effort. In consequence, companies aiming for the fourth level in the cultural dimension should work on creating trust and motivating for ongoing information sharing on multiple levels.

The *readiness to listen to scouts and external sources* is an important prerequisite for using information from SF activities, as most insights have sources outside the company. The lack of this readiness is also an important barrier to corporate foresight. A similar phenomenon has been investigated in innovation-management research. It has been shown that groups that work together for a long time continuously decrease their communication and collaboration with external colleagues (Katz and Allen 1982:7). Companies that have a long track record of working in an isolated fashion should therefore be alert to this threat and work on ways to encourage the building and maintaining of external networks.

The element *informal communication* measures the role and effectiveness of informal communication for the diffusion of future insights. For companies emphasizing the cultural approach to corporate foresight, this element is crucial for transferring information and insights to decision makers and ultimately taking appropriate actions. In companies where this element is well-developed, the openness to talk to anybody is often expressed like this:

> All [the communication] is extremely cooperative, open, and direct. This I strongly believe. And now I am repeating myself, but I am totally convinced that this is an important factor contributing to our success.[18]

In addition to the individual tendency to build networks to outside sources, the *attitude of the organization toward the periphery* has to be influenced in a way that triggers a continuous scanning of the environment by all employees.

Willingness to test and challenge basic assumptions is a major role of foresight, and Blackman and Henderson point out the importance of double-loop doubting for foresight. They emphasize that it is important not only to challenge basic assumptions but also to challenge the underlying mental models that are used to build consistent expectations about the future (Blackman and Henderson 2004:263).

Such crucial expectations or assumptions are made in every investment decision, sometimes on the basis of sound data and in other cases on the basis of intuition. In order to generate value from foresight activities, there must be an internal demand for it, and decision makers need to be encouraged to make their basic assumptions explicit, track them, and challenge them frequently.

4.3 Usage Logic

Past research has two definitions of corporate foresight. A narrower view defines corporate foresight as a process executed by a dedicated team and linked to other functions and processes, such as strategic management and innovation management (Becker 2002:7; Burmeister et al. 2004b:12; Müller 2008:25). The wider definition of corporate foresight defines it as an organizational ability (Slaughter 1999:287; Tsoukas and Shepherd 2004b:10). This research follows the second definition and understands corporate foresight as an organizational ability that allows for the identification and assessment of discontinuous change, triggering management actions and ultimately ensuring the long-term survival of a firm.

---

[18]*Translated from German by the author. Original quote: "Alles [die Kommunikation] ist extrem kollegial, extrem offen und extrem direkt. Das ist, glaube ich wirklich. Und jetzt wiederhole ich mich, aber ich bin fest davon überzeugt, dass das ein ganz großer Faktor ist, der zu unserem Erfolg beiträgt".*

4.3.1 The Trade-Off Between Structure and Culture

In consequence, the understanding of this research includes any capability that allows the company to survive in the light of discontinuous change. Through cross-case analysis, two directions for building high corporate foresight ability have been identified:

- The *structured* approach, in which corporate foresight is a task that is executed according to a process by dedicated units and in which the response to discontinuous change is achieved by linking the foresight process to other corporate functions through follow-up processes.
- The *cultural* approach builds on involving a much larger proportion of employees and making them accountable for detecting and responding to weak signals on discontinuous change. The organizational reaction is not triggered by dedicated foresight and follow-up processes but through traditional processes such as new-business development processes and corporate entrepreneurships, in which individual employees are motivated to take the initiative to explore new business fields.

The head of the global research centers of one company explains the trade-off between the *structural* and *cultural* approach like this:

> To explain that a little bit from the organizational perspective: We do not have a staff unit that is full-time dedicated to it [strategic foresight]. Everyone in this building has it in his job description to look outside for change.[19]

In the definition of the maturity model, I aim to capture both directions by including both structural and cultural elements. Figure 4.4 shows the elements that reflect the two directions.

It can be seen that the *structural* approach is composed of the dimensions: *information usage*, *method sophistication*, *people and networks*, and some elements of *organization*. The *cultural* approach includes all elements of the *culture* dimensions, and from the *organization* dimension come the elements accountability and incentives.

If corporate foresight abilities can be built with either cultural or structural elements, then the overall corporate foresight ability of a firm can be represented in a diagram with two axes: the *culture* axis, on which all elements of the cultural approach are scored, and the structure axes, on which all elements of the structural approach are scored. Combining the two axes creates a corporate foresight ability index with two dimensions.

Figure 4.5 shows this index, which can also be used to identify four idealized cases, which were given the following names:

[19]*Translated from German by the author: Original quote: "Um mal ein bisschen etwas organisatorisch zu erklären an dieser Stelle. Wir haben keine Stabsstelle, die das hauptamtlich macht. Alle die hier im Gebäude sind haben ihrer Job Description nach andere Aufgaben als jetzt quasi nach außen zu gucken, was passiert denn da so".*

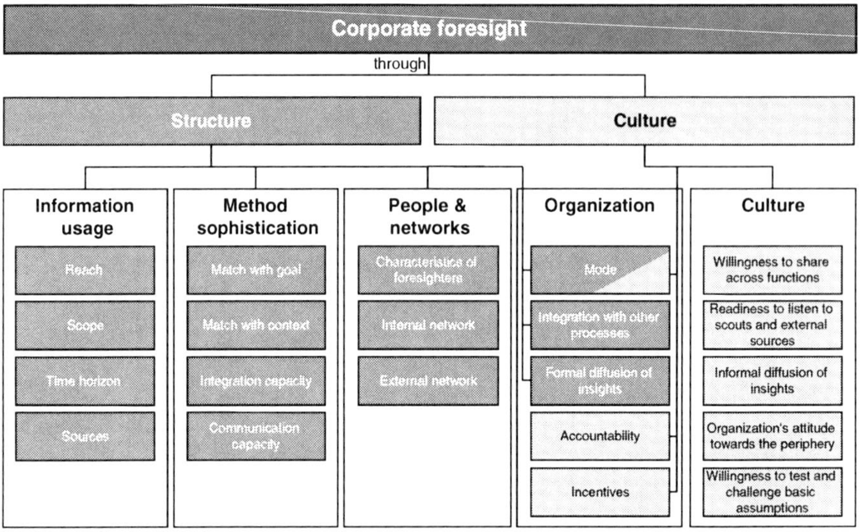

Fig. 4.4 Elements of the structural and cultural approach

- The *Foresight Company*, for practices that build strongly on cultural elements and involve large parts of the employees of the company.
- The *Hyperactive*, for companies which are strong on both structural and cultural elements. A case that is not expected to be encountered, because the effort would be too high, and formal and informal processes would be expected to clash frequently, when future insights are generated through the two ways simultaneously.
- The *Ignorant*, for companies that are strong neither in the structural nor in the cultural dimension and thus are expected to lack the ability to succeed in times of discontinuous change.
- And the *Systematic Foresighter*, for companies that are strong in the structural elements of corporate foresight, such as having formalized processes, strong method portfolios, and strong information usage.

How the cultural can substitute for the structural elements was also commented on by a foresight manager:

> What I mean by expert network is also that you actually do not need to analyze electronic information sources, you don't need future research. If every employee – and we have about 10,000 to 20,000 employees in R and D, who are travelling around the globe, and everyone has contacts – lives it [foresighting and scanning the environment] and aims at transferring [insights], then you don't need this whole process.[20]

[20]*Translated from German by the author. Original quote: "(...) man braucht letztlich keine Zukunftsforschung. Wenn jeder Mitarbeiter selber das verkörpert, und letztlich jeder von uns, und wir haben vielleicht so 10.000, 20.000 in der F&E. Wenn die weltweit unterwegs sind und jeder hat irgendwo Kontakte weltweit und wenn man das auch wirklich explizit lebt und auch transferiert, dann braucht man diese ganzen Prozesse nicht".*

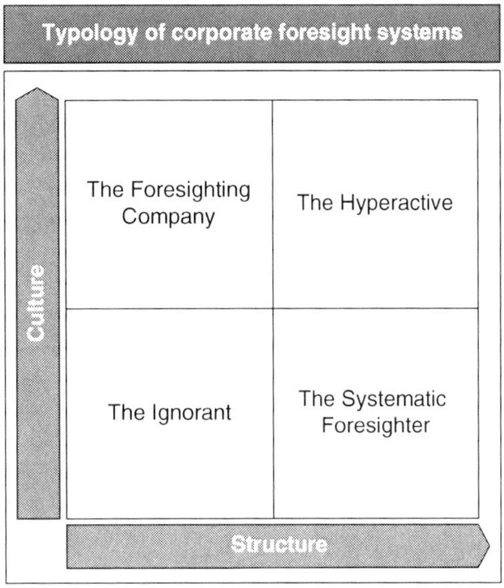

Fig. 4.5 Theoretical types of foresight practices

The conclusion is that companies may have a choice of which of the two approaches they want to use to build their corporate foresight system. In the sample of case studies, none of the company was following only one of the two possible ways in a clear fashion. On the one hand, respondents from companies dominated by the structural approach pointed out that they feared that the individual employee is being discouraged from scanning the environment, because the impression is given that foresight is a central function exclusively performed by dedicated units. On the other hand, companies that followed more the cultural approach with incentives in place to encourage every employee to scan for weak signals in the environment still had formalized foresight processes feeding, for example, into the strategic planning or innovation process.

4.3.2 *Process Dimension*

In the interviews, the respondents repeatedly emphasized the need to establish a process understanding in order to implement corporate foresight. I therefore aimed to link the maturity model to the process dimension.

In 1984, Daft and Weick proposed a process model which was designed to guide organizational interpretation of the environment. It consists of three steps: (1) *scanning*, or data gathering, (2) *interpretation*, where data is given meaning, and (3) *learning*, where the organization takes action (Daft and Weick 1984:286). By following these steps, organizations can translate weak signals on emerging change into managerial actions. In our research, we used the model of Daft and Weick as a guiding frame and aimed to validate its applicability to studying and designing corporate foresight systems.

Through cross-case analysis, we identified five relevant barriers that correspond to the *five procedural barriers* to corporate foresight:

- Change is not detected by organizational sensors
- Change is not judged as relevant by foresighter
- Decision makers are not convinced about relevance of change
- Response strategies are not planned and/or decided
- Responsible persons for acting are not convinced and prevent change

Asking the informants about their activities to overcome these barriers made it possible to develop an extended five-step process model (see Fig. 4.6). For each barrier, the process model shows the activity and corporate foresight capabilities that are needed to surmount it. For example, to prevent external change from going undetected, organizations need to ensure that they (1) scan the entire environment, (2) define accountabilities for sensing weak signals, (3) hire and develop foresighters with ideal characteristics, and (4) promote the four characteristics of a corporate culture supportive of "corporate foresight." The process model implies that a high level of corporate foresight capabilities increases the probability of successfully surmounting the barriers.

When comparing our model with the conceptual model of Daft and Weick, two new steps have been introduced. While *identify*, *assess*, and *act* are similar in the old model, *convince* and *plan* are new. Their introduction is a result of the emphasis of informants that failure to translate weak signals into actions is often a result either of a failure to convince decision makers or a failure to convince the responsible persons to act (steps 3 and 5).

Most informants agreed that *identifying* emerging change is not the primary challenge. Organizations generally felt confident that knowledge about major

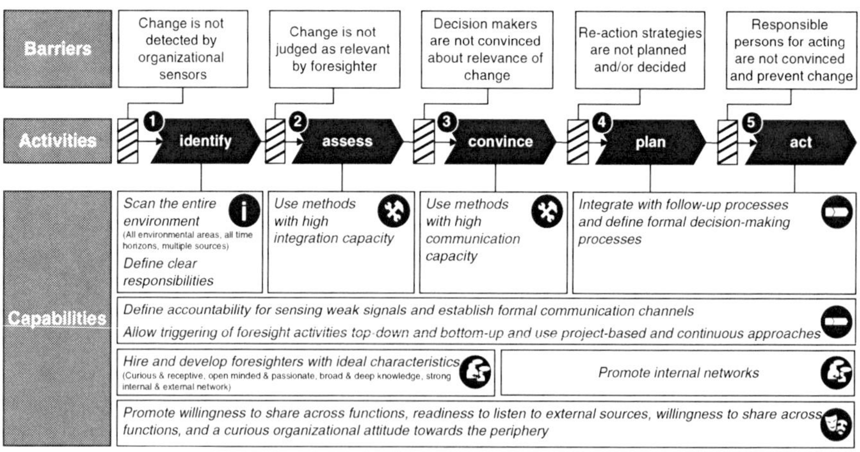

Fig. 4.6 Procedural barriers and capabilities of corporate foresight

changes exists in the company. All organizations in our sample that had dedicated foresight units expressed confidence that these units are able to detect all major changes. Equally optimistic was the judgment on their ability to *assess* importance and the potential impact of change. Informants reported on a variety of methods that were used to support the interpretation process and that ensure that the emerging change is well understood.

But many companies stated that even though change is successfully identified and interpreted, they fail to *convince decision makers* about its relevance. This failure often resulted in strategic issues being neglected. Companies that reported having little trouble getting the buy-in of senior management reported providing for a high level of participation of decision makers.

The *planning* step was considered to be comparably easy and straightforward. Generally speaking, for each emerging change whose relevance has been confirmed by senior management, a response strategy is developed. But it was emphasized that the success of this step should not be judged by planning quality but rather by the success of the execution of the plan. Informants provided many examples of plans not being executed because the buy-in of responsible persons has not been secured. Therefore, as in the third step, the success of the fifth step depends on ensuring a high level of participation of stakeholders in the preceding step.

To further validate the process model, it is useful to make a careful appraisal of its explanatory value in the Kodak case. When digital cameras made their appearance on the market in the early 1980s, Kodak not only knew about the change, but it had even developed its own digital sensors 5 years earlier. Kodak also knew about the possible disruptive potential of a shift toward digital photography. That means that in the process model, steps one through four had been taken.

Top management was convinced that digital photography was a substantial threat and that counteracting the threat required radically changing the company. But top management failed to convince middle management (i.e., the people responsible for executing the strategic change) that the threat is serious, that restructuring of the old business would not save the company, and that a new business needed to be built in the new field of digital photography (Lucas and Goh 2009:54).

The Kodak example thus provides an additional argument for the extension of the process model and at the same time emphasizes the importance of developing capabilities to surmount the barrier of convincing internal stakeholders.

4.3.3 Usage Procedure

When using the maturity model to design or enhance a corporate foresight system, it is important to understand that not all companies should aim at attaining the maximum in each element of each capability dimension. In doing so, the company would invest too much effort and potentially slow down other processes in the company. *The aim should rather be to strive toward the optimum level given a certain context.*

To identify the optimal design for a corporate foresight system, the maturity model proposes that companies choose

1. An *overall target maturity level*
2. A *structural* or *cultural approach*
3. *Maturity levels* for *individual capabilities*

Following these three steps requires the company to make an assessment of its context using the elements that have been presented in Sect. 4.1.1. In the three steps, different context elements will be the basis for recommending design characteristics for the corporate foresight system.

4.3.3.1 First Step: Choosing the Overall Maturity Level

In the first step, the choice of the *overall target maturity level* is influenced by the context elements: *company size*, *nature of strategy*, *complexity of the environment*, and *industry clockspeed*. Table 4.19 can be used as a guide to choose the overall maturity level. In the first two columns, the context elements are given. The last two columns show the design recommendation.

It can be seen that for a *large company*, the maturity level is recommended to be high. The logic is that the larger the company, the more it is preoccupied with internal processes rather than with the outside world. This was pointed out by multiple respondents, who said that the dominance of internal processes prevents systematically innovative initiatives and responses to discontinuous change. In addition, large companies form stable, self-reinforcing systems. Therefore, an internal customer pointed out, a high effort of corporate foresight is crucial to breaking up the stable system and planting the seeds of change. He explained that the goal of corporate foresight should be to

> Wake people up and show them things outside their view of the world.[21]

For the element *nature of strategy*, the maturity model follows Porter's generic strategies:

- *Focus strategy*, i.e., targeting a specific or niche market
- *Cost leadership strategy*, i.e., copying other products or services and offering them at lower cost
- *Differentiation strategy*, i.e., aiming to be the innovation or quality leader with superior products or services (Porter 1980)

[21]*Translated from German by the author. Original quote: "Wachrütteln, Dingen außerhalb des eigenen Weltbildes zeigen".*

Table 4.19 Design guide for the overall maturity level

If context		Then capability should be	
Element	Operationalization	Dimension (element)	Design recommendation
Company size (high)	Revenue Number of employees	Overall	High maturity level
Nature of strategy	Differentiation strategy	Overall	High maturity level
	Cost leadership	Overall	Medium maturity level
	Focus strategy	Overall	Medium maturity level
Complexity of environment (high)	Industry, channel and market structure Enabling technologies Regulations Public visibility of industry Dependence on public funding and political access Dependence on global economy	Overall	High maturity level
Industry clockspeed (high)	Rate of introduction of New products New processes New organizational structures	Overall	High

For the maturity model, it is assumed that companies following a focus strategy and a cost leadership strategy will need overall a medium maturity level and companies with a differentiation strategy need a high maturity level. Companies with a differentiation strategy were said to need to constantly scan for superior technologies, products, services, or business models as well as for substitution products and disruptive technologies. Cost leaders can put less effort into foresighting, as they can follow the innovation leader and need only to scout for changes affecting their production cost. Companies following the focus strategy have a narrower market and thus a medium maturity level can be expected to be adequate.

The logic of the recommendation for firms in *complex environments* and *high clockspeed industries* is straightforward. Both context factors imply a high level of uncertainty and thus generate the need for powerful corporate foresight systems and thus high maturity levels.

4.3.3.2 Second Step: Choosing Between the Cultural and Structural Approach

After having chosen the overall target maturity level, a company needs to decide in the second step whether it wants to emphasize the *structural* or the *cultural approach* to corporate foresight. For this choice, no clear recommendation has emerged from the case studies. As was explained in the previous Sect. (4.3.1), none

Table 4.20 Design guide for choosing between cultural and structural approach

If context		Then approach should	
Element	Operationalization	Emphasize	Reason
Corporate culture	Empowering the individual (high)	Cultural elements	Individuals starting their own innovation initiatives and reaching top management attention quickly is the fastest way to respond to discontinuous change In such an environment the cultural capabilities effectively promoted the impact of CF

of the companies had foresight practices that were purely composed of elements from the cultural or structural dimensions. Respondents from companies building more on the *cultural elements* claimed that the reason is a good match to their corporate culture that is open and supportive and aimed at empowering individual initiative. It can therefore tentatively be concluded that firms with such a corporate culture should be able to establish strong cultural capabilities for corporate foresight. This logic is also given in Table 4.20.

The logic was derived from a company at which every respondent pointed at the effectiveness of the company's desired traits, which they were looking for in every employee and which were used for performance assessment in the annual review of the employees. Two of these traits were "external focus" and "imagination and courage."

In the personal annual review, every employee has to comment on how he or she intended to develop and use these traits and to explain the extent to which this has added value to the company. Every respondent from this company agreed that new initiatives from individuals receive strong support and can be brought effectively to the attention of top management in a timely manner.

The head of strategic marketing explained the effect of reviewing these traits regularly during the annual performance review:

> People are always visible, and whether you are on a team or you are a manager, there are tools to do the performance review, and there is a lot of focus on growth.

A project manager added that the openness to listen to people is the key to empowering the individual. For his company he explained that

> The organization is very open toward people who come and say, 'I've heard something. Can we not change the way we do it?' Or 'I believe this to be interesting [for our company].' In such cases, they will get attention.[22]

[22]*Translated from German by the author. Original quote: "Die Organisation ist sehr offen dafür auch wenn von unten einer kommt und sagt 'ich habe das und das gehört, kann man das nicht anders machen?' oder 'wäre das und das interessant?', dann wird dem auch zugehört".*

Companies building more on the *structural elements* seemed to rely generally more on formalized processes than on individual initiatives and open communication. Their performance relies on clear responsibilities. They typically follow the logic that a task should always be executed by the person who is best qualified, thus arguing that foresighters should do the foresighting and business managers should run the business operations. Companies building on individual empowerment build more on the logic that the performance can be maximized by giving the task to the employee who is the most motivated.

Thus it can tentatively be concluded that it can be recommended to companies with corporate cultures built on personal empowerment to emphasize the cultural capabilities and companies with corporate cultures built on clear processes and clear responsibilities to favor structural elements.

4.3.3.3 Third Step: Choosing Maturity Levels for Individual Capabilities

In the third step, the *maturity levels* for *individual capabilities* are chosen. From the cross-case analysis, it was concluded that customizing the corporate foresight system should be done only in the capability dimensions *information usage* and *method sophistication*. This conclusion follows two arguments: First, the case studies indicated no clear pattern of interdependencies between context and the other three capability dimensions, and second, the informants did not comment on deliberate customization efforts in the other three dimensions. The context elements, which influence the choice of capability maturity levels in information usage and method sophistication, are *source of competitive advantage* and *industry clockspeed.*

Table 4.21 shows the individual recommendations. For companies that gain their *competitive advantage* through technological leadership, it is recommended to

Table 4.21 Design guide for choosing maturity levels for individual capabilities

If context		Then capability should be	
Element	Operationalization	Dimension (element)	Design recommendation
Source of competitive advantage	Technology leadership Customer and service orientation	Information usage (scope)	Emphasize scanning areas that are not the source of competitive advantage
	If both sources are equally important	Method sophistication (integration capacity)	High level
Industry clockspeed (high)	Rate of introduction of New products New processes New organizational structures	Information usage (reach)	High level
		Method sophistication (communication capacity)	High level

closely assess the scope of information usage and emphasize foresight activities in the areas political, customer, and competitive environment. This follows the logic that firms building on technological leadership are already well-informed on changes in the technological environment. This was confirmed by all companies. Thus, firms should, as a rule, build strong corporate foresight abilities only in the areas that are not the source of competitive advantage.

In support of this recommendation, Paap and Katz have shown that technology-based companies are generally good at spotting emerging technologies but often lack the ability to identify shifts in market drivers and customer needs (Paap and Katz 2004:13).

For companies that operate in highly competitive environments – in which they have to simultaneously compete through technology leadership and customer and service orientation – it is recommended to emphasize the integration capacity of their method portfolio. This will enable them to use corporate foresight to moderate and facilitate an early strategic discussion about the next generation of products and services.

For companies that operate in a highly volatile environment (i.e., a high industry clockspeed) it is recommended that they pay special attention to the reach of information usage and the communication capacity in their method portfolio. Both capability elements should be developed to a high maturity level. The communication capacity plays a particularly important role in high clockspeed industries, because the time for interpretation of weak signals is shorter and responding quickly will be possible only if the insights have been created with the participation of relevant stakeholders from multiple perspectives.

4.3.4 Conclusion on Usage of the Maturity Model

Through the cross-case analysis, building on the qualitative recommendation of the informants and previous research, it was possible to build a framework that (1) allows one to measure the corporate foresight ability level and that (2) can be used as a guide to design corporate foresight systems. For guiding the design and/or improvement of the corporate foresight system, a three-step process has been defined. This process is dominated by the choice of the target maturity level. In addition, the customization by emphasizing culture or structure and by emphasizing individual capabilities helps adapt the foresight system to a different organizational or environmental setting.

When implementing new corporate foresight systems, companies will face additional choices, such as choosing the appropriate methods and choosing the appropriate sources of information. These choices cannot be guided by the maturity model because they depend on factors (among them the availability of resources, knowledge about method usage, and access to data sources) that can be assessed only at the individual company level.

But overall, the Maturity Model of Corporate Foresight should be suitable to helping companies improve their ability to detect discontinuous change and produce adequate responses. Being able to measure the corporate foresight ability should also help trigger more benchmarking activities and broaden the academic discussion on the topic.

To add to the knowledge about what can be done to improve corporate foresight abilities, the next chapter will present best-practice approaches in the corporate foresight dimensions.

Chapter 5
Best-Practices in Corporate Foresight

The following chapter presents eight best practices. They are structured along the capability dimension of the Maturity Model of corporate foresight. The structure of the chapters is given in Fig. 5.1.

Each best practice is discussed in a three-part structure. The first part presents contextual factors and the motivation for the particular design of the approach. The second part contains a detailed description of the approach and points out critical design characteristics. The third part evaluates the practice by using points of reference from other cases and from literature. This comparison with previous research also helps increase generalizability (Eisenhardt 1989:533).

5.1 Networks of Scouts (Information Usage)

5.1.1 Context and Motivation

The first best-practice example has been identified in the telecommunication industry, which is in absolute terms one of the highest R and D spending industries (Pouillot and Puissochet 2002:33; BITCOM 2009:2). In the case studies, it was discovered that three out of four network operators used an approach that involves building networks of scouts to gather foresight information. Using people to gather data was believed by companies from other industries to be a rather ineffective way of acquiring information and increased the curiosity to look deeper into this approach, which seemed so popular among telecommunication network operators.

Similarities in context factors of these three companies are (1) a large company size (all companies generate more than 40 billion euros in annual revenue), (2) an innovation leader strategy, (3) consumer understanding as the major source of competitive advantage, and (4) the perception that they are in a complex and high clockspeed environment.

Another commonality is that all companies had a high alertness toward discontinuous change in their environment. This was attested by the information that the industry overall has seen major disruptions in the past and expects to be confronted

R. Rohrbeck, *Corporate Foresight*, Contributions to Management Science,

DOI 10.1007/978-3-7908-2626-5_5, © Springer-Verlag Berlin Heidelberg 2011

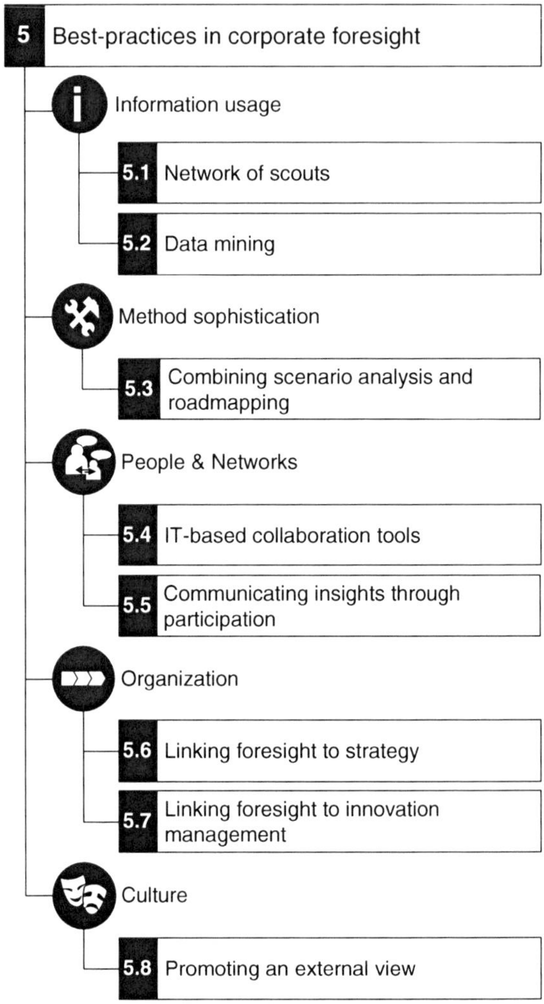

Fig. 5.1 Structure of best practices

with major disruptions in the future. Examples of such disruptions included the emergence of mobile telephony and the emergence of the Internet.

When in 1979 NTT – the incumbent Japanese telecommunication operator – introduced its first mobile telecommunication service, its European and North American counterparts still perceived mobile telephony as a threat to their fixed-line business (Agar 2003:34). The mood changed in the following years, and in 1984 the French and German governments signed an agreement to develop a common standard for mobile telephony (GSM Association 2008:1). One informant said that his company has survived the mobile telephony disruption entirely because it was still a state-owned company and had a comfortable monopoly in the telecommunication market. If not, he would have expected that smaller rivals would have won the race of becoming the dominant player in the mobile telephony market.

The second major discontinuous change frequently mentioned was the emergence of the Internet. From the network operator's perspective, the Internet meant the loss of the dominant position for services offerings that required a network. It allowed small companies to offer services that used to be highly integrated vertical silos. An example for such a service is the voice call, which formerly required building and maintaining a large network and physically connecting customers one another. Today, the Internet offers this connectivity to anyone who has access to it. And small software-based companies, such as Skype, a voice over Internet protocol (VoIP) provider, can offer voice call services over the Internet with comparably small investment and operating costs (Pradayrol and Cyrot 2008:4).

Many informants agreed with Rupert Murdoch, the chairman and CEO of News Corporation, a global media company. Murdoch pointed out that:

> The world is changing very fast. Big will not beat small anymore, it will be the fast beating the slow.

The informants explained the major disruptive potential of the Internet as an increase in the capability of small companies to compete on equal terms with large incumbent companies.

These two experiences of discontinuous change have created in telecommunication operators a deep-rooted perception that they are in need of building corporate foresight abilities – and thus increase their chance of identifying future disruptions early and being able to produce adequate and effective responses in a timely manner.

The major difference between the companies was the corporate culture. The difference ranged from one company being almost the perfect example of empowering individual initiative and demanding that initiatives are brought quickly to top management attention to another company with a tight net of specific processes that had to be observed to bring issues to the attention of top management. The third company can be characterized as somewhere in the middle.

When asked about the reason and motivation behind using people to gather foresight insights rather than databases or the Internet, one informant pointed to the importance of direct communication among people:

> 80% of all information is channelled through people.

He went on to explain that if you use databases, then the outcomes are usually written reports in text or presentation format. In his opinion to be able to use the foresight insights to trigger management action you need to provide not only the facts but also contextual information, which should be tailored to the needs of the decision maker. In consequence, using people who have firsthand evidence of weak signals on future changes is the only way to convince management to make major changes in the company. This view is shared by research (Galbraith et al. 2006:673) and backed up by the finding that knowledge transfer is positively influenced by social proximity (Sorenson et al. 2006:994).

Another reason was given by an informant of a different company who had much experience in using the Internet as a basis for scanning for weak signals. He explained that using automated search engines requires a good knowledge about the taxonomy of certain knowledge domains. The taxonomy, he said, is the knowledge about specific terms and their meaning as well as an understanding of the relationships between these terms.

He gave the example of *Web 2.0*, a term that at that time was widely known and whose meaning was clear to everyone working in the telecommunication industry. He pointed out that when the term was first introduced – to explain the phenomenon that increasingly users of Internet services were providing their own content rather than consuming content provided by media companies – it was competing with other terms, such as *crowd sourcing* and *user-generated content*. For a foresight project, he explained further, aimed at providing knowledge about this phenomenon, it would have been almost impossible to build information gathering entirely on automated searches in databases or on the Internet. Without the knowledge about the relationship of competing terms, it would have only returned information about a fraction of the overall phenomenon.

The informant also pointed out that in the emergence phase of new issues, human cognition will always be essential. While an automated search approach involves a large effort to set up – for defining the taxonomy and selecting adequate sources – the human scout is able to readjust his search approach faster and more efficiently. In addition, the human scout would also capture more contextual information, which allows him to create a rich understanding of the phenomenon, rather than identify for example only the number of citations of certain terms in certain media types.

From the assessment of the context and the motivation, it can be concluded that companies that use scouts to gather foresight insights have a high level of alertness about future disruptions and perceive themselves to be in a complex and volatile environment, but that they differ in corporate culture. The two primary motivation sources that drive the use of scouts for foresight are (1) the superior ability of humans to foresight in environments of unclear terminologies and (2) the additional advantage that scouts can transport rich information directly to decision makers.

5.1.2 Description of Practice

Surprisingly, all three companies had independently chosen to build their foresight system on the basis of scouts. Even more unexpected was the finding that the setups of the scouting approach also had much in common. The description of the practice will be done by first describing the commonalities between the approaches and then by describing the differences.

The first commonality is that all three companies had built their scouting network following a network architecture similar to a neuronal network (see Fig. 5.2).

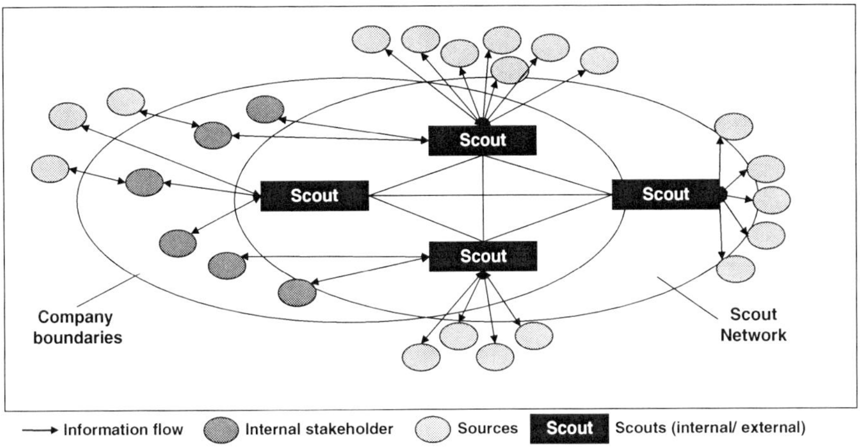

Fig. 5.2 Generic scout network

In such a network, scouts serve as information nodes or information hubs that search for information in their network and communicate it to their direct contacts. One informant also emphasized the importance of having a tight network among the scouts. The reasons are (1) that they need to communicate frequently to validate weak signals and (2) in order to be an interesting contact for their sources they should also be able to trade information gathered by other scouts.

Second, all companies used both internal and external scouts. It was reported that the downside of using external scouts is their limited knowledge about the needs of their internal stakeholders, which limits the usefulness of their information. It was emphasized that if external scouts are used, they need to be familiar with the organization they work for in order to (1) know how new issues are dealt with, (2) how information is channeled within the organization, and (3) what the strategic innovation priorities are.

> Each scout has to be able to not only understand the technology, but he must also be an expert in the innovation priorities of the company's business lines.

The primary reason for using *external* scouts is the establishment of scouting operations in new regions, such as Asia, where the European-based companies have little knowledge about the market and are typically not well connected. Another reason was that for some locations the companies did not feel the need to have a full-time scout, so hiring a consultant for 2 days a week was judged preferable in a certain region.

Another commonality was that all three companies aimed at establishing a worldwide scouting network with operations that go beyond the traditional triad of the United States of America, Europe, and Japan. Figure 5.3 shows the active scouting locations of the three companies.

The figure has been aggregated from three internal presentations that have been made available by the companies. The resource investment in the regions – represented

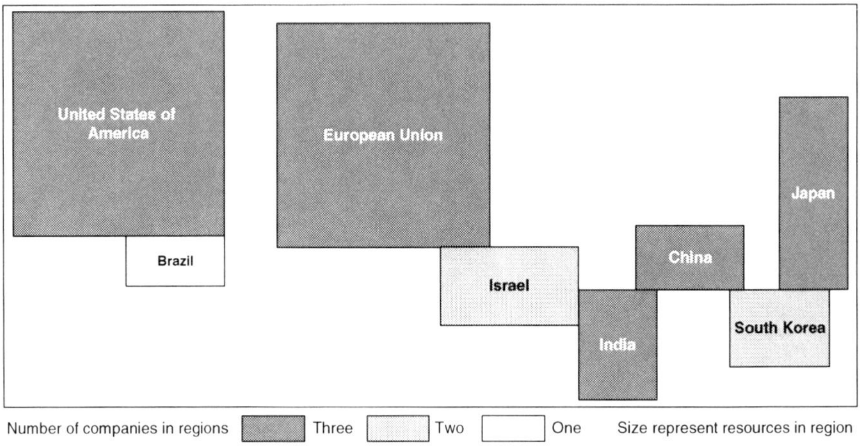

Fig. 5.3 Global reach of scouting networks

as the size of the rectangles in the figure – was available only for two companies and had to be estimated for the third on the basis of the information given in the interview. Therefore, the interpretation of the figure should be done with care. Nevertheless, it gives some indication of the distribution of the scouting effort in the different regions.

Particularly interesting is that, in addition to the traditional triad, all companies have established scouting operations in China and India. As the primary reason for this extension, informants pointed to the large R and D spending of the two countries and in the case of China the recent ambition to develop national standards for telecommunication and consumer electronic products. In addition, two companies have established scouting operations in South Korea and Israel, because both countries have telecommunication specific strengths. South Korea is the most important lead market for telecommunication services, because of its high broadband penetration, and Israel is a lead market for Internet and telecommunication security.

One difference between the companies is the way in which they disseminate the information. The company with the corporate culture based on empowerment of the individual relies on regular workshops in which the strategic foresight unit challenges R and D projects with future insights. Its primary aim is to enhance product concepts and ensure state-of-the-art R and D project outcomes. The company with the most rigid processes has not established any formal process links between the foresight process and follow-up processes. The dissemination is organized through a report which is published every 4 months and is distributed as a printed version to the top management and as an electronic online version to other interested employees. Both process oriented companies use graphical overviews to enable browsing through the different issues that have been reported by the scouts.

All companies also commented on the importance of designing motivation schemes for the scouts as well as the sources of information. One scout pointed out that in order to maintain his personal network he needs to be interesting for them. If he talks for instance to public research to collect information, then he needs to offer either information on the technological interests of its company or facilitate collaborative R and D projects. Table 5.1 shows a collection of motivation sources of the different actors in the scouting network.

For internal scouts, the primary motivation is recognition as being a valuable source of information and strengthening their own internal networks. Monetary rewards in the bonus schemes have been reported only in one case. For external scouts, the motivation is either direct payment (as a flat fee or per relevant technology) or business development opportunities. One company reported that for one of its consultants, scouting is the primary way to acquire consulting projects dealing with strategic technology assessments.

For academic sources, the primary driver to share knowledge about emerging issues is the chance to do a joint research project and to be recognized as an expert in a particular field. No company reported paying an academic source for information. For industry sources, the motivation is often business development, particularly if the industry source is a supplier to the telecommunication operator. Suppliers judge providing information to their customer a good opportunity to influence their innovation planning and to get early feedback on their product concepts. In addition, lateral information disclosure among companies in the same position in the value chain is seen as a good way to start collaborations and a convenient approach to validate internal foresight results.

A company from the automotive sector has taken the idea of networks of scouts even further and planned to establish so-called "scouting rings" of their own scouts in different regions and different industries. The concept structure of such a scouting ring is shown in Fig. 5.4.

There were two primary reasons for inviting other companies to such collaborative scouting activities. First, it was expected that most emerging issues, such as for example the trend toward health and sustainability oriented lifestyles, have an impact on all industries. Therefore, it was expected that all companies would be interested in establishing a foresight mechanism designed to identify the issue and

Table 5.1 Motivation sources in scouting networks

Actor in scouting network	Used incentives
Internal scouts	Recognition Strengthening of internal network Monetary reward in bonus scheme
External scouts	Payment per relevant technology Payment of periodical fee Business development opportunity for consultants
Academic sources	Chance for joint research projects Recognition
Industry sources	Business development and sales Collaboration opportunity Validation of internal foresight insights

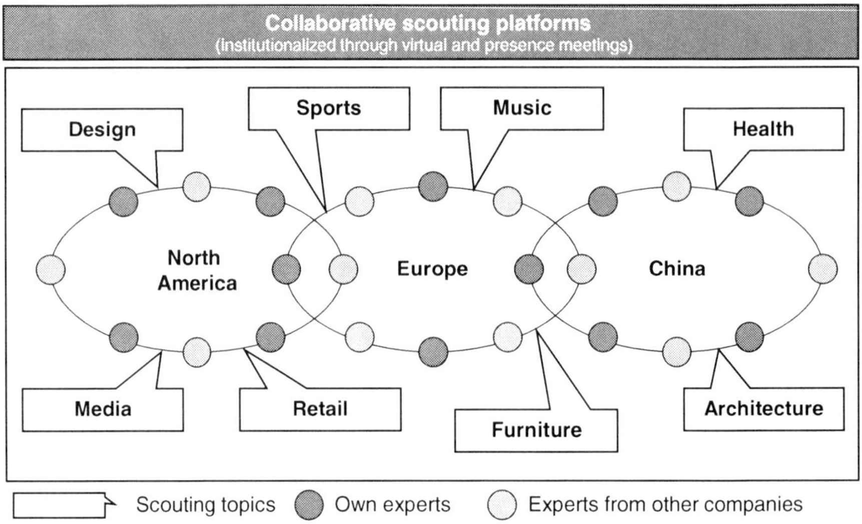

Fig. 5.4 Collaborative scouting platforms

in addition it would offer to all participating companies the benefit of shared costs. The second reason was the expectation that the detection of weak signals on emerging issues should be easier from multiple points of view, particularly if all industries with a strong consumer orientation could be brought into the radar rings.

In the end, this initiative was not brought to life, for operational reasons. But the strong interest from other companies showed the appeal of the approach. The idea to be able to get early feedback on weak signals that have been detected by internal foresight activities was reported to be very appealing. It can therefore be regarded as a promising extension to a company's internal network of scouts.

5.1.3 Evaluation

From the assessment of the context in which scouting is used, it has become clear that the information and communication industry (ICT) has a particular need for corporate foresight. Past studies have confirmed the perception of the informants that the ICT industry is in a high-velocity environment (Wirtz et al. 2007:295), which implies a high volatility of business models as well as frequent changes in the competitive landscape (Pradayrol and Cyrot 2008:4). The market for Internet based services and products is characterized by a high volatility, which translates for the companies into a need to build processes that enable them to produce fast responses (Buganza and Verganti 2006:393).

In that context, building a foresight system on the basis of networks of scouts should make the channeling of information faster and more flexible (Monteiro 2006:13).

In addition, the possibility of transporting rich information – including contextual information – should provide a benefit in environments with unstable terminologies and frequently emerging issues. An expected additional benefit is that the same scouting network can also be used for sourcing the technology (Bodelle and Jablon 1993:26–28; Steensma and Fairbank 1999:20), by either starting joint R and D projects, licensing, or acquisition (Vanhaverbeke et al. 2002:741; Vrande et al. 2006:347; Lichtenthaler 2008b:148). It can also be expected that having a worldwide network of scouts might increase the capability of the firm to form R and D collaborations, which have been shown to positively influence innovation performance (Faems et al. 2005:238; Bader 2008:311; Hurmelinna et al. 2005:347).

Scouts can also support in the process of "issue selling," which includes explaining relevant aspects of an issue to a specific target person to ensure his or her buy-in and promotes implementation (Dutton et al. 1997:407). Through direct communication, the process of strategic decision making can also be expected to be faster, which has been shown to increase its success (Baum and Wally 2003:1107).

It can be concluded that using networks of scouts yields a competitive advantage in specific contexts. These contexts include high external complexity (with unclear interdependencies between emerging issues), high industry clockspeed (where search queries would need to be changed frequently to focus on new issues), and high fuzziness of terminology (where the search keywords change frequently). In such a context, it is advisable to include scouts as a means of information gathering, possibly as a complementary component to an automated IT-based scanning.

5.2 Data Mining (Information Usage)

When assessing corporate foresight capabilities, one differentiation can be made between issue driven and undirected foresight (Krystek and Müller-Stewens 1993:177; Reger 2001b:539). Issue driven means that the foresight activity starts with a concrete question. For example, a company might be interested in knowing how good the prospects for the commercialization of a certain technology are. An example for undirected foresight is the scanning for emerging trends without having a hypothesis on what these trends might be.

For corporate foresight, both issue driven and undirected activities are essential (Krystek and Müller-Stewens 1993:177). While using networks of scouts can be used for both the directed and the undirected information gathering, data mining is used for directed issue driven foresight only (Porter and Cunningham 2005:18; Reger 2001b:539). Data mining uses text analysis tools and science and technology databases to inform technology, innovation, and R and D project managers (Cunningham et al. 2006:915; Daim et al. 2006:981) and be the basis for the use of other foresight methods such as technology roadmapping (Yoon et al. 2008:51).

5.2.1 Context and Motivation

The company in which the data mining best practice was analyzed is a utility company from the energy sector. In 2007, the company had annual revenues of more than 20 billion euros. It has neither a clear innovation leader nor a clear cost leader strategy. The source of competitive advantage is customer proximity and internal processes. The complexity of the environment is high. It is primarily driven by the complexity in the technological and political environment. Although the environment was perceived as not particularly volatile, the informants pointed out that most of their technology investment decisions have large financial impacts.

The primary reasons for developing the data-mining approach was rapidly increasing of complexity in the technological and political environment and three major changes in the environment.

- First, the *liberalization of the energy market*, which began in 1996 with the European Union (EU) directive 96/92/EC (Franz et al. 2006:3). This liberalization led to increased competition in the market, as retail and wholesale customers gained the right of free choice of their supplier (Seefeldt et al. 2007:31).
- Second, the need for *innovation and investment*. This need is triggered by the growth in energy consumption at a rate of 1.22% per year (EC 2007:58; Schulz et al. 2005:31). Meeting this need is further impeded by the decommissioning of almost half of the currently running power stations until 2030 (EC 2007:62) and an aging electricity infrastructure. These needs are expected to trigger major investments in the energy sector. In its World Energy Outlook 2008, the International Energy Agency expects $831 billion to be invested in the European electricity system between 2007 and 2015 and another $1.428 billion between 2016 and 2030 (IEA 2008:151). In addition to the renewal of existing infrastructures, innovation is also needed to develop new fields such as hydrogen for transport and energy storage (McDowall and Eames 2006:1236).
- Third, the increasing *emphasis on sustainable energy use*. On December 17, 2008, the European Parliament (EP) passed an energy package that sets the legally binding target to cut greenhouse gas emissions by 20%, increase the share of renewable energy to 20%, and to improve energy efficiency by 20% by 2020 (European Union 2008).

In order to stay abreast of such changes in the environment, it was decided that new capabilities need to be developed. The ability to assess new issues and the ability to propose response strategies was judged to be vitally important. For this, data mining was identified as a powerful tool.

In the first step, the data-mining approach has been designed to support the management of the R and D portfolio. The head of the R and D portfolio management explained that in order to make investment decisions he needs to know (1) how important the key technologies are for the financial results of his company and (2) how strong the internal technological capabilities are in comparison to their competitors. The data-mining approach is primarily expected to deliver the capability to assess the technological position of the company and expected to help in identifying start-up companies with particular technological competencies for collaboration or acquisition.

In the second step – which was due to be taken after the completion of this case study – it was planned to extend the use of the tool to a general intelligence tool. In this use, it will be made available to all functional top management for issue-driven information gathering.

5.2.2 *Description of Practice*

To design and implement a data-mining approach – or as it is called in the company, an intelligence tool – the company collaborated with a specialized start-up company. When asked why a small company was chosen as the supplier of the tool, the head of the project said that the market for such intelligence tools is still not very developed and the two options available to them were (1) to hire a university professor who had developed his own solution or (2) work with the start-up company, which has previously worked for the French government and thus had good references to implement complex data-mining systems.

At the time of the interviews, the system was still in the trial phase. The setup had been completed 3 months previously, and two initial projects have successfully been completed with the use of the data-mining system. In the case study, it was possible to question the developers of the system as well as three employees of the energy company. This made it possible to analyze the running system as well as capture the project sequence of the first test trial.

From the overall six-step data-mining process, Fig. 5.5 shows only the first four steps that are relevant to the information use capability of corporate foresight. The fifth step is the development of the final report and the sixth step the use of the

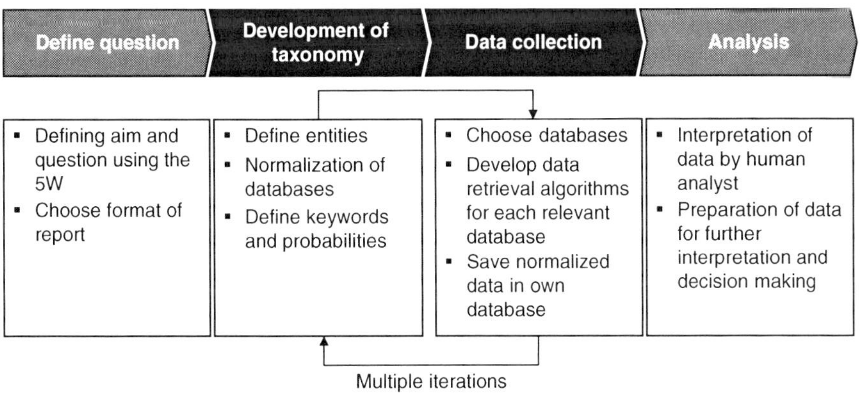

Fig. 5.5 Information gathering in data mining

answer. For the assessment of the practice and the understanding of the capability strength in terms of information use, the first four steps are sufficient.

The data-mining process starts with the *definition of the question*. In our case, the question was: Which companies are the technology leaders and which companies are the biggest producers of micro algae? These micro algae were of interest because they feed on the climate threatening carbon dioxide (CO_2) and in addition can be used to produce bio-fuel.

The first step in the processing of the request is the definition of the research aim. For that, the general rule is to use the 5W (who, what, when, where, why), a set of questions that clarify the request intention and research aim. In addition, the format for the final report is defined. The format can range from a simple yes or no answer to a board level presentation and a written report. In this case, the format was an approximately 20-page presentation, which would be used to decide on R and D investments in micro algae.

The second and third steps are the core of the data-mining approach and set it apart from other information-gathering techniques. The two major mechanisms of the *taxonomy definition* are the careful definition of entities (i.e., an object of the database which can be put into relationship with other objects of a database) and the normalization of data. In the normalization process, the terminology in the databases is compared. If entries with the same meaning have different names, then these terms are modified in order to match. The definition of entities and the normalization allows cross-linking databases and database objects. This provides the ability to represent and explore data visually.

To better understand the use of entities and the normalization procedure the initial project was further investigated. In the project on micro algae for CO_2 reduction and bio-fuel production, four entities had been defined:

- *Pilot plants* that had been installed to test the effectiveness of the micro algae to consume CO_2.
- *Researchers* that hold patents or have authored publications on the micro algae production or their use for CO_2 reduction.
- *Technologies* that are used in the context of micro algae production within factories.
- *Companies* which are associated with micro algae pilot plants that employ researchers or are mentioned in publications or patents.

For finding relevant data, about 100 information sources have been used. They included patent and publication databases, a market intelligence database, specific databases on research projects, and specific Web sites that provided information on particular aspects of micro algae, such as the CO_2 consumption of different species.

In order to make sure that the tool will only retrieve relevant data, additional keywords have been defined that need to appear together with the search keyword. For example, publications that were searched for with the search keyword *algae* had to include also the keyword *CO_2 consumption*. By assigning each additional keyword a weight, the user can adjust the search mechanism to give an appropriate number of search results.

Overall, the two steps of defining the taxonomy and retrieving the data took approximately 3 months and included multiple iterations. But this comparably long time was also a result of being the first trial run. After the data-mining tools are fully set up and after multiple relevant databases have been integrated, the process duration is estimated to come down to 2–4 weeks.

When asking whether the tool is worth the money and effort to set it up, an analyst who used to do information gathering manually explained:

> It is a tool with which the intelligence analyst can look for relations between different databases. . . . So it is much easier for your work you have to do as an analyst. You don't have to go to Google and have to read everything. [Google] gives you all the information but also just one piece of it at a time.

The major advantage of data mining is that it gives the data some meaning by linking one piece of information to another. It thus makes it possible to outsource some of the cross-linking to an automated mechanism, which previously had to be done by the analyst.

The head of the intelligence unit confirmed the importance of understanding the links and associations among bits of information to answer complex questions quickly. He also pointed to the time savings in the fourth step, where the analyst has to prepare the final report, which gives an account of the final interpretation of the data.

In this fourth step, data mining allows the user to graphically navigate the retrieved data. An illustrative example of the visual exploration of the data is given in Fig. 5.6. The figure has been composed on the basis of the demonstration and the explanation by the software architect. It illustrates how the visual exploration was used to identify links and draw conclusions on the strengths of companies and on the characteristics of pilot plants.

In order to navigate between the four views given in Fig. 5.6, the user needs only to click on one of the entities.

- The first view shows how, for a selected *technology*, the data-mining tool can identify related companies and pilot plants and related researchers who had developed aspects of the technology.

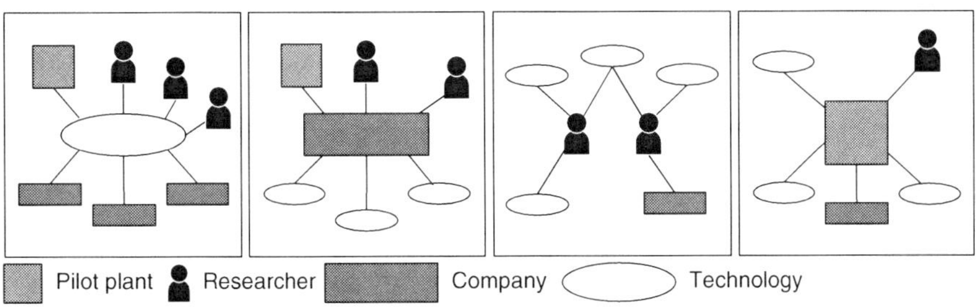

Fig. 5.6 Visual exploration in data mining

- From the first view, the user can proceed to the second by clicking a *company*. The tool will then show the researchers, pilot plan, and technologies that are associated with it.
- The third view can be used to show the associations of a selected *researcher* with other researchers or companies or which technologies he has helped to develop.
- The fourth view shows the association of a pilot plant. These can include companies that own the pilot plant, companies that have built the pilot plant, and technologies that have been employed.

In addition, clicking on one of the entities allows one to open the documents that are the basis of the identification of the link as well as additional documents on the entity. The major benefit of the graphical exploration is being able to use the knowledge about the associations to gain insights into the research question. In the micro algae case, it was reported to have created much value to know which technologies are most frequently used in the pilot plants as well as to know which companies are building pilot plants and which companies have the most experience with the preferred technology. In addition, information on the strengths of the competitors can be generated, including their technological capabilities, employed researchers, pilot plants, and production plant capacities.

5.2.3 Evaluation

From the case study, multiple advantages of data mining in comparison with other forms of IT-based searches have been identified. They include:

- Possibility to cross-link all entities of the database (companies, technologies, researcher, etc.)
- Visual exploration of the data, which makes it possible to discover interdependencies of entities and thus make better decisions (for example, discovering that the needed technology can be bought from the original researcher, rather than from a supplier company which is licensee to the researcher).
- Usability by even an analyst with limited domain knowledge, because some of the interpretation is done automatically.

Therefore, data mining can be expected to be a valuable tool for enhancing decision making on technology investments (Stillman 1997:15) and can also be used as a tool to support an established technology planning process (Petrick and Provance 2005:171; Probert et al. 2003:1183) such as technology planning with roadmaps (Lischka and Gemünden 2008:208; Phaal et al. 2003:52; Wells et al. 2004:46).

Against these advantages, the high costs of setting up a data-mining system have to be considered. In the case study, the overall set-up effort was estimated to be 2 years calculated in full-time equivalents. At an average cost of €150,000 per year, this would translate into an effort of €300,000 for setting up the tool plus the effort from the internal customers, who need to help in defining the taxonomy and finding adequate databases.

This effort should pay off in time savings in future foresight projects. The investment should also make for better decision making. The latter payoff is difficult to quantify, but was the major reason for installing the data-mining system. In the case study, the results have been praised by the internal customer as being of remarkably high quality. Thus, it can be tentatively concluded that the data-mining approach has contributed to decision quality. The time-saving aspect has also been confirmed, but considering that the research is typically done by junior researchers, it is not possible to confirm an overall cost-saving potential.

In conclusion, data mining can be characterized as an approach that is more powerful than other alternatives such as Web searches with classic search engines, but which is also associated with high investment costs. No clear pattern of favorable context factors has been identified. But it should be emphasized that companies wishing to establish a data-mining system should have the necessary resources, both for hiring external support as well as more importantly ensuring sufficient participation of internal staff. The internal staff is particularly important because it is needed to define taxonomies and make sufficient internal marketing to be sure that the tool is used by as many internal stakeholders as possible.

5.3 Combining Scenario Analysis with Roadmapping (Method Sophistication)

In the case studies, methods have been identified as critical for the interpretation ability of a company. Particularly, methods that make it possible to integrate data from different domains and time horizons without oversimplifying the issue have been identified as important for interpretation capacity. In addition, the communication capability of the method was commented to be of high importance when it comes to disseminating gained insights, making sure that the insights trigger actions, and for getting the buy-in of internal stakeholders.

Multiple companies in the sample have built internal corporate foresight methods to suit their specific needs. Some of these have extended or combined multiple methods to build an integrated method. Two companies have combined roadmapping and the scenario technique for project-based foresight activities. Some documented examples exist in which scenario analysis and roadmapping have been combined in national foresight exercises (Saritas and Aylen 2008:15; Saritas and Oner 2004:27; Quist and Vergragt 2006:1027) and in a corporate context (Strauss and Radnor 2004:51; Pagani 2009:382; Andersen et al. 2004:311).

The best-practice description will focus on the approach of the company with the most experience, which will be called Company A. The other company will be called Company B. The similarities and differences in the two approaches will be discussed in the Sect. 5.3.3.

5.3.1 Context and Motivation

Both companies are large, with annual revenues of more than 60 billion euros and more than 230,000 employees. Both companies have, therefore, the resources necessary to run large-scale foresight projects and might also have a particular need to employ methods with a high degree of structure. This need for a structured method in large companies was highlighted by the head of a business unit with more than 500 million euros in annual revenue:

> It is important to employ a structured method. I believe our company grows so strongly [the company has tripled its annual revenue in the last six years] that a more structured approach is needed.[1]

When asked what the value of a more structured method is, he pointed to the enhancement of transparency, which as a consequence speeds up decision processes and increases the commitment of internal stakeholders:

> I believe that transparency is an important argument. It you don't have transparency, decision processes are delayed, because not all people have participated and they might question the decision. There will also be less commitment overall in the company, because there is no understanding of why it has to be done this way. The art of leading large companies is to align all the employees [to a common goal].[2]

In addition to the need for a structured approach, both companies draw their motivation to engage in such large-scale foresight processes from their strategic aim to be an innovation leader. In that respect, the foresight projects were designed to make it possible to drive internal innovation efforts and in addition make it possible to influence other companies to follow their vision of the future.

The corporate culture of both companies can be described as process oriented. The companies' management systems are built on clearly defined roles and responsibilities. Rather than empowering the individual and encouraging individual initiatives, the companies believe in top-down strategy making. One example is the approach through which Company A defines new business fields. It follows an approach based on mega trends. These mega trends are identified on the corporate strategy level and are then translated into business opportunities that each division has to follow. For example, the mega trend aging society was translated into a strategic goal to develop more innovations in the field of driver assistance systems

[1]Translated from German by the author. Original quote: "Es ist wichtig eine strukturiertere Methode zu haben. Ich denke, unsere Unternehmung wächst so stark zurzeit das eine strukturiertes Vorgehen nötig ist."

[2]Translated from German by the author. Original quote: "Ich denke, dass Transparenz für mich ein wichtiges Argument wäre. Wenn die Transparenz nicht gegeben ist, verzögert das Entscheidungsprozesse, weil die [Entscheidungen] dann vielleicht in Frage gestellt werden - von Leuten die nicht beteiligt waren. Es gibt auch weniger Commitment von der Firma insgesamt, weil nicht verstanden wird, warum etwas gemacht wird. Ja die ganze Kunst große Unternehmen zu führen ist es, dass der Sack voller Flöhe unidimensional aufgerichtet wird."

in order to enable older customers to stay mobile longer. The business unit operating in the automotive industry then had to follow this strategic aim.

In consequence, bottom-up initiatives are not encouraged and are subject to close assessment concerning their fit into the corporate strategic goals that have been defined top-down.

Concerning the complexity and volatility of the corporate environment, the companies score high in both. Both companies have a global presence and thus high external and internal complexity. In addition, Company A has a corporate structure which – at the time of the interview – includes business units operating in six different industries. Concerning volatility, Company A had a history of reorganizing its business portfolio, moving in and out of industries and restructuring its portfolio of equity holding by frequent mergers and acquisitions. Recently, the company even had to abandon its heritage and founding industry when its operations in the telecommunication division did not meet the required profitability goals.

The primary source of competitive advantage of Company A is technology leadership, for which the company spent 5.3 billion euros in R and D in 2006 (Department of Trade and Industry UK (DTI) 2006:8). Of its total R and D expenditure, 95% is spent within the business units and 5% in a central technology unit. This central unit is responsible for developing key technologies for the long term and drive innovation activities with a high level of synergy between the business units.

For Company B, the primary source of competitive advantage is customer orientation and innovation leadership. But in contrast to Company A, the innovation leadership of Company B is built more on innovative services and business models and only to a smaller extent on technological innovations.

Another important context factor of Company A is that it has installed a central technology unit, which has been asked to develop long term-strategic technologies as well as technologies with a high degree of benefit and synergy for multiple business units. This central technology unit is also responsible for the foresight projects and has developed the best-practice approach which will be described further on. For its foresight projects, it has four primary goals:

- Identification of the technologies with high growth potential
- Identification of technologies with high disruptive potential
- Identification of future customer needs
- Identification of new business models

In addition, the projects aim to enhance the collaboration of the corporate technology unit and the business units by facilitating a strategic dialogue on future technologies, future products, and future markets.

5.3.2 Description of Practice

The aim of facilitating collaboration between business unit and corporate technology unit is also reflected in the project organization (see Fig. 5.7).

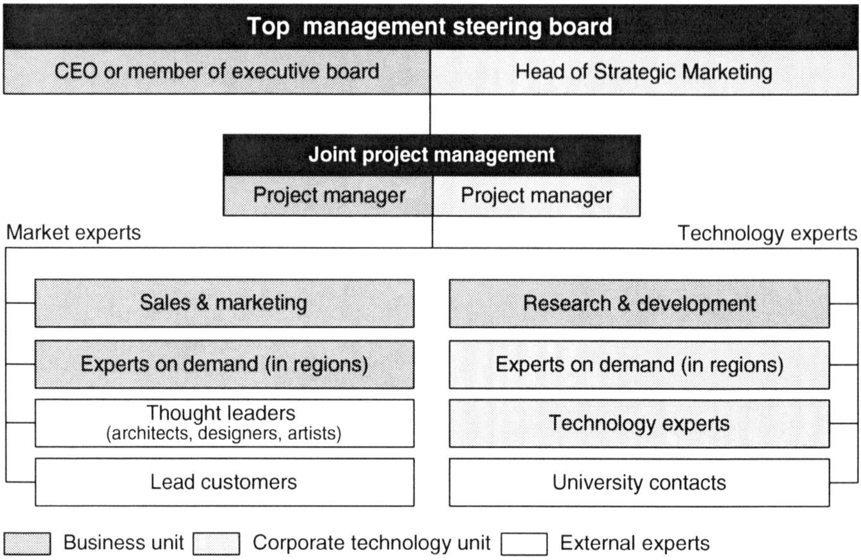

Fig. 5.7 Project organization

The project organization has three primary characteristics:

- *Steering by top management*: The steering board always includes the head of the business unit and a senior representative of corporate technology. This is usually the head of strategic marketing of corporate technology, who is also the method owner of the combined method of roadmapping and scenario analysis.
- *Collaborative project management*: The project has two project managers, one from the business unit and one from corporate technology.
- *Joint staffing from business unit and corporate technology unit:* Both business unit and corporate technology unit provide experts with complementary knowledge and expertise.

These three characteristics have been said to play an important role to ensure the buy-in of the business unit. This buy-in is needed to ensure the acceptance of the recommendation of the foresight project and to ensure that actions will be confirmed and taken.

The project duration of these scenario analysis and roadmapping projects is approximately 6 months. The overall effort can be estimated to be 2–4 years, calculated in full-time equivalent (FTE). The project team usually includes two *full-time project managers*, four to six *core team members* (who work 40–80% of their total time), and *experts on demand* from the business unit and the corporate technology unit. In addition, *external experts* such as thought leaders, lead users, and university contacts are to complement the internal knowledge about customer requirements and technology-related information.

The underlying process of the approach has some degree of freedom. That means that the process is not followed in the same way in every project. The process is often customized to fit the specific goals of the business units. To understand the level of customization, two projects have been studied that have been chosen because they were particularly different from one another. From the analysis of the procedure of both projects, a generic process framework has been developed. In Fig. 5.8, this process framework is used to analyze the similarities and differences between the two projects.

In Project 1, the process starts with a situation analysis, which includes the current R and D portfolio and the current R and D roadmap. In contrast, Project 2 starts not with the analysis of the current situation, but with the development of the scenario analysis. These different starting points give the projects a very different character. While Project 1 is an extrapolation from today into the future, Project 2 is a scenario-based retropolation, which uses future scenarios to give directions for today's planning. That means that Project 1 is more based on today's contingencies while Project 2 challenges today's assumptions with possibilities for the future.

Concerning the scenario analysis, both projects follow the same sequence in which trends and drivers are identified, hypothesis are generated, the scenarios are developed, and the scenarios are used to derive implications for today's management.

The outcome, however, is very different. Project 1 was used to derive knowledge about technology gaps and to initiate new R and D projects. It thus has (from the point of view of the business unit) a very concrete and tangible outcome. The outcome of Project 2 is the identification of future business opportunities and future key technologies. But these results are only documented in the project report and not directly integrated into the business unit's processes. Likewise, the technology roadmap with the future key technologies is not directly linked to the

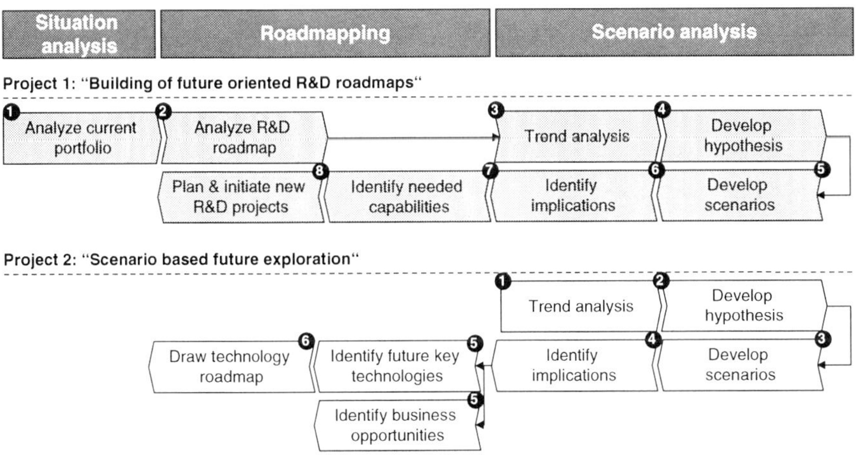

Fig. 5.8 Generic process

technology management of the business unit. It has thus a weaker link to the operational management but produces more recommendations for long-term strategic (technology) planning.

In consequence, a "Project 2"-like approach is suited to identify new issues outside today's current view of the world and a "Project 1"-like approach is useful to challenge and extend the current planning of the business units.

In conclusion, in the description of the approach it can be noted that the two concrete examples have been cases of extreme customization. Most projects follow an approach that is a mixture of both examples. Common characteristics of all projects in this company are

- *Creative countercurrent* of extrapolating current activities and retropolating from future scenarios
- *High degree of participation* of foresight customer (the business unit) in the foresight activity (run by the corporate technology unit)
- *Long and iterative process* to make sure that the whole organization – top management, middle management, and expert-level employees – of the foresight customer get involved.

The last point was said to be particularly important to ensure a tangible outcome of the foresight activity. The method owner said that

> There is always a discussion on how fast we can do such a project. I believe I would be able to deliver one – given the knowledge of all the people in our company – in 14 days. But this would not serve the purpose, because the people who have to introduce the change in the organization need to acquaint themselves with the new mindset.[3]

This view was shared by all informants in the company. They emphasized the importance of giving all involved parties enough time to discuss and challenge the insights generated by the project. Failing to provide enough time was associated with the threat to trigger a not-invented-here syndrome, which might inhibit the use of the insights.

An additional strength of the approach run by Company A was the integration of regional expert knowledge. For the integration, three different strategies were used (see Fig. 5.9).

First, internal experts in the regions were identified through regional sales offices and through the business unit's and corporate technology unit's contact networks. These experts were used as experts on demand and contacted when their expertise was needed.

The second strategy to integrate experts was through a regional workshop where core team members were physically present. These workshops were run by at least

[3]Translated from German by the author. Original quote: "Es gibt immer Diskussion, wie schnell man so ein Project machen kann. Ich meine, ich könnte Ihnen ein solches Projekt, bei dem Wissen das die Leute in unserer Firma haben, innerhalb von 14 Tagen machen. Aber das wäre nicht zielführend, weil die Leute die Veränderungen im Konzern herbeiführen müssen, sich an die alternative Denke gewöhnen müssen."

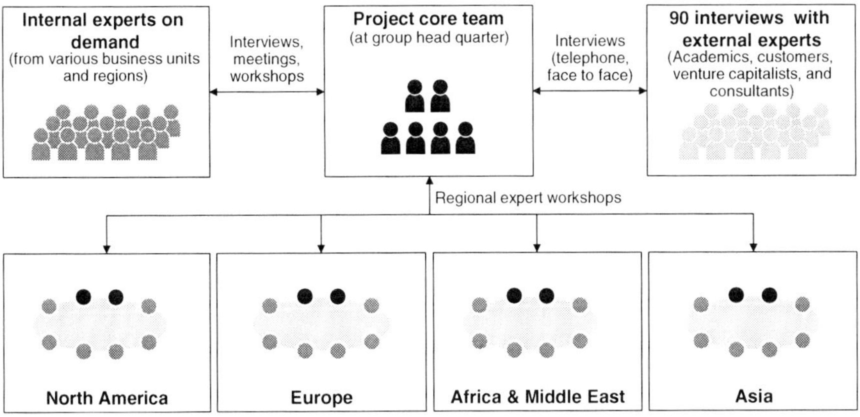

Fig. 5.9 Integration of regional expert knowledge

two representatives of the core team. The duration was 2–3 days. The invited participants were often from different business units in the region but always internal, so that confidential information could be shared freely. Informants identified three benefits of using internal experts to capture information from the regions:

- Ease of identification of experts
- The ability to talk about confidential information
- The possibility of later using the same channels to initiate joint innovation initiatives

The third strategy was the integration of external experts through interviews. These interviews were conducted either by telephone or face to face. Experts had primarily four backgrounds: (1) academics from public research, (2) customers, (3) venture capitalists, and (4) consultants. For the identification of suitable experts, multiple channels have been used, including personal contacts of the core team, contacts of the business units, and relevant experts identified through Web searches.

5.3.3 *Evaluation*

From the context analysis, it has become clear that the motivation to run these large-scale foresight projects is derived from large company size and diversified corporate structures. These characteristics trigger the need to align and direct the company. They do, however, not directly translate into the need to run these kinds of foresight projects. But with the presented methodology, Company A has introduced a systematic planning approach that makes it possible to plan for the future and that delivers the additional benefit of facilitating the alignment of multiple business units and the alignment of corporate technology to the business unit.

One reason for the long-term success of the approach – and for earning it the label "best practice" – is the intelligent integration of the business unit into the foresight effort. The approach by which the company allows for participation on many levels (steering board, project management, and expert level) ensures effectively the use of the foresight insights. Inviting the top management of the business units ensures top management sponsorship of the necessary measures to deal with external change. Inviting the operational level into the project prevents the not-invented-here syndrome, which might hinder the implementation of needed change. In addition, the integration of regional knowledge leverages the benefit of the company's size and global presence.

Concerning the development of the scenarios, Company A and B follow different approaches. Company A uses most-likely scenarios, forcing the project team to agree on one scenario, which is used in the planning stage as the point of reference. Company B produces multiple scenarios, thus following the more traditional approach made popular by Royal Dutch Shell (see also Brenneman et al. 1998; Mayring 2002; Schoemaker and Heijden 1992), where alternative futures allow the company to identify the robustness of its strategic decisions.

The advantage of using multiple scenarios is that they are closer to reality, in which future outcomes are also not predefined (Fink et al. 2005:365–366). In addition, the knowledge of possible developments can be used to define measures that enhance the probability that the future moves in a favorable direction and to define countermeasures if current developments move in an unfavorable direction (Gruber and Venter 2006:976). Scenarios are also a means to integrate more creativity and imagination into strategic decision making, which has been shown to positively influence decision making success (Brockmann and Anthony 2002: 449; Szulanski and Amin 2001:537).

The advantage of using most-likely scenarios is that they are easier to communicate in a network of multiple stakeholders. Particularly the strategic-planning process, which includes budget planning, is difficult to integrate with a future exploration that delivers uncertain and ambiguous recommendations. Another reason that Company A has chosen this approach is the goal to influence other stakeholders, including other companies as well as political bodies. To do so, a clear vision has been expected to be better suited to ambiguous future scenarios.

In conclusion, it can be said that the scenario technique enhances the ability of the company to understand the inherent uncertainty of the future. The combination of the scenario technique and roadmapping allows the company to reflect on the uncertainty in planning the future, as has been expected from previous studies (Drew 2006:241; Strauss and Radnor 2004:57). Judged from the two case studies, it can also be concluded that the two methods effectively complement each other. While roadmapping has its strengths in the integration of multiple perspectives and information, the scenario technique has its strengths in dealing with uncertainty and facilitating the communication about future insights. In addition, the two methods can be expected to be a powerful tool that can help firms plan their entry into a new market (Bayus et al. 2007:139).

Concerning the question of in which corporate context the combined method is recommended, no clear pattern has emerged. One factor limiting the implementation of such an approach is the high cost and the high internal effort. Therefore, the approach would be expected to be more suitable to large companies with a sufficient budget. Another reason to not employ such a combined method would be if the company is operating in an environment of limited uncertainty. Then it might be sufficient to plan the future by using only roadmaps. For other companies that are faced with high levels of uncertainty and that have sufficient funds available, using such a combined approach of scenario technique and roadmapping is recommended and will enhance its corporate foresight capability.

5.4 IT Collaboration Tools (People and Networks)

In 2001, based on interview data among 26 large multinational companies, Reger argued that foresight move toward being more "need driven", meaning that foresight is more directed by the needs of internal customers (Reger 2001a:550). In addition, he saw a trend toward using central IT tools in order to facilitate the foresight process, including collection, interpretation, and communication (Reger 2001a:551).

Using IT tools such as the Internet, intranet, and specific software should provide higher efficiency and make communication more flexible and scalable. For example, an internal customer of foresight, who needs to decide whether a certain technology should be developed internally or sourced externally could put this question into a foresight IT system. This question could then be read by a theoretically infinite number of technology scouts worldwide. Relevant information gathered by the technology scouts could be entered into the IT system, where the internal customer could collect the answer to his question. In addition, the IT system could include a discussion area where the technology scouts could exchange their views on the question and collaboratively work on the answer, and by doing so improve the quality of the final decision

Particularly the use of virtual networks has become easier by the creation of so-called Web 2.0 Internet services. Initially, *Web 2.0* was used as a term to describe primarily the emergence of user-generated content, which can be defined as (1) content made publicly available over the Internet, (2) which reflects a certain amount of creative effort, and (3) which is created outside of professional routines and practices (Vickery and Wunsch-Vincent 2007:9). Today, it has been extended to include the emergence of smart Internet services which allow for building and maintaining social networks for searching for and managing large amounts of data, including personal information services, which filter and deliver information in predefined areas of interest.

It can therefore be hypothesized that using IT tools as an integral part of corporate foresight systems should positively influence the overall corporate foresight ability. Particularly promising could be the use of new functionalities made available by the emergence of the smart Internet services in Web 2.0.

5.4.1 Context and Motivation

And indeed, as predicted by Reger, the companies in my sample had implemented a number of IT-based foresight tools for specific purposes, including tools that have emerged within the Web 2.0 phenomenon. The widest range of tools and the highest levels of use were found in the telecommunication operator's foresight units.

These companies all perceived themselves to be in a complex and fast-clockspeed environment, in which the primary source for competitive advantage is speed (Monteiro and Sull. 2006:1; Chen and Watanabe 2006:731) (more specifically, the speed in combining emerging technological capabilities with new customer needs in order to be the first to introduce a winning product or service). Consequently, the nature of their strategy was stated by all four telecommunication operators to be based on innovation leadership. Their company size measured in number of employees ranges from 17,600 to 251,000 and their revenue from five billion to 62 billion euros (annual reports, 2008).

5.4.2 Description of Practice

From the interviews, ten IT-collaboration tools have been identified. In addition, these tools have been classified according to which phase of the corporate foresight process they are being employed. The differentiation was made between data gathering (dg), interpretation (in) and communication (co), following the three-step process logic introduced by Daft and Weick (Daft and Weick 1984:286). An overview of the IT tools is given in Table 5.2.

The first tool, *news reader*, was used in all companies to collect relevant information on predefined topics. One example is the so-called RSS-feed, in which RSS stands for really simple syndication. These news feeds make it possible to subscribe to news tickers or specific Web sites to collect information on specified topics of interest in an automatic fashion. In this way, the total news content is filtered to best meet the user's specific information needs. The user gets only the information which is most relevant to him and in an aggregated format. This results in an increase in personal productivity.

Another source for data gathering is *internal libraries,* which are accessible through the intranet of a company and which give all employees access to reports and studies that have been bought by the company. Particularly in a large company in which most relevant reports are bought, this gives foresighters access to valuable information in an effective way.

Table 5.2 IT collaboration tools used for foresight activities

Tool	Description	Used for dg	Used for in	Used for co
News readers	Software program that extracts information on predefined topics from a selection of Web sites	√		
Internal libraries	Online libraries in which all studies and reports are stored centrally to give access to all employees	√		
Document management platforms	Systems that store electronic documents centrally in order to enable work on them collaboratively. Includes the functionality to check in and check out documents to prevent version conflicts	√	√	√
Corporate directories	Listing of all employees, which allows searches for internal experts and internal stakeholders	√	√	√
Instant messaging	Form of communication that allows the sending of text messages as well as other documents instantaneously and thus speeds up communication and interpretation of information		√	√
Tagging platforms	Systems that assign keywords to any kind of electronic information or files. These keywords can then be seen by other users of the system, helping to identify the relevance of information from different perspectives		√	
Instant Delphi analysis	Software program which runs a Delphi-like analysis with multiple rounds and among a group which is connected over the Internet. Such an analysis is usually completed within 1 or 2 days		√	
Wikis	Web page that can easily be edited by anyone and is used to collaboratively create knowledge. Each user can add information to complete information entered by previous users or to correct wrong information		√	√
Mailing lists	Predefined groups which are known for their common need for specific information. The list is the basis for the dissemination of information to these groups			√
Blogs	Web sites used to regularly post new information, commentaries, graphical elements, and videos. Particularly suited to communicate information in fast-changing domains			√

dg data gathering, *in* interpretation, *co* communication

All four companies had also installed a central *document management system (DMS)*, to facilitate collaboration. Through such a system documents can be accessed and worked on by many employees. This allows the foresighters to collaboratively collect and interpret information and communicate their insights. In the old way of working, a foresight report would have been divided into chapters written by different foresighters and integrated into a single document just before publishing. A DMS facilitates the collaborative working on smaller sections while preventing version conflicts. In addition, DMS can be used for the dissemination of foresight insights. A DMS not only allows for the distribution of the report to a wider audience at a low cost but also facilitates the distribution of backup material on the future topics, such as original articles and video interviews with key informants.

Another IT tool which facilitates all three phases of foresight and was available at all four companies is a *corporate directory*. Corporate directories allow searching for internal experts as well as internal customers for foresight. The four companies had installed corporate directories that offer different degrees of information on the employees. In the least developed corporate directories, only contact details and the job title were available. In the most developed corporate directories, a complete personal profile was available, including the work area, projects, and fields of expertise of the employee. This provided data allows searching for specific skills or expertise and thus allows creating new contacts or expert networks within the company.

One Web 2.0 IT tool which is used by all companies (although to different extents) is *instant messaging (IM)*. Today's instant messaging tools make it possible to send not only text but also pictures, videos, and any kind of document instantaneously over the Internet or intranet. Some IM systems also provide virtual white boards, where two users can jointly draw diagrams while being connected. IM has greatly increased the frequency and speed of communication. The head of corporate strategy of one company noted that whereas 7 years ago he would have communicated with the CEO about the strategy only two times a year through a formal exchange of written documents, he has communicated with him on the day of the interview already three times in the last 2 h.

A novel way of interpreting information was also introduced in the Web 2.0 environment under the name of *tagging platforms*. Tagging describes the action of assigning keywords to information or electronic documents. While the function is rather simple, the impact for the efficiency of foresight has been described as being profound. Collaborative tagging facilitated by a central platform makes it possible to identify the relevance of new information from different perspectives. For example, a technological development could mean from the point of view of an engineer an efficiency gain, while from the point of view of a product manager it could enable new functionalities. On a tagging platform, the foresighter could tag the new information with the keywords *new product A* and *efficiency gain for technology 1*, thus enabling the distribution of the information to his two internal customers.

One company employed within its IT tool suite a tool to run what it called an *instant Delphi analysis* among groups within their virtual personal network. This functionality was employed to consolidate opinions on trends within the group of foresighters. One user would ask a question, and within 1–2 days the Internet-based Delphi would run a predefined number of rounds to produce a consolidated answer among the virtual expert panel. The key and barrier for this tool is the participation. When sufficient participation is achieved it is a very effective tool. But if the foresighters fail to generate sufficient participation, the tool will not generate a consolidated opinion.

Another tool discussed under the headline of Web 2.0 is the *wiki*. The inventor of wikis derived the name from the Hawaiian word for fast. A wiki is a Web site that makes it possible to create and edit interlinked Web pages in an efficient fashion and integrate the viewers of the Web site as authors and editors.

The most prominent example of a wiki is the user-generated encyclopedia Wikipedia. In the corporate foresight context, two of the four companies employ wikis to collaboratively create knowledge on new topics. The wiki tool makes it easy to work on one issue with many people. Thus, new information about an emerging issue can be added and edited collaboratively and in an effective and efficient manner. One company uses the wiki tool as a foresighter-collaboration tool and publishes its foresight insights directly through the wiki pages to the internal customers and in a second version externally.

Another simple but powerful IT tool is a mailing list. For inter-personal information exchange, e-mail has become the primary communication channel. Likewise, *mailing lists* have become the preferred communication channel to distribute information in a one-to-many mode. All four companies use these mailing lists to disseminate their foresight results. Only very few foresight insights are still being sent as hard-copy reports, mostly to high level executives and specific reports that cover a long time horizon and a broad topic range. All other foresight insights are generally made available through document management systems and mailing list.

To disseminate time-critical information, *blogs* are starting to being used in the context of corporate foresight. Blogs were originally employed as online diaries used to communicate opinions to specific target groups. Today they are Web sites that are used to regularly post new information on specific topics (Kumar et al. 2005:160). Like wikis, the blogs are easy to use and thus allow the owner of information to communicate them in an effective and efficient manner. One company uses blogs to facilitate monitoring of topics on which they have been asked to regularly provide updates on any development in this domain.

In order to establish some knowledge about the implementation cost, the informants were also asked to describe their implementation effort as measured by hardware investments, software and application development, and the effort needed to motivate and educate internal users. On the basis of the qualitative descriptions, Fig. 5.10 has been developed. Given that it has no quantitative basis, the interpretation of the figure should be done with care. Nevertheless, it can be seen that some IT collaboration tools need less implementation effort than others, and it is shown in which phase of the foresight process the tools can be used. Thus, the figure should provide practitioners some guidance on finding appropriate IT tools to extend and improve their corporate foresight systems.

5.4.3 Evaluation

Overall, it can be concluded that IT tools yield the potential to increase both efficiency and effectiveness of a corporate foresight process. They can help focus the information collection and facilitate interpretation, particularly by allowing the *integration of multiple foresighters and internal stakeholders into the interpretation* process. IT tools can be effective communication channels, thus allowing a larger number of participants, which in turn can be expected to positively influence the

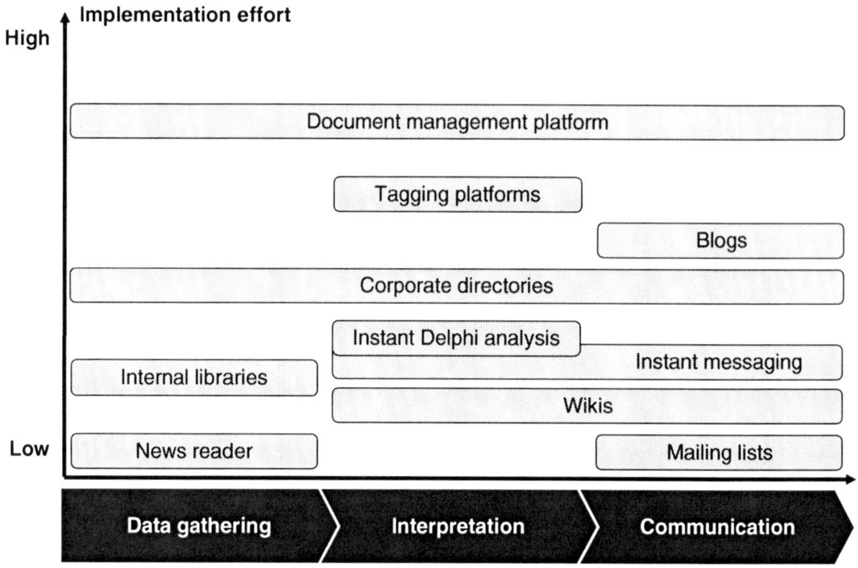

Fig. 5.10 IT collaborations tools and implementation effort

performance and success of the corporate foresight activity (Neill et al. 2007:731; Björk and Magnusson 2009:662) and making it possible to disseminate the information to more internal customers.

From the context analysis it can be concluded that companies that (1) operate in a high clockspeed environment, (2) follow innovation leader strategies, and/or (3) operate in a complex environment have a particularly high motivation to employ IT tools. In one company, a wiki was used for tracking the founding and growth of start-up companies. This platform was maintained by a cross-functional working group, including staff from the foresight department, marketing, mergers and acquisitions, and R and D. The result is a more comprehensive and more detailed information base on start-ups than could be found in any of the other companies. In addition, the information in the wiki is subject to regular reviews and consolidation by internal experts and stakeholders, making it much easier to trigger actions, such as starting collaborations with start-up companies and preparing for the acquisition.

Concerning the cost of implementation of such tools, all respondents emphasized that the costs of developing and installing the tools have gone down considerably in recent years, making most tools available even to small and medium-sized enterprises (SME). But particularly for large companies the real cost of implementations is the cost of promoting their use and surmounting individual barriers of use. Some tools, such as new readers, yield benefits even if they are only employed by one individual foresighter. But most tools need to be used by most if not all relevant stakeholders to produce the desired benefit. Thus, the decision to employ IT tools for foresight should always be made taking into account the necessary promotion cost and the probability of achieving widespread use.

Implementation of such tools should only be pursued if a clear understanding exists on how the relevant stakeholders can be motivated to utilize them. For example, a wiki will only be successful if all relevant information owners, foresighters, and internal customers use the wiki as their major point of reference. To achieve this, all potential participants have to be persuaded to use the wiki as their personal knowledge management tool. They should be motivated to put all information with relevance into the wiki or use the wiki to link to the relevant information sources through hyperlinks.

Many companies reported activities of implementing IT tools for corporate foresight, but only a limited number among them reported getting a significant benefit out of them. Even fewer companies reported that all relevant stakeholders do participate in using and promoting the tools. Nevertheless, all respondents agreed that the degree of IT tool use will increase and contribute significantly to the success of top-performing companies. Thus, it can generally be recommended that the use of IT tools should be considered by all companies, but the decision to implement them should be made for each tool individually.

5.5 Communicating Insights Through Participation (People and Networks)

Many studies have highlighted the need to ensure a high degree of participation of the decision makers or internal customers in the foresight exercise (Van der Helm 2007:3; Harroussi 2004:4; Scapolo 2005:1059; Oner and Gol 2007:451) otherwise the risk is that the foresight insights will never be used to trigger actions (Schwarz 2005:22). Participation increases the decision-making speed (Zehir and Ozsahin 2008:709), promotes a constructive dialogue to plan the future (DenHond and Groenewegen 1996:33), and increases the likelihood that foresight results will trigger actions (Cuhls 2003:93; Salo 2001:696; Konnola et al. 2007:609), because foresight is particularly for top management a learning process in which the will to take action needs to be built over time (Costanzo 2004:219).

In the case studies, several respondents added that often future-oriented decisions are taken based on "gut feeling" rather than on data. In these cases, it is particularly important to involve the decision makers in the foresight exercise and to confront them with tangible insights such as lead customer statements and prototypes that utilize emerging technologies.

5.5.1 Context and Motivation

A company from the automobile sector has developed a particularly comprehensive set of mechanisms to communicate insights while ensuring a high degree of participation of internal customers. The company has a global presence in all major automobile markets. It has a workforce of 370,000 employees and annual revenues of 114 billion euros (annual report, 2008). The source of competitive advantage is a mix of innovation leadership and customer proximity. Characteristic of the organization is also a complex organizational structure, which includes in addition to a functional and regional structure a structure of multiple brands. The respondents pointed to this complex structure as the reason for a corporate culture built on a strong belief that clear and well-executed processes are needed to ensure corporate success.

The primary motivation for the foresight activities which were analyzed in the case study was to get a better understanding of customer needs in an important foreign market. This aim was proposed in response to a drop in sales, which had been attributed to the lack of appeal of recently introduced car models.

The goal of the foresight project was to increase customer understanding, critically review the model portfolio, and propose new features and new car concepts that would better suit the requirements of the customers in the foreign market.

5.5.2 *Description of Practice*

In order to bring internal customers as well as internal stakeholders into the foresight project, it was decided to create a team, led and coached by the foresighters, but whose team members were recruited from other functional units in the company. The team recruitment was done trough a company-wide selection process. The result was a team of 23 employees on which all major functional units were represented by at least one team member.

After an initial on-boarding week, the whole team moved for 18 months to the foreign country in order to immerse themselves in the culture and lifestyle. The whole team lived together in a large house in one of the major cities of the country. The city was selected because it was particularly diverse culturally. This allowed the team to study all relevant subcultures without having to travel to different cities and regions in the country. To gain the possibility of working on unusual time schedules, certain degrees of freedom were negotiated for the work contracts directly with top management and the trade unions.

Given the size and budget of the project, it was particularly important to show outcomes directly from the beginning of the project. In addition, the aim of the project was to help in deciding on fundamental change of the strategy of market cultivation in the foreign country. Particularly for such far-reaching decisions, it was believed to be critical to involve internal customers in the project and spread the insights through multiple channels in order to trigger an organizational learning process. From the activities mentioned by the nine informants, seven primary mechanisms were identified (see Table 5.3).

Table 5.3 Mechanisms for facilitating communication and participation

Mechanism	Example
Integrate functional units into project team	Company-wide selection process is used to form a project team that includes 23 employees representing all major functional units
Internal customers gather real-life evidence	Internal customers and stakeholders of foresight results are involved in the gathering of information and thus get real customer testimonials and firsthand evidence
Making information as tangible as possible	To ensure that the future-related information is as tangible as possible, lead users, prototypes, and interviews with lifestyle visionaries were captured and communicated through blogs, pictures, short videos, and audio recordings
Representations of future customers	To communicate customer preferences and customer profiles, real-world representations were composed of 200 personal items that are typical of the consumer group
Physical future living spaces	In the project, future living spaces of the year 2020 were built jointly with 40 other companies from different industries. These living spaces were used for corporate board meetings in order to transfer insights about the future and to make future scenarios perceivable
Encourage word-of-mouth communication	During the 18-month project duration, various groups from the company were invited to get firsthand insight from lead users and thought leaders. This encouraged the sharing of information within the whole company by word-of-mouth communication
Using virtual communication channels	The gathered insights were documented using videos, audio recordings, pictures, and written reports. All information was made available through the intranet and updated regularly. The daily blog had 6,000 readers per month

The first mechanism, *integrate functional units into the project team*, has been emphasized for its role in bringing the functional units full-time into the project. The project manager explained that

> It is important that the people are 100% on the task, . . . and not that they consider the task only as an afternoon task in addition to their operational responsibilities. Then it makes no sense![4]

Therefore, the 23 employees were put on leave for their duties and responsibilities in the operational units and assigned full time to the foresight exercise. With the representation of all major functional units, it was ensured (1) that the team had a strong multi-disciplinary profile that brought different perspectives to the foresight task and (2) that the foresight insights would have maximum communication penetration by being transferred by word of mouth in all participating functional units.

[4]Translated from German by the author. Original quote: "[Es ist. . .] wichtig, dass die Menschen hundertprozentig dabei sind [. . .] und nicht, dass man die Aufgabe nur als Nachmittagsaufgabe neben seiner operative Tätigkeit sieht, dann macht es keinen Sinn."

Another mechanism is the *gathering of real-life evidence by the internal customers*. The project used nine primary data-gathering methods. They included overnight stays at customer homes in order to immerse themselves in their lifestyle and trend emergence through talking to trendsetters. One such trend was the so-called LOHAS-trend, the trend toward a lifestyle of health and sustainability, which triggered new markets for wellness, organic food, and energy efficiency. Particularly the sub-trend toward energy efficiency has supported the success of the hybrid cars, which have emerged as an important new car model category.

To encourage the internal customers to gather data on their own, it was said to be important to coach them with experts in the different methods. The project leader emphasized that

> What has been always very helpful was to give the teams of internal experts, which often have been recruited from departments with no customer contact, a structured guide and provide for intensive coaching.[5]

These teams were directed to collect information as tangible as possible. This includes the use of photos, short videos, and audio recordings of interviews with lead users or lifestyle visionaries. The project manager pointed out the importance of capturing the original testimonials to transport authentic evidence:

> Intensive written documentation of interviews is important, as well as the use of videos and audio recordings to capture original customer testimonials, in order to have them for later use.[6]

These testimonials, together with additional information from traditional market research, were used to development *representations of future customers*. These representations are composed of approximately 200 items that are typical of the consumer group. These items were identified in ten categories:

- Entertainment and media
- Sports and leisure
- Health and beauty
- Nutrition
- At home
- Car and mobility
- Mindset and motivation
- Technology and gadgets
- Fashion and accessories
- At work

[5]Translated from German by the author. Original quote: "Was sich immer als sehr hilfreich erwiesen hat, ist dass man den Teams, die auch aus internen Experten zusammengesetzt sind, die häufig aus kundenfernen Bereichen stammen, für die Interviews strukturierte Hilfen an die Hand gegeben hat und sie intensive gecoached hat."

[6]Translated from German by the author. Original quote: "Wichtig ist eine möglichst intensive Mitschrift, oder aber auch die Möglichkeit per Film oder Tonaufnahme zusätzlich den O-Ton mitzuschneiden, so dass man diese sehr wertvollen Informationen weiter benutzen kann."

The representations are used to transport tangible insights into future customer groups. This gives engineers and product designers insights into the needs of the diverse portfolio of customers. This provides them with guidance for adapting future products and services to the needs of their customers, rather than letting the product designers and engineers pursue their own preferences.

To channel future insights directly to top management, a large installation of *physical future living spaces* was created. These living spaces were built together with 40 other companies and installed in a large warehouse. They were also used to host board meetings and helped to transfer insights into future scenarios, thus broadening the perspective of top management and enhancing the future orientation in current decisions.

While future insights can be transferred to top management via such focused events, transferring knowledge in a broader fashion into the whole organization requires relying on *word-of-mouth communication*. This was encouraged by inviting groups to the project house and by making demonstrations of insights back in Germany. By showing the tangible insights, such as the customer testimonials and lead user prototypes, other employees of the company were confronted with foresight results on a more emotional level and thus more likely to start relaying the information. The second professional foresighter in the project explained:

> It is important to communicate results on a tangible and emotional level. Many people approach you after such presentations and tell you: "This is very interesting. How can I help transport these insights? How can I contribute?"[7]

To further enhance the reach of foresight insights, the project used a daily blog – an online diary which was described in Sect. 5.4 – which was made available on the intranet. Such *virtual communication channels* target a large audience at a limited cost. The blog consisted of textual descriptions of insights as well as pictures, videos, and audio elements to transport tangible insights and real customer testimonials. This blog attracted around 6,000 readers per month and thus helped spread the foresight insights even further into the company.

5.5.3 Evaluation

Compared to other companies in my sample, this portfolio of mechanisms to ensure communication of insights and participation of internal stakeholders is particularly comprehensive. Its effectiveness has to be assessed using the results of the project and its impact on decision making.

---

[7]Translated from German by the author. Original quote: "Es ist wichtig wirklich auf einer anfassbare, emotionale Ebene Ergebnispräsentation zu bringen. Viele Leute kommen danach zu einem und sagen: Das ist ja interessant! Kann ich helfen das zu transportieren? Wie kann ich mich da mit einbringen?"

As described in the context and motivation section, the primary goal of the project was to review and enhance the product portfolio and increase sales and customer appeal in the foreign market. By questioning the internal customers of the project, five results from the foresight project have been identified:

- Better understanding of the brand image in the market, e.g., it was shown that the brand was perceived to be female.
- Restructured product-portfolio. The analysis indicated, for example, that the current models were outside the so-called sweet spots (i.e., market positions with a particularly high-demand).
- Three new car concepts that addressed the specific customer needs in this market.
- New engine strategy, to address specific needs in the market.
- Decision on creating a local manufacturing site.

Overall, these five results show that the foresight project had an important impact on the company. Given the considerable investment, it is difficult to decide whether the project should be considered an overall success. This judgment remained controversial, with some informants judging it highly successful and others judging it too expensive.

The conclusion for other companies should be that the different mechanisms employed in this project yield the potential to improve the impact of foresight activities. In addition, most of these mechanisms are not particularly expensive. Using for example blogs to communicate insights has a negligible cost but can significantly enhance the reach of the foresight insights. Likewise, foresight insight presentations can yield the potential to motivate more people to participate in the future exploration activities, even if they are not assigned the task and are not expensive.

It can therefore be recommended to experiment with some of the mechanisms in order to enhance the use of corporate foresight results, thus increasing the return on investment on the foresight activity.

5.6 Linking Foresight to Strategy (Organization)

For many scholars, foresight activities are primarily aimed at enhancing strategic management and strategic decision making (Choo 1996:329; Slaughter 1997:13; Liebl 2005:121; Müller 2008:2). Others add that foresight is essentially an executive board task which cannot and should not be delegated (Krystek 2007:52). But empirical studies have shown repeatedly that the overall level of use of foresight insights for strategic decision making remains low (Liebl 2005:123; Burmeister et al. 2002:3; Gruber et al. 2003:286).

In the case studies, three primary barriers for the use of foresight results have been pointed out by the informants:

- Foresight insights are often characterized by a *high level of uncertainty*, but for strategy making empirical data and forecasts are preferred.
- Managers are expecting to make *decisions based on facts*, but foresight identifies possibilities and often increases the number of options, making it seem more a hindrance to than a help in strategy making.
- Foresight insights are often seen as *"just another piece of information,"* without making clear the value for strategic management.

Nevertheless, multiple companies reported that foresight plays a role in strategic management and adds value to the processes of strategy development and strategic decision making.

However there has been no clear best practice that emerged from the analysis of the case studies. Most companies used foresight to enhance their strategic planning at certain points in their process. In addition, multiple companies reported having different strategic-planning processes for different time horizons:

- A *short-term* planning process, which plans the next fiscal year and includes a small amount of strategic planning. It has more the character of identifying top-level goals and short-term opportunities. But particularly the discussion between the business units (BU) and the corporate level was described as a strategic-planning process.
- A *medium-term* planning process, which plans 3–5 years ahead and is focused on evaluating current markets. The result is often a strategic plan which shifts emphasis from one business field to another.
- A *long-term* planning process, which looks 15–25 years ahead, plans the road toward future markets, and proposes measures to deal with potential disruptions.

Although it might be more intuitive to expect corporate foresight to be performed only on the long term, most scholars report corporate foresight having a role in both the long term and medium term (Ruff 2006:281; Gruber and Venter 2006:972; e Cunha et al. 2006:949). Others expect the time horizon of corporate foresight to be dependent on the industry (Becker 2002:14–15), and a third group even emphasizes the importance of foresight for the short-term planning, because the corporate sensing system has inherent blind spots and foresight is needed to regularly scan these areas (Day and Schoemaker 2004a:118–119; Winter 2004:165).

This study takes the view that corporate foresight can and should play a role in all time horizons of strategic planning. And through the case studies it has been possible to identify successful strategic-planning processes that utilize corporate foresight in all three time horizons.

5.6.1 Short-Term (1 Year)

The case study which provided information on the integration of corporate foresight in the short-term strategic-planning process is from the energy sector. The company is an energy producer with a corporate and business-unit structure. The business units are structured along the value chain reaching from mining and generation to sales (annual report, 2008).

The primary respondents, the head of corporate development and the head of strategic planning, perceived the company to be in a low-clockspeed and medium-complex environment. Their major sources of competitive advantage are optimal processes and customer proximity. The primary source of uncertainty is the political environment, which strongly influences the demand by setting energy-efficiency targets and introducing new laws. In addition, politics also influences the operating costs through regulation and may disrupt the business model through anti-trust laws. For example, an ongoing political discussion – at the time of the interview – was directed at forcing energy producers to sell their energy transport networks in order to increase competition.

As a consequence, the company's primary aim in corporate foresight was to enhance the scanning of the political environment. While a certain amount of scanning of the environment is expected to be done by the business units, the major workload of political foresight is done on the corporate level.

For the short-term planning, the company follows an annual planning cycle which is subdivided into strategic planning in the first half of the year and financial planning in the second half (see Fig. 5.11). The planning is done by multiple iterations between the corporate and business unit level.

In a first step, the business units review the financial data from last year to identify strong and weak business segments within their portfolio and establish a need for change. In addition to this internal analysis, the business units generate strategic options by interviewing business managers and by discussions among the strategy managers in the units. Both analyses are integrated with a workshop, where the strategic manager has discussions with the BU's top management. Using the insights from the workshop and further analysis, the strategy manager of each business unit writes a business unit strategy.

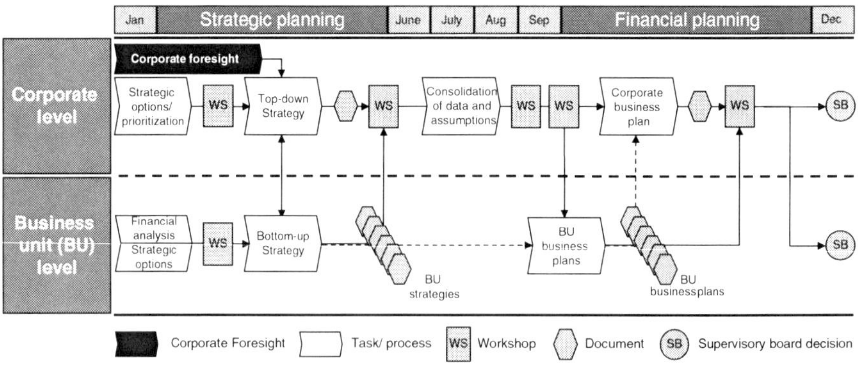

Fig. 5.11 Linking short-term foresight to strategic planning

On the corporate level, the first step is an open brainstorming-driven top-management workshop, which identifies strategic options and uses a scoring mechanism to prioritize them. As a first task of corporate foresight, the strategy unit on the corporate level generates future insights, primarily through desk research and interviews with industry leaders. This first part of corporate foresight is integrated with the political foresight unit to compile a consolidated future outlook. The strategy unit uses both the prioritized strategic options and the corporate foresight insights to produce the top-down strategy.

The integration of the top-down and bottom-up strategy takes place roughly 5 months after the kick-off of the strategic planning. The integration is done in an initial workshop in which the corporate and BU strategies are reviewed and discussed. After the workshop, the corporate strategy unit consolidates the data and basic assumptions from both planning levels. Two subsequent corporate workshops use the data and assumptions to finalize the strategic planning and to break down the strategic goals into operational goals that form the basis for the financial planning in the business plans.

The business planning takes place again separately on both levels and is integrated through a final workshop at the end of the year. The final decision on the strategic and business plans takes place in the supervisory boards on the corporate and on the business unit level.

5.6.2 *Medium Term (3–5 Years)*

The integration of foresight insights into the medium-term strategic planning was observed also in a case in the energy sector, but this time in a manufacturing firm. The company in question has a global reach with a presence in 160 countries. It offers a comprehensive portfolio ranging from oil and gas, fossil, nuclear, and renewable energy applications as well as transmission and distribution systems. The business units are organized in a matrix structure consisting of a regional dimension which encompasses the whole energy business in a certain region, and a product line dimension (annual report, 2008).

The primary respondents, the head of the German business unit and the head of the corporate R and D centers, described the corporate environment to be of medium complexity and characterized by a high clockspeed. The primary source of competitive advantage of the company is technological leadership.

The aim of the medium-term strategic planning is to make a complete review of the business units in order to produce a sales forecast. To generate such a forecast, an environmental scanning exercise is integrated into strategic planning. It provides insights on future developments that may influence sales and business in general. A strong emphasis is put on integrating all relevant internal actors into the process and to use the data available for insights into the company. Such data include the local knowledge about future projects (e.g., for new power plants), insights from lost sales pitches, and information about technology use in products of the competitors.

Similar to the situation of the energy producing company, the business of energy manufacturers is also highly dependent on political decisions. For that reason, this company has a political foresight team of five employees who work full-time on the anticipation of changes in the political environment and in public opinion as well as on monitoring legislative procedures. This team builds on approximately 20 additional managers in different business units, which assume the political foresight responsibility only part-time.

The medium-term strategic-planning process in this company has a time horizon of 3 years. Concerning the scope, the medium-term planning is primarily focused on the market and the political environment. Given that the company pursues a technology leadership strategy, it might be surprising that this area is missing in the scope. This was explained to be because future technologies are managed through a separate process led by the three global corporate R and D centers.

The medium-term strategic-planning process can be divided into three steps: (1) data gathering, (2) aggregation and interpretation, and (3) the model-based forecast (see Fig. 5.12).

In the first step multiple actors are gathering data.

- The *strategic marketing unit* buys and analyzes studies on market developments, including forecasts from market research institutes and universities.
- The *sales unit* gathers feedback on expected sales developments in the different regions, using sales and marketing managers as input sources.
- The *political foresight* unit aggregates all information on changes in regulation and legislation that may have an impact in the next 3 years.
- The business unit's top management uses their personal contacts to high level politicians to collect additional insights into emerging issues and ask for predictions of outcomes of the current legislative discussions.

In the second step, a workshop with representatives of the four units is organized to discuss and consolidate the insights into future developments. In this workshop,

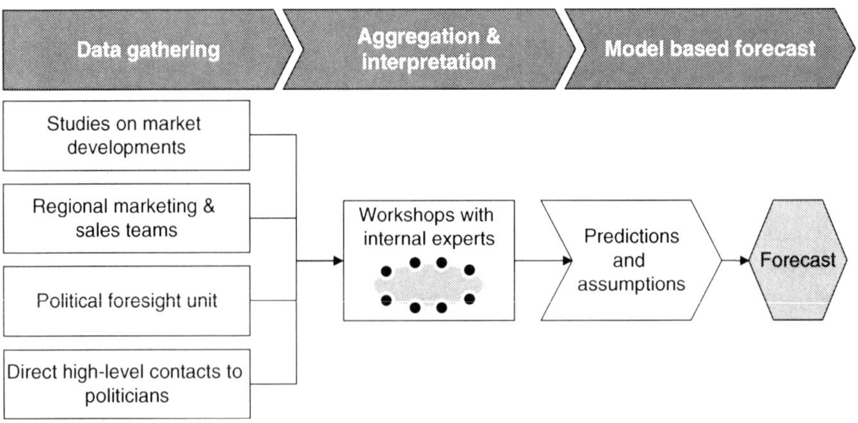

Fig. 5.12 Linking medium-term foresight to strategic planning

the predictions of the different teams are discussed and validated. In addition, there is a check: are the different anticipated developments consistent with each other? Their probability is also predicted.

In the third step, the predictions and assumptions are further analyzed and additional data is collected and processed. Should the predictions be proven wrong by hard evidence, the assumptions are adjusted. After all the predictions and assumptions have been validated, they are used to feed a prediction model that generates sales figures for different business fields and regions. The model also tests the sensitivity of the sales prediction to changes in the assumptions.

5.6.3 *Long Term (15–25 Years)*

A good example of how corporate foresight is used for the long-term strategic-planning process was observed at the same company as in the medium-term strategic planning: the energy-systems manufacturer.

The case offered the opportunity to observe an example of a successful corporate foresight exercise which resulted in the entry of the company into a new and promising market. However it does not qualify as a best practice, because it is not an established practice that is repeated regularly. Although the outcome has been judged by all participants as successful, it has not been repeated in the same way.

The process can be divided into three steps (see Fig. 5.13). The starting point of the exercise was the initiative of the executive board, which was started to look into new and promising business fields. To that end, a team of an external foresight consultancy was hired and asked to gather and provide information about a pre-selected field. This intelligence development was done by gathering studies, internal field research, and interviews with leading experts.

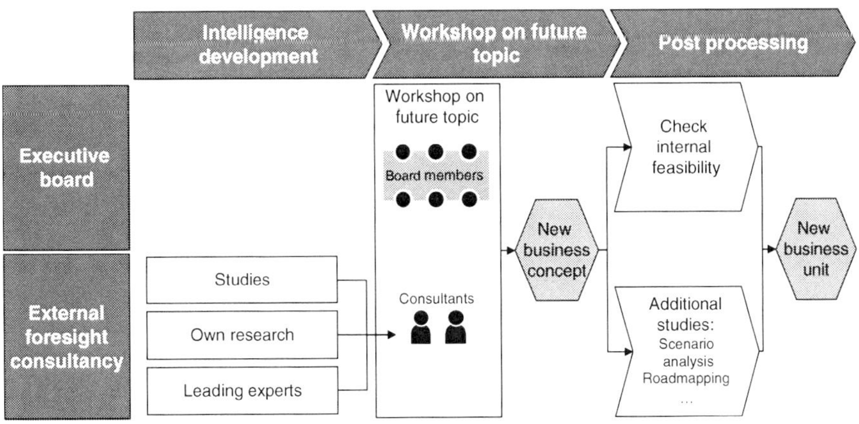

Fig. 5.13 Linking long-term foresight to strategic planning

In the second step, the consultants presented the results from the analysis, using as many visual presentation techniques as possible. The visualization of the insights was judged to be success-critical and allowed the executive board to intellectually immerse themselves into the new business field. In the workshop, much room was left for discussion among the board members. The discussion was moderated by the consultants. The board members were asked to judge which internal assets could add to the success if the company chose to enter the new business field. The workshop resulted in an agreement that the business field is promising.

In the post-processing of the workshop, the consultancy developed an initial business concept that contained both the market data and the internal assets that had been identified by the executive board members. This business concept was used as a basis for the third step.

In the third step, the consultancy worked further on studies that explored the new business field. The scenario analysis was used to understand possible developments in the field and to identify drivers and barriers. Building on the insights from the scenario analysis, a roadmap was drawn to plan milestones and critical developments that needed to be monitored or influenced.

On the company side, the outcome of the workshop was used as the basis for an internal project that made a feasibility study for the development of the new business field and planned initial steps.

The final outcome was the founding of a new business unit that today is highly successful.

5.6.4 Evaluation

Through the case studies, a variety of possibilities have been identified that build corporate foresight into the strategic-planning processes. No best way has emerged. It has rather become clear (1) that companies tend to customize their strategic planning and thus also tailor the foresight input to their needs and (2) that strategic planning and strategic decision making still rely heavily in most companies on internal data, thus leaving a gap that needs to be filled by corporate foresight.

Although most top-management respondents agreed that strong environmental scanning should be part of any strategic-planning process, most also had difficulties clearly pointing out the value from corporate foresight.

From the barriers to integration of foresight in strategic planning, it has become clear that many corporate executives feel more comfortable making a decision on the basis of data and facts – even if they are neither complete nor conclusive. Having corporate foresight input is often perceived more as a hindrance to making the decision and at times makes the executives more uncomfortable with their final decision. In consequence, corporate foresight will only be ubiquitously applied for strategic management if the mindset changes in corporate boardrooms.

The good news for companies that are willing to use foresight to improve their competitiveness and enhance their strategic management is that the cases also provided multiple examples of the successful use of foresight. The examples identified clear value contributions, such as the exploration of new business fields and the initiation of new product development projects.

It can therefore be tentatively concluded that there is a high potential for the application of foresight in strategic management, but that there are also multiple barriers that need to be overcome. As described in the previous Sect. (5.5), a high level of participation is crucial to the use of foresight insights. Likewise, participation – such as the participation of the executive board in the concept development for the entry into a new business field – is very important for ensuring the stable integration of foresight in strategic management.

5.7 Linking Foresight to Innovation Management (Organization)

In times of radical change and discontinuities, it is expected that companies that are the first to perceive and understand a trend will be in a position to gain a competitive advantage (Krystek and Müller-Stewens 1999:175; Liebl 2005:12; Rollwagen et al. 2008:355). Having the knowledge about the emerging trend would give the company the possibility of acting early and of producing an adequate response. The response can be expected to involve the innovation management of the company (Gruber and Venter 2006:172; Ruff 2006:286).

One initial hypothesis could therefore be that corporate foresight should be directly linked to the innovation process (Stuckenschneider and Schwair 2005: 779; Martinet and Ribault 1989:229). Investigating this hypothesis, respondents were asked to comment on the relationship and possible process links between corporate foresight and innovation management. From the analysis of the responses, it has become clear that in most companies the relationship between foresight activities and innovation activities is complex and that links exist on various levels.

Given the complexity of the interaction of innovation and foresight activities, it was aimed to identify generalizable interaction patterns. To do so, all cases were compared and clustered. This clustering has been made by identifying individual activities and clustering them. Through this process, three major clusters have been identified and analyzed. It has been concluded that these clusters can be described as roles of corporate foresight, which are played to enhance the innovation capacity. The three roles derived from the clustering are depicted in Fig. 5.14.

Using a four step innovation process as a frame of reference, the three roles can be positioned at the start of the innovation funnel (initiator role), outside the innovation funnel (strategist role), and along the innovation funnel (opponent role). In these three roles, different activities are conducted to boost the innovation capability of the company:

- In the *initiator* role, corporate foresight triggers innovation initiatives by identifying new customer needs, new technologies, and the new product concepts of competitors.
- In the *strategist* role, corporate foresight guides innovation activities by vision creation, providing strategic guidance, consolidating opinions, assessing and repositioning of innovation portfolios, and identifying the new business models of competitors.
- In the *opponent* role, corporate foresight challenges the innovators to create better and more successful innovations by questioning basic assumptions, challenging the state-of-the-art of current R and D projects, and scanning for disruptions that could endanger current and future innovations.

5.7.1 The Initiator Role

From Fig. 5.14, it can be seen that corporate foresight in the initiator role directly feeds into the innovation process. The *initiator* role triggers new innovation initiatives, including new R and D projects, new processes, and business-model innovations. By doing so, it feeds the innovation funnel, which in turn is the basis for an increase in the quantity and quality of innovative output.

Most companies that have a corporate foresight system with a strong emphasis on the initiator role have also installed direct process links to the innovation process. Only two companies did not have such a direct link, preferring instead to communicate the insights through the Intranet, mailing lists, and a printed report. These companies aim to use corporate foresight for creating input but leave the responsibility for taking action with the individual innovation managers, who have to propose, for example, new innovation projects.

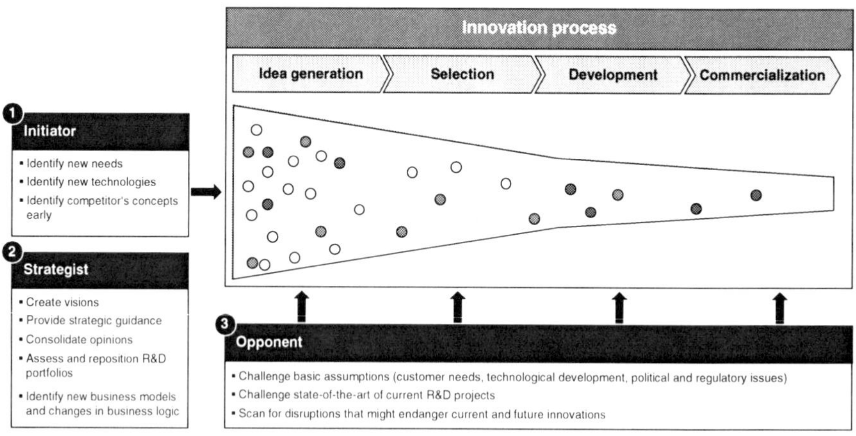

Fig. 5.14 The three roles of foresight in innovation management

Concerning the areas of foresight activity in the initiator role, three distinct input clusters have been found (Table 5.4):

- *New customer requirements*, which are identified by analyzing cultural shifts and collecting the needs of lead customers.
- *New emerging technologies*, which are identified by scanning the science and technology environment.
- *New competitors' concepts*, which are identified by monitoring the activities of the competitors.

Table 5.4 Linking foresight to innovation management (initiator role)

Impact of initiator role	Description	No. of references	Quotes
Identify new needs	Socio-cultural change and/or change in lead customer needs generate new requirements that in turn trigger innovation	123	In particular, I feel that we need to be dialogue-oriented. Just placing a questionnaire in front of the customer is not good enough[a] Today, products need not only to have a good usability; they need to be cool. I sell shampoo only through emotions; the ingredients are of no interest[b]
Identify emerging technologies	Scanning science and technology enables companies to create new products and brace against disruptive and substitution technologies	84	We have ten strategic areas. In each we define the reach, scope, and technology surveillance interest Technology watch is a continuous process; it is used for R and D projects
Identify competitors' concepts early	Monitoring the activities of competitors is the basis for anticipating their future actions and plan their own innovation activities	56	We need to be alert that there are constantly new business ideas and new start-ups. Technology foresight is easy for us, but exploring future changes by competitive intelligence is much more complex and much more difficult

[a]Translated from German by the author. Original quote: "Vor allem glaube ich an diese Dialogorientierung. Das man nicht nur einen Fragebogen hinlegt, sondern wirklich mit ihm diskutiert und sich mit ihm auseinander setzt"

[b]Translated from German by the author. Original quote: "Es geht nicht nur drum wie mache ich Sachen möglichst einfach bedienbar, sondern die müssen noch cool daher kommen. Ich verkauf heute ein Shampoo nur noch über Emotionen, die Inhaltstoffe interessieren keinen Menschen"

From the number of references in each cluster, it can also be observed that the customer perspective was mentioned the most in our sample, although most capabilities were identified in the technology domain. The reason appears to be that most companies still struggle to implement customer foresight activities in their environmental scanning systems. The continuous monitoring of the movements of the competitors has been reported only by a few informants and was mostly focused on monitoring the start-up environment.

Overall, the initiator role has been said to be crucial in times in which the company wants to move into new business fields and in times of discontinuous technological change. In a situation in which a company is aiming to stabilize or extend its position in the current business field (incremental innovation), it was judged by the respondents to be sufficient to rely on the intelligence gathering which takes place by the engineers in the business units. In such a situation no specific corporate foresight activity is needed. But where innovation moves into new business fields and makes use of new technologies (radical innovations), informants expressed the need of a top-down corporate initiative to gather the needed information.

5.7.2 *The Strategist Role*

The *strategist* role is not directly linked to the innovation process. It is rather played by corporate foresight for defining strategic guidelines, identifying new strategic innovation areas, and scanning for disruptive business models. More specifically, the strategist role has been created by clustering five distinct activities, which have been described in Table 5.5.

The first cluster is the impact of supporting the *strategic review of R and D portfolios*. In the foresight activity, emerging innovation opportunities are identified and compared with current R and D priorities and budgets. If a realignment is needed, the foresight activity provides the needed arguments for taking decisions on re-allocating R and D investments.

Another function of the strategist role is *providing strategic guidance*. One company produced visualizations of future product-use scenarios and used them to direct and align thinking and working throughout the company. Providing these visualizations is thought to promote common goals and to help in the synchronization of innovation efforts.

In addition, corporate foresight can help in the identification of the potential and disruptive power of *new business models and business logic*. One company used scenario analysis to explore possible changes in its home market in the next 15 years. In the scenario analysis, one scenario, judged to have a high probability, described a market configuration in which 15% of all value creation would be achieved through networks of companies. In consequence, the company formulated a strategic ambition to engage more in collaborations with other companies and build internal value-creation networks. On top of the proactive identification and development of new business models, corporate foresight efforts could include

Table 5.5 Linking foresight to innovation management (strategist role)

Impact of strategist role	Description	No. of references	Quotes
Assessing and repositioning of innovation portfolios	Corporate foresight provides the future insights to change innovation portfolios	68	(Our technology intelligence) supports the analysis of our project portfolio We use the information (from foresighting) for our product planning for the coming years (On the basis of the foresight insights) we have changed the product portfolio in China and the United States and introduced four new cars in China and three in the United States[a]
Providing strategic guidance	Future insights are used to define strategic directions	58	Our most important goal when we do scenario analysis is that we need an overall goal and strategic guardrails This (scenario technique) allows you to align the whole wagon . . . to set the ship on a long-term course[b]
Identifying new business models	Foresight exercises challenge current business models and provide insights into alternative ones	38	(Engaging) in value-creation networks has been one of the major outcomes of the scenario project Blackberry is an example (of a latent need) that no company has expressed the need for. But it is certainly a new trend to enhance the individual's efficiency
Consolidating opinions	The process of creating future insights is often used to trigger discussion and consolidate opinions throughout the company	30	(The goal) is primarily to form opinions. That means we throw something to the people and leave them alone with it (The goal is) to consolidate an internal market view (with our market forecasts)
Vision creation	Corporate foresight creates pictures of the future to create a common understanding of future directions	23	With future topics, there is no certainty. And that is why you gain safety if you stay unspecific, if you describe (the future) in a picture and not in a precise mathematical description

[a]Translated from German by the author. Original quote: "(Auf der Grundlage der Frühaufklärungsaktvitäten) haben wir in China und in USA das Produktportfolio geändert, in China 4 neue Fahrzeuge, in den USA drei neue Fahrzeuge"

[b]Translated from German by the author. Original quote: "Und dadurch (Szenarioanalyse) kann sich der gesamte Karren in eine Richtung ausgerichtet werden. Das heißt wir bringen das Boot langfristig auf Kurs"

the scanning for new (and rival) business models and changes in business logic, which have the potential to threaten the current business activities.

Other companies commented also on a benefit derived from the process of corporate foresight. By engaging multiple internal stakeholders, an internal discussion is triggered that helps to *consolidate opinions*. These opinions include probability of trends, judging the size of a business opportunity, and validation of market forecasts. One company regularly runs a foresight activity that involves its foreign subsidiaries and local marketing staff to make predictions about new emerging market segments. This activity is judged as very successful for facilitating a cross-regional discussion and for consolidating the different opinions on market developments.

A further impact is *vision creation*, which differs from providing strategic guidance, because it is left unspecific. Several companies said that with foresight insights they aim for a certain fuzziness in order to emphasize the uncertainty and ensure that the visions inspire the company to create the future by working in the direction of the vision, rather than demotivating through a rigid goal definition.

5.7.3 The Opponent Role

The *opponent* role has an impact throughout the innovation process (see Fig. 5.14 earlier in the document). The opponent role was derived by clustering three activities (see Table 5.6).

In the role, the primary aim is to *challenge the ideas and basic assumptions* of innovators. Such assumptions can be in the field of customer needs, technological developments, and regulatory issues. They are typically built on views of the world that are undisputed within the company, but which are discussed more controversially outside the corporate environment.

By monitoring such assumptions and reporting expected changes, corporate foresight facilitates re-adjustments of innovation activities within a project or triggers the cancellation of projects when they are judged to be likely to fail to produce a competitive product.

In addition, corporate foresight plays the opponent role when it identifies technologies, products, or changes in the consumer needs domain that have *disruptive potential*. These changes were said to yield their disruptive potential particularly because they come from a domain outside the scope of the current business activity. They are often alternatives or substitution products that build on technologies that are outside the technological areas currently used by the company.

The third major impact of the opponent role is to ensure the *state-of-the-art of R and D projects*. One company judged this to be the major aim and impact of all corporate foresight. This company employs a unit of six full-time employees who scan the environment, discuss and process the collected information, and use the generated insights for workshops with R and D project teams. The team's major impact is the regular participation in new project presentations, project milestone

Table 5.6 Linking foresight to innovation management (opponent role)

Impact of opponent role	Description	No. of references	Quotes
Challenging basic assumptions	The foresight activity challenges current innovation activities to adjust to external changes	18	(One outcome is) to wake up people and show them things outside their worldview If a (scientific) study proves that mobile telephony triggers cancer, then our business model is gone forever That's true, if we do not have this scenario approach, then we also do not challenge our premises
Scanning for disruptions that could endanger current and future innovations	Corporate foresight provides information about wild cards, i.e., potential disruptive change	18	There might be glowing wallpaper, or people do not have money anymore to consume energy; such things could be disruptive Environmental factors such as pollution or drying-up of all oil wells; in such cases, we do not need to think about cars anymore. Transportation, yes, but not about petrol or diesel engines
Challenging the state-of-the-art of current R and D projects	Foresight projects show how current R and D projects need to be refocused to adapt to changes in the environment	15	(As a consequence of the foresight activity,) we have changed the engine strategy and moved toward smaller 4-cylinder engines, whereas before everybody said, 'You are crazy (to propose such a thing)'

meetings, and review workshops. At these workshops, they challenge the current activities with what they have observed in the environment or what is already available in lead markets.

5.7.4 *Evaluation*

Through cross-case analysis, I was able to identify three roles that corporate foresight can play in innovation management. The quotes of the interviewees also captured testimonies on how corporate foresight positively influences the innovation capacity of a company. This is a clear extension of the knowledge about the value creation of corporate foresight.

Multiple examples – such as Kodak's failure to respond effectively to the threat of digital photography – highlight the need to establish effective mechanisms that allow companies to respond to disruptive change in a timely manner. Here the activities associated with the strategist role should enable companies to enhance their ability to identify and exploit the windows of opportunity that arise from disruptive change and which allow them to move into new business fields.

Most companies that used corporate foresight in a strategist role had a strategic innovation and strategic technology management unit, which are the primary internal customers for the foresight insights. A clear recommendation from the case studies is to involve members of these boards directly in the activity or ensure for multiple iterations and discussions before the final implications are presented.

The opponent role has been observed in the case studies as being played through face-to-face workshops with R and D project teams. As this practice has been said to be successful by both the foresight manager and the internal customers, it can be recommended to establish the opponent role in a similar fashion.

Concerning the initiator role, it has not been possible to conclusively judge what kind of link is more effective in triggering actions (1) a formal link to the innovation process or (2) dissemination of foresight insights in a broadcast fashion. Even though the formal link to the innovation process ensures that the innovation opportunity will be evaluated, it does not guarantee that the decision makers within the innovation funnel's gates will be convinced that the opportunity should be pursued. In companies that relied exclusively on broadcasted foresight information dissemination, it is not certain that it reaches R and D or product managers and that they will take action. But broadcasting foresight insights reaches more internal stakeholder, thus increasing the chance that the organization will be more receptive and responsive to innovation opportunities.

The tentative conclusion is that companies should pursue a multi-mode dissemination strategy, meaning that they should establish process links and at the same time broadcast the foresight insights through mailing lists, the intranet, blogs, wikis, and internal document management systems.

5.8 Involving Every Employee to Manage Discontinuous Change (Culture)

In past research, scholars interested in understanding how companies manage discontinuous change were primarily focused on identifying the formal processes (Becker 2002:7; Burmeister et al. 2004a:24; Coates 1985:30; Horton 1999:5). Only more recently have scholars started seeing the management of discontinuous change more as an ability that may be managed as a process, but which may also be developed without a process (Slaughter 1998:382; Krystek and Müller-Stewens 1999:175; Tsoukas and Shepherd 2004a:138).

5.8.1 Context and Motivation

One company in our sample reported having no corporate foresight capabilities at all, but it is one with a track record of having been able to reinvent itself repeatedly, thus having demonstrated its ability to manage discontinuous change in the past. More than 150 years old, this U.S.-based company company is active in multiple industries and in 160 countries (annual report, 2008). The company follows a technology leadership strategy and sees its technology strength also as their primary source of competitive advantage. To develop the technological competencies, the company spends more than 450 million euros on R and D and runs four global research centers with more than 3,000 employees (annual report, 2008). The global research centers also facilitate a cross-divisional technology exchange platform to identify synergies in R and D as well as commercialization of their products.

Concerning the environment of the company, the informants rated the complexity to be between medium and high and the industry clockspeed to be high. It has thus been surprising that the informants reported that no formal corporate foresight processes are in place. It was attributed to the fact that the company is primarily business driven and in consequence does not look far into the future, but is more focused on improving business performance in today's markets.

Another important characteristic is that the company operates exclusively in B2B markets and in markets that are highly dependent on the political environment. In the case study, the informants reported that on several occasions political shifts have deeply affected the company's revenues, forcing the company to reposition itself strategically.

5.8.2 Description of Practice

The first 10 min in the first interview revealed the paradox that the need to develop abilities to proactively manage discontinuous change was widely recognized but that no active foresight processes were in place. The first respondent, who was the head of one of the corporate research labs, knew the term *corporate foresight* and was able to define it, but was insistent that no such processes were regularly being executed. But he explained that most employees are asked to have an external view and particularly the employees at the corporate research lab are continuously scanning the environment:

Table 5.7 Five personal "growth traits" that foster foresight ability

Personal trait	Description derived from interviews
External focus	Employees are expected to actively look outside the company boundaries and continuously scan the periphery
Clear thinking	Describes the ability to translate strategy into action. A clear thinker communicates clearly and concisely
Imaginative	Employees should use their creativity to identify opportunities and take risks to make them reality and thus add to the company's competitiveness
Inclusiveness	The ability to connect and inspire other people to invest their efforts in new topics and the ability to create an environment of trust
Expertise	Employees should strive to continuously enhance their domain, functional, and industry knowledge, allowing them to make better judgments on opportunities and threats

> To explain that a little bit from the organizational perspective: We do not have a staff unit that is dedicated full-time to it (strategic foresight). Everyone in this building (the corporate research lab) has it in his job description to look outside for change.[8]

In the following interviews, the notion that all employees are expected to identify discontinuous change and propose appropriate managerial actions was stated repeatedly. All six informants pointed at so-called "growth traits" which in their opinion played a crucial role in preparing the company for the future. An overview of these five "growth traits" is given in Table 5.7.

When questioned on the use and impact of the "growth traits," all respondents explained and confirmed that they are often mentioned in day-to-day work and tracked every year in the personal annual review. Indeed, every respondent had them memorized and was able to describe them. Compared to other companies, this is remarkable. In most other companies, the employees were not able to name the corporate values, code of conduct, or the traits that are promoted as part of the corporate culture.

Looking closer at the five growth traits, a high degree of similarity can be observed in the desired characteristics of foresighters, which have been discussed in Sect. 4.2.3 (see also Table 4.16). These desired characteristics, which have been identified through the case studies as well as from the literature review, have a good match with the personal "growth traits" identified in the case study. Four out of five growth traits have corresponding items in the desired characteristics of foresighters (see Table 5.8).

The *external focus*, which is central to the work as a foresighter can be matched with the strong external network, which is desired for foresighters. In the interview, it was explained that all employees are asked to create and maintain personal networks and within their annual review have to comment on what they were able

[8]Translated from German by the author. Original quote: "Um mal ein bisschen etwas organisatorisch zu erklären an dieser Stelle. Wir haben keine Stabsstelle, die das hauptamtlich macht. Alle die hier im Gebäude sind haben ihrer Job Description nach andere Aufgaben als jetzt quasi nach außen zu gucken, was passiert denn da so."

Table 5.8 Matching "growth traits" and the desired characteristics of foresighters

Personal trait	Desired characteristics of foresighters
External focus	Strong external network
Imaginative	Curious and receptive
Inclusiveness	Open-minded and passionate
	Strong internal network
Expertise	Broad knowledge
	Deep knowledge

to gain from them. The external focus can therefore be expected to effectively promote the inflow of environmental information and thus support the insight generation on discontinuous change.

The personal trait *imaginative*, which is designed to support out-of-the-box thinking, also resembles the desired characteristics of foresighters to be curious and receptive. If imagination is promoted among all employees, then it can be expected that this will foster the foresight ability overall.

The personal trait *inclusiveness* aims to foster the ability to connect and convince people and can be judged crucial to creating change in a large organization. Argued from the opposite direction, it can be expected that even with a well-established process for corporate foresight, successful change management can only be achieved through leadership and inclusiveness. This trait also matches with having strong internal networks and being open-minded and passionate.

The fourth personal trait which can be matched with the desired characteristics of foresighters is *expertise*. The expertise should enable employees to make better decisions and produce better results. For foresighters, it is expected that they should have a mix of deep domain knowledge and broad knowledge about technological areas and markets.

Overall, this matching of personal traits that are promoted and tracked by the company and the desired characteristics of foresighters leads to the conclusion that the company has introduced a successful mechanism to make every employee part of a large foresight system. In so doing, the company has fostered its ability to detect and respond to discontinuous change.

In a corporate foresight process, the next step would be to trigger action, by proposing measures to meet the threats from discontinuous change and initiate actions to exploit the arising opportunities. Without such a process in place, the hypothesis is that even if discontinuous change is identified by the employees, the risk remains that appropriate actions will not be taken.

Confronted with this hypothesis the respondents pointed to the corporate culture as an important catalyst for taking action. If for example an employee has insights into external change that opens windows of opportunities for innovation, he is expected to take action himself. To empower him and give him free space for taking action, he can negotiate time off from his normal duties directly with his superior. This gives him the opportunity to work on his idea and produce a business concept that can be taken further. In addition, the corporate culture fosters communication across divisional boundaries and across hierarchical boundaries. The head of corporate research explained that

> It makes no difference . . . whether it is the CEO of a business unit or somebody on operational-level or somebody in between. . . . It is our business philosophy to listen carefully to people and to provide everybody with profound feedback.[9]

The director for corporate business development confirmed the perception about the importance of networks and fast communication across hierarchical boundaries:

> As far as I am concerned, [the company's] internal network and fast communication across hierarchies is the crucial success factor.[10]

Additional confirmation came from the manager for strategic marketing and competitor analysis for Europe/North America/Russia and North Africa:

> Yes, it's a flat organization and information travels fast.

It can thus be concluded that if discontinuous change has been identified, then there is a high likelihood that this insight will be disseminated fast through the organization using informal communication channels. In addition, the open and communicative corporate culture will also enable the employees to get information and support in an effective and efficient manner.

Another obstacle to the ability to manage discontinuous change is that decisions – such as the decision to move into a new business field while cannibalizing exiting businesses – can only be taken at the top-management level. The hypothesis would therefore be that the described bottom-up approach to managing discontinuous change meets barriers when it comes to high impact decisions.

Possibly for that reason the company has installed an executive-board program to explore new growth areas. The case study revealed that the program is well-known throughout the company and has widespread support. The program was introduced in 2004 and by 2007 has already created $14 billion in revenues (corporate Web site, last accessed on April 26, 2009). Its success was attributed to the willingness of business units to cooperate and the backing of the corporate executive board. In order to illustrate the persuasive power of this executive board backing, the principal of the power market economics explained what happens if a business unit leader refuses a request for support:

> . . . then what I would say is, "Why don't you explain that to [first name of the CEO]?"

What this statement underlines is that since the program is installed by the top management and known as a CEO initiative, there is no natural limitation in terms of amount of support or size of funding for any given initiative. This in consequence means that initiatives which are started bottom-up can grow to become new

[9]Translated from German by the author. Original quote: "Es spielt keine Rolle [. . .] ob das jetzt der CEO von einer Business Unit ist oder ob das jetzt jemand auf der Arbeitsebene ist oder irgendwo dazwischen. [. . .] Es gehört zu unserer Unternehmensphilosophie, dass man zuhört und sich Mühe gibt und den Leuten ein vernünftiges Feedback gibt."

[10]Translated from German by the author. Original quote: "Aus meiner Sicht ist der ganz entscheidende Erfolgsfaktor von [der Firma] eine extreme Vernetzung und die extrem schnelle und unhierarchische Kommunikation."

business fields with multiple millions of euros in revenue using the framework of the program.

5.8.3 Evaluation

This last case has brought more insight into the cultural dimension of the foresight ability. It allows for an understanding of how companies trigger responses in times of discontinuous change, without following a structural corporate foresight logic.

Given the track record of the company, which has a history of 150 years through which it had repeatedly reinvented itself, when faced with external discontinuous change, it can be concluded that such a cultural approach to corporate foresight can also be successful.

The case study has also revealed three primary mechanisms on which the company builds its foresight ability:

- *Putting every employee on the lookout*, by defining and tracking five personal "growth traits" which oblige every employee to fulfill some foresight duties and at the same time promote and reward foresight-supporting personal strengths.
- *Creating a corporate culture that promotes cross-divisional and cross-hierarchical communication.*
- *Executive-board programs* that allow bottom-up initiatives to grow fast and allow them to be transformed into new business ventures.

It can tentatively be concluded that these three mechanisms combined could be sufficient to ensure high corporate foresight ability. This would be a clear extension to the current knowledge about corporate foresight.

For companies aiming at enhancing their foresight ability, it can be concluded that particularly the support of a corporate culture that enhances communication within the company should prove valuable. Even if the company has chosen to build its foresight ability on the structural approach by using clearly defined processes, better communication should enhance the probability that the foresight insights create value.

Chapter 6
Discussion and Conclusion

6.1 Managerial Contributions

With the presented literature analysis in mind, I began this research with the hypothesis that most firms still lack effective systems to identify, interpret, and respond to external change. This is troubling, because corporate foresight capabilities are closely associated with the ability of a firm to retain its competitive advantage in times of discontinuous change (Levinthal 1992:427; Teece et al. 1997:509; Eisenhardt and Martin 2000:1105; Helfat and Peteraf 2003:1007) and its ability to ensure long-term survival (Stubbart and Knight 2006:79; Anderson and Tushman 1990:604; Audretsch 1995:441). Even though I was able to identify various best practices in specific capability dimensions, none of the firms had implemented a comprehensive, stable, and effective corporate foresight system. Most companies had mature practices in one or two capability dimensions but few capabilities in the others. Thus, the overall implementation level is still troubling and raises serious concerns about the ability of firms to retain their competitive advantage in times of discontinuous change.

The great need of managers for advice on how to build organizations that stay successful in times of discontinuous change is also emphasized by the many management guides that deal with the problem. Books such as *Dealing with Darwin* (Moore 2006), *The Tipping Point* (Gladwell 2001), *Clockspeed: Winning Industry Control in the Age of Temporary Advantage* (Fine 1998), *Peripheral Vision: Detecting Weak Signals That Will Make or Break Your Company* (Day and Schoemaker 2006), and the classic book by Peter F. Drucker, *The Age of Discontinuity* (Drucker 1992), all give advice about the challenge of managing and organizing firms to ensure their long-term competitiveness. What these books also document is that there are no recommendations commonly agreed on.

- Moore uses evidence from Cisco to propose a *set of methods and tools* to enhance innovation management in growing, mature, and declining markets (Moore 2006).
- Gladwell shows with compelling examples how *viruses and innovation adoption respond to similar mechanisms* that can turn them into epidemics or popular

R. Rohrbeck, *Corporate Foresight*, Contributions to Management Science,
DOI 10.1007/978-3-7908-2626-5_6, © Springer-Verlag Berlin Heidelberg 2011

products. His advice is to monitor and promote these mechanisms in order to create the next "blockbuster" product (Gladwell 2001).

- Fine employs evolutionary theory to propose that companies need to *develop product, process, and supply chain simultaneously* in order to be able to adapt in time to changes in the environment. He also emphasizes that particularly in volatile industries, the competitive advantage of a firm will erode quickly, and such companies therefore need to build capabilities fast and frequently move into new business fields (Fine 1998).
- Day and Shoemaker assert that companies need to *develop sensors* that are dedicated to detecting weak signals *in areas that are otherwise blind spots* in the corporate scanning systems (Day and Schoemaker 2006).
- Finally, Drucker's work illustrates that the challenge of dealing with discontinuous change has a long tradition. His book, first published in 1969, taught its many readers that *discontinuous change is occurring, and both governments and companies are struggling to deal with it* (Drucker 1969). The book is still being sold; it was reprinted in 2008, its eighth edition.

That the topic still generates so much interest from readers seems to indicate that managers feel that there are still missing pieces in the jigsaw puzzle of managing discontinuous change. To improving this situation and helping companies build organizations that are more agile and robust, this research contributes in several ways.

Contribution 1. *Providing a* maturity model that allows benchmarking and planning the improvement *of corporate foresight practices.*

Contribution 2. *Describing* best-practices in their application context*, allowing managers to learn from comparable firms and design corporate foresight systems according to their contingency factors.*

The cross-cases comparison also showed that the corporate foresight ability can be built on either *structural* or *cultural* foundations. This in itself is also an important result, with implications for management practice. Firms interested in building up or enhancing their corporate foresight ability should first assess the strengths in their corporate culture and then design their foresight system accordingly. Firms with a corporate culture that promotes individual initiatives and empowers the individual employees (often found in American firms) should build their corporate foresight system more on cultural elements, while companies whose corporate culture is built more on execution of carefully designed processes (often found in German firms) should more often utilize the structural elements of the corporate foresight maturity model.

In addition to management of corporate foresight, there are several contributions to the wider perspectives of (1) managing discontinuous change, (2) gaining and retaining a competitive advantage in turbulent times, and (3) ensuring long-term survival.

For *managing discontinuous change*, it has been shown that foresight systems can detect discontinuous change and effectively channel information into and through the organization. Corporate foresight can also contribute to the identification of activities that are needed to successfully respond to discontinuous change (Siggelkow and Rivkin 2005:101).

Contribution 3. *Corporate foresight systems support* management of discontinuous change *by detecting change and by channeling information into and through the organization.*

To *gaining and retaining a competitive advantage in turbulent times*, this research contributed insights on how companies use foresight to identify and assess emerging technologies (realization potential) and combine these with the identification of changes on the demand side (such as customer needs or changes in the socio-cultural, competitive, and political environment). Combining technology orientation and market orientation has been found to have a positive effect on the performance of a firm (Paladino 2009:616; Leenders and Wierenga 2002:305; Perks et al. 2009:640). Thus, the integration of technology and market foresight can be expected to also have a positive effect. The combination of technological realization potential and market opportunity can then be used to identify needed strategic resources (Wernerfelt 1984:171; Barney 1991:99) and create breakthrough innovations (Kim and Mauborgne 2005; He et al. 2008:368; Darby and Zucker 2003:1).

Contribution 4. *Corporate foresight systems support* gaining and retaining a competitive advantage *in turbulent times by identifying needed strategic resources.*

To *ensure the long-term survival* of firms, research has shown that companies that die do so because they fail to alter their organizational structure in time (Stubbart and Knight 2006:79; De Geus 1997a:2–6). There are also indications that strategic renewal may be helped by a certain degree of formalization of the front end of innovation (Poskela and Martinsuo 2009:671). In this research, I have shown that the major obstacle is not the identification or interpretation of discontinuous change, but the inertia and ignorance of internal stakeholders – particularly top and middle management. A key to ensuring the management buy-in and acceptance of a need for action is the participation of middle and top management in the foresight exercise (Gerbing et al. 1994:872). Participation makes it possible to challenge top management's dominant business logic and their basic assumptions about the future (Schwarz 2005:22; Van der Helm 2007:4). Participation is also expected to help in turbulent times, in which companies rely more on emerging strategies than on long-term planning (Wiltbank et al. 2006:981).

Contribution 5. *Corporate foresight systems* help ensure the long-term survival of firms *by challenging dominant logic and basic assumptions and creating a need for action.*

It is my hope that, in particular with the maturity model and the individual best-practice recommendations, this research will contribute to the enhancement of management practices and to building more agile and robust organizations. Both the good participation and engaged discussion at our corporate foresight conferences showed that the results were well-received in the community of corporate foresight professionals. It has yet to be seen whether the maturity model will also lead to an increase in interest in building corporate foresight abilities at the top management level.

6.2 Theoretical Contributions

In the literature review, I pointed out two major shortcomings in the research on corporate foresight.

- First, a strong informant bias, which results from the *failure to collect evidence from the users* of corporate foresight results. This resulted in a limited view on the impact of corporate foresight and carries the risk of overestimating the true impact, because the responding foresighters may have an interest in overstating the value of their work.
- Second, a too *narrow definition of corporate foresight* as a set of methods (Porter et al. 2004:287; Schwarz 2009:291; Salo et al. 2003:235) or as a process (Amanatidou and Guy 2008:539; Becker 2002:12; Horton 1999:5; Müller 2008:25; Müller-Stewens and Müller 2009:9). In consequence, other important elements that contribute to the corporate foresight ability of a firm (Slaughter 1998:382; Tsoukas and Shepherd 2004b:10) may have been overlooked.

To address the methodological shortcoming, particular emphasis was placed on interviewing internal stakeholders. Of the 107 interviews, 42 (40%) were conducted with internal customers. By collecting unbiased accounts on examples in which corporate foresight has created value for the company, I was able to identify twelve distinct impacts and cluster them into three groups:

- *Reduction of uncertainty* with the impacts: (1) early warning, (2) challenging basic assumptions and dominant business logic, (3) trend identification, prediction, and interpretation, and (4) improving decision making.
- *Triggering internal actions* with the impacts: (1) new R & D projects (innovation management), (2) change product portfolio (marketing), (3) new business development (corporate development), and (4) support strategy decision making (strategic planning).
- *Influencing others to act* was a group of impacts that has not been mentioned in previous research, but for which clear evidence was identified in the case studies. Through corporate foresight, firms were able to (1) influence other companies to for example follow into new business fields and (2) influence legislation on the national and European Union level.

In addition to these three groups, I also identified two *secondary impacts*: (1) the support for public and investors relations units to communicate the vision and long-term strategy and (2) organizational learning, for example raising awareness about technological issues or shifts in customer preferences.

The identified impacts have also been useful in a follow-up quantitative study. In this study, it was shown that top-performing companies use corporate foresight more often than average companies as a means to influence others to act (Rohrbeck et al. 2009c:29). This finding is particularly interesting, because using corporate foresight as a basis to influence others has not been mentioned in the literature, but it seems to play an important role in management.

Contribution 6. Extension of knowledge on value creation *from corporate foresight by identifying 12 distinct impacts.*

Following the hypothesis that current definitions of corporate foresight – focusing on methods and processes – is too narrow, I was able to identify a range of additional elements. Of the 21 individual elements of the corporate foresight maturity model, 12 have been newly identified, described, and validated by various informants from several companies and industries. The 21 elements have been further clustered into five capability dimensions to facilitate their management and improvement tracking.

In addition, it was possible to use a cross-case analysis to identify four maturity levels for each of the 21 capability elements. By combining maturity levels, capability dimensions, and capability elements, it was possible to build a *comprehensive maturity model for corporate foresight* and make operational the extended understanding of corporate foresight as an organizational ability.

Contribution 7. Extending the understanding of the corporate foresight ability *by identifying twelve new capability elements and combining them with nine previously found capability elements in a comprehensive maturity model.*

Following a contingency logic, it was possible to formulate normative guidelines for designing corporate foresight systems. These recommendations use six contingency factors that have been identified through a cross-industry analysis: (1) company size, (2) nature of strategy, (3) corporate culture, (4) source of competitive advantage, (5) complexity of environment, and (6) industry clockspeed.

This is valuable, because it has been shown that various factors affect the design choice for corporate foresight systems (Müller 2008:368–369) and because designing a corporate foresight system has to be regarded as an optimization problem. More capabilities will enhance the ability of a firm to respond to discontinuous change, but it will also come at a price: the cost of running the corporate foresight system. Thus a company in a stable or uncontested environment should not waste resources by building corporate capabilities of a high maturity level. On the basis of the analysis of contingency factors 1, 2, 5, and 6, the maturity model gives a normative recommendation on the desired overall maturity model. Contingency factor 3 (corporate culture) is used to recommend the emphasis in the design of the corporate foresight systems on either structural or cultural elements. Contingency factors 2 and 6 are used to recommend a focus in the information retrieval and the method usage.

Contribution 8. *Development of* normative recommendations for building corporate foresight systems on the basis of an analysis of contingency factors.

Another contribution to theory is the linkage of corporate foresight capabilities to their value creation. On the basis of evidence of value creation from corporate foresight, seven hypotheses can be proposed:

H1:. Overall information usage positively influences overall value creation.
H2:. Communicative capacity of employed methods positively influences the ability to trigger actions and influence others to act.
H3:. Combining methods such as scenario analysis and road mapping positively influences overall value creation.
H4:. IT collaboration tools enhance the ability to integrate a high number of stakeholders and thus positively influences the value creation from triggering actions.
H5:. The degree to which foresighters match the ideal characteristics (curious and receptive, open-minded and passionate, broad knowledge, deep knowledge, strong external network, strong internal network) positively influences the overall value creation.
H6:. Value creation of corporate foresight systems that are built on cultural or structural means is moderated by corporate culture.
H7:. Overall cultural capabilities positively influence the overall value creation.

Contribution 9. *Proposition of seven hypotheses that link corporate foresight abilities to value creation.*

To increase the implementation of corporate foresight systems, it is not only important to study its elements, its context and its value creation, but also to link it to the other functions of a firm (Gruber et al. 2003:287; Hines 2002:337). It can be expected that corporate foresight can only be established as a regular function, if it can be identified how it complements existing activities such as strategic planning or innovation management.

Through the cross-case analysis, it was possible to identify best practices on linking corporate foresight to innovation and strategic management. It was possible to identify (1) how corporate foresight can be integrated into short, medium, and long-term strategic planning and (2) what roles can be played by corporate foresight to enhance the innovation capacity of a firm. The identification of the roles emphasizes that corporate foresight can contribute in different ways and that different value impacts can be expected:

- *Initiator* role, which triggers innovation initiatives by identifying new customer needs, new technologies, and new product concepts of competitors.
- *Strategist* role, which directs innovation activities by vision creation, providing strategic guidance, consolidating opinions, assessing and repositioning of innovation portfolios and identifying the new business models of competitors.

- *Opponent* role, which challenges innovators to create better and more successful innovations by questioning basic assumptions, challenging the state-of-the-art of current R & D projects, and by scanning for disruptions that could endanger current and future innovations.

Contribution 10. *Identification of best practices that* link corporate foresight to innovation and strategic management.

A further step to linking corporate foresight to other corporate functions was made by extending the literature analysis beyond future research to include literature on strategic management and innovation management.

The analysis showed a lack of cross-referencing between these three management research disciplines, indicating a low level of cross-fertilization and, more importantly, the lack of an effort to compare and consolidate their knowledge bases. Through this extended literature review, I was able to identify similar phenomena that have been studied from these three perspectives under different names, but which are in fact similar. In addition, the integration of the French literature made it possible to integrate a rich, but detached, body of knowledge on future research. Both extensions of the literature review should provide future research with a richer theoretical base.

It was also possible to link important current research streams to the research on corporate foresight, including (1) environmental scanning and peripheral vision, (2) corporate change and ambidexterity, (3) decision making, (4) radical innovations and open innovation, and (5) management of disruptions. This will promote cross-fertilization and further extend the theoretical basis of research on corporate foresight.

Contribution 11. Extension of the theoretical basis of future research *by integrating findings from strategic management and innovation management research as well as French literature.*

As is typical for a young research stream, corporate foresight lacked the established basis of management theories that can be found in more mature research areas. A particular emphasis, therefore, was made in the literature review on analyzing the suitability of three major management theories for application to corporate foresight research. It was possible to confirm the applicability of the contingency theory, the resource-based view and the theory of dynamic capabilities. It is my hope that other researchers will follow suit by applying these theoretical frameworks and thus produce results that are more generalizable and that can complement each other more easily.

Contribution 12. Extension of the theoretical basis of corporate foresight research *by proposing contingency theory, resource-based view, and dynamic capabilities as guiding theoretical frameworks.*

6.3 Limitations and Future Research Directions

In the contributions section, it was shown how I have addressed the shortcomings of previous research in order to add to existing knowledge. By its very nature, research, no matter how well-designed and well-executed, will always carry limitations with regard to interpretation and generalizability of results. It is, therefore, a good practice to highlight the limitations in order to suggest future research directions. It is my hope that these insights will be used by other researchers as guidance on engaging in interesting research projects that will increase understanding of corporate foresight.

A primary – and from my perspective most important – limitation is that this research was conducted in a cross-sectional design. This design has been chosen because it made it possible to interview many companies in many industries, thereby making it possible to identify the large number of additional elements in corporate foresight systems. It was therefore suited to my research aim.

However, the downside of cross-sectional designs is that they do not make it possible to investigate dynamic developments over time. In particular, the question "Does corporate foresight contribute to the ability of a firm to survive discontinuous change?" is difficult to answer with a cross-sectional design. To come closer to an answer, a longitudinal research design would be more appropriate. By studying a firm at various points in time, it would be possible to judge its corporate foresight ability first and in subsequent points in time the ability of a firm to retain its competitive position in times of discontinuous change.

For this study, it was decided that advancing the research field would require ensuring that all relevant elements of a corporate foresight system have been identified. With my large sample encompassing several industries, I have a high degree of confidence that this has been achieved.

Recommendation for Future Research 1. *Use a longitudinal design to answer the research question: Does a firm's corporate foresight ability positively influence its ability to retain its competitive position when faced with discontinuous change?*

Another limitation is that some companies in our sample had only recently built or improved their corporate foresight practices. In consequence, there is a risk that not all value creation potential can be observed. By asking internal customers (who have not yet experienced all potential contributions of corporate foresight), the true impact of corporate foresight could be underestimated. To reduce this risk, internal customers were asked when describing value creation examples to also specify the concrete corporate foresight results upon which the value creation had been built.

For follow-up quantitative studies, it would be important to control for this risk, either by asking for the time a certain corporate foresight practice has been in place or by allowing for a 6-month lag between sending the questionnaire to the manager and sending the questionnaire to the internal customer of corporate foresight.

Recommendation for Future Research 2. *Use a cross-sectional design to investigate value creation of corporate foresight. Capture data from two respondents in* *each firm: Foresight manager and internal customer. Allow for a time lag of 6 months between sending the questionnaire to the manager and sending it to the internal customer.*

A third limitation may arise from research that measures the dependent and independent variable from the same source. This limitation is also referred to as single-informant bias. In my research, I aimed to minimize this risk by questioning the foresight manager on capabilities and internal customers on value creation. This approach should have greatly reduced the single-source bias. However, given that both respondents are from the same company, there remains a risk that statements are not fully objective, limiting the interpretation and generalizability of findings, particularly in the cross-case analysis.

For follow-up research, I would, therefore, recommend employing suitable strategies to reduce the single-source bias. A general strategy is to introduce an external data source, independent of the informants. Finding such a data source is no easy task in the field of corporate foresight, as the value contribution is difficult to quantify and thus no data are available in public databases. It is my hope that the value-creation categories that I proposed in the maturity model will help in the search to find suitable variables and adequate data sources.

One possibility to tackle the challenge would be to choose an industry that has been affected by a discontinuous change and select a sample of similar companies of the same size and position in the value chain. By collecting data on their corporate foresight system at the time of the discontinuous change and their competitive position before and after the change, it may be possible to assess the impact of the corporate foresight system on the ability of a company to retain its competitive position in times of discontinuous change.

Recommendation for Future Research 3. *Use an external data source for value creation from corporate foresight. One possibility is to assess the competitive position of a firm before and after a discontinuous change.*

A fourth limitation is the limited breadth of coverage of industries. This research covered a wide range of industries, including automotive, electronics, semiconductors, energy, fashion, and banking. It also covered different positions in the value chain, from supplier to manufacturer to service company. However, it did not cover insurance and reinsurance companies, which have been known to have strong foresight capabilities (Käslin 2008).

The exclusion of the insurance and reinsurance industry has been done for two reasons. The first reason is that Käslin very recently studied and described the corporate foresight systems of two major reinsurance companies (SwissRe and Münchern Rück) and two major insurance companies (Zurich Financial Services and Allianz Group). The second reason is that there is a fundamental difference in the nature of corporate foresight systems in the insurance industry compared to any other industry. Whereas other industries use corporate foresight to shelter their business from discontinuous change, the business of the insurance industry is the risk arising from discontinuous change.

The consequence is that insurance companies can be considered often as best-practice cases for information usage and method sophistication, with particular strengths in prediction methods and tools. But comparing cultural, people and network, and particularly organizational aspects would fail, because for most industries these follow the logic of a corporate function, while in insurance companies they have the character of a production process for insurance products.

Nevertheless, the recommendation to extend research to other industries can be given. It could be particularly interesting to study corporate foresight in the fashion or music industry. The challenge in these industries is speed, as new trends emerge, mature, and fade in quick succession.

Recommendation for Future Research 4. *Extend corporate foresight research to the fashion and music industry.*

Another recommendation for further research concerns one of the fundamental dilemmas of corporate foresight: how to scan for weak signals without spending too much time on them, overestimating the trend behind them (Neugarten 2006:902–903) and without discarding important ones, because of initial low signal strength (Ilmola and Kuusi 2006:908).

Weak signals scanning systems carry the risk of having the same effect as magnifying glasses. A bug observed through a magnifying glass can look like a huge monster while actually being only 5 mm long and harmless. Similarly, weak signals brought to the attention of top management by describing them as a strategic issue carry the risk of being amplified to a point where they are judged as life-threatening discontinuities, while they in fact are only minor turbulences.

To tackle this problem, several solutions have been proposed, including not filtering at all (Ilmola and Kuusi 2006:908), deliberately relying only on qualitative data (Schwarz 2005:22), allowing for serendipity in issue identification by looking sideways (Neugarten 2006:903), and doing the interpretation only at the top-management level (Krystek 2007:52). However, the dilemma has not been solved by these recommendations and thus invites further research.

Recommendation for Future Research 5. *Aim to solve the dilemma that weak signals need to be amplified to be recognized as a trend, but that the amplification carries the risk of overestimating the true impact of the trend or of suppressing weak signals on other trends.*

It is my hope that my contributions will help to advance the research field of corporate foresight and that they will help practitioners design and implement better corporate foresight systems. In the last 3 years, I have become convinced that corporate foresight is an important ability for any firm, and I can say with certainty that, being a young field, corporate foresight is also a rewarding field for researchers.

Chapter 7
Appendix

7.1 Interview Guideline

Before each interview, a brief introduction of the aim of the study and its relevance to management practices was given.

Interview guideline

Question	Comments
Introduction and context	
What is your position within the company?	Including differentiation in: (1) internal customer, (2) activity manager, (3) activity team
How complex is your industry?	Factors include: (1) # of competitors, (2) complexity of customer segmentation, (3) reliance on political environment, (4) technological complexity of product
How high is your industry's clockspeed?	Factors include: (1) major changes in your industry in the past three years, (2) technological change, (3) business model change, (4) customer behavior and needs change
What do you associate with the term corporate foresight?	If unfamiliar: use terms such as future orientation of a firm or dealing with disruptions in the environment
What is your relation to corporate foresight activities in your company?	If unable to answer: ask about relation to strategic management, innovation management, marketing and corporate development
How do you judge your company's need for corporate foresight?	Follow-up: Why?
Is the need for foresight increasing of decreasing?	Follow-up: Why?
Information usage	
Which information source do you use in order to anticipate and monitor future developments?	Differentiate: (1) internal vs. external, (2) formal vs. informal, (3) restricted sources that yield a competitive advantages vs. easily accessible sources. *(Use template)*

DOI 10.1007/978-3-7908-2626-5_7, © Springer-Verlag Berlin Heidelberg 2011

Where do you search for future related information?	Differentiate into: (1) current business, adjacent business and white spaces, (2) technological, customer, competitor and political environment *(use template)*
Which time horizon do you consider in your foresight activities?	Try to standardize by product lifecycles (2, 3–4, 5 and beyond) or else by years (2–5, 5–15, 15 and beyond)
Method sophistication	
Which methods do you use to gather, assess and disseminate future related information?	Differentiate into: (1) market-oriented, (2) technology-oriented, (3) cross-functional *(Use template)*
Do you use methods which facilitate internal and external communication?	Example: roadmapping which through its process promotes cross-functional and cross-hierarchical communication
How do you select foresight methods?	Are they chosen regarding (1) aim of foresight exercise, (2) context of the company
People & networks	
What are desirable characteristics of foresighters?	Example: Strong internal network
How are foresight insights diffused within your company?	Differentiate into: (1) formal vs. informal, (2) rapidly vs. slowly, or (3) not at all
Organization	
How are foresight activities started (triggered) in your company?	Differentiate into: (1) top-down vs. bottom-up, (2) issue-driven vs. continuous
Please describe the process of a typical foresight activity	Using the generic process as reference *(use template)*
Please name units which are involved in foresight activities within your company	Differentiate into: (1) level: strategic, tactic, operational, (2) market-oriented, technology-oriented or cross-functional *(use template)*
Where are foresight units positioned in the organizational structure?	Please draw the organizational structure *(use template)*
Is the responsibility for foresight clearly assigned?	
Are there incentives in place to reward an external future oriented view of the employees?	
Are foresight activities linked to any other processes or departments?	Possible answers include: (1) innovation management, (2) marketing, (3) corporate development, (4) controlling, (5) strategic management
Culture	
How important is corporate culture for foresight success?	
Please name important characteristics of corporate culture	
Value contribution	
Which benefit do you expect from foresight activities?	Examples include: (1) reduction of uncertainty, (2) warning on discontinuities, (3) influencing the future
Which benefits have foresight activities created in your company? Please name concrete examples	Follow-up: If possible, ask for quantification of benefit

7.2 Context Questionnaire

Context

I	COMPANY PROFILE					
1	**Name of company**					
1	**Position in company**					
2	**Industry** (e.g. Energy, Telecommunications, etc.)					
3	**Number of employees**	☐ <500	☐ <5.000	☐ <50.000	☐ <200.000	☐ >200.000
4	**Annual revenue in 2007 (€)**	☐ <10 Mio	☐ <100 Mio	☐ <1 Bill	☐ <10 Bill	☐ >10 Bill
5	**Investments in 2007 (€)**	☐ <1 Mio	☐ <10 Mio	☐ <100 Mio	☐ <500 Mio	☐ >500 Mio
6	**Type of market**	☐ B2B (Business to Business) ☐ B2C (Business to Consumer) ☐ B2B and B2C				
7	**Market share** (average if more than one business or country)	☐ <10%	☐ <20%	☐ <40%	☐ <60%	☐ >60%
8	**Business activities**	☐ Regional	☐ Trans-regional	☐ Germany	☐ Europe	☐ World
9	**External company perception**	☐ Environment friendly company ☐ Innovative company ☐ Socially responsible company ☐ Customer and service oriented company				
10	**Differentiation characteristic** 1. Technological leadership 2. "We have the deepest understanding of our customer's needs" 3. "Our are sold together with a customer experience"	☐ Technology ☐ Consumer understanding and use oriented products ☐ Products combined with emotions				

II	NATURE OF YOUR STRATEGY		
1	**Focus of your strategy**		
	Narrow (protected niche)	☐☐☐☐☐☐☐	Broad (global)
2	**Growth orientation**		
	Modest	☐☐☐☐☐☐☐	Aggressive
3	**Number of business to integrate**		
	Few	☐☐☐☐☐☐☐	Many
4	**Focus on reinvention**		
	Minor	☐☐☐☐☐☐☐	Major (50% revenue must come from new products in three years)

III	COMPLEXITY OF YOUR ENVIRONMENT		
1	**Industry structure**		
	Few, easily identifiable competitors	☐☐☐☐☐☐☐	Many competitors from unexpected sources
2	**Channel structure**		
	Simple and direct	☐☐☐☐☐☐☐	Long and complex
3	**Market structure**		
	Fixed boundaries and simple segmentation	☐☐☐☐☐☐☐	Fuzzy boundaries and complex segmentation
4	**Enabling technologies**		
	Few and mature (simple systems)	☐☐☐☐☐☐☐	Many converging (complex systems)
5	**Regulations (federal, state, etc.)**		
	Few or stable	☐☐☐☐☐☐☐	Many or changing rapidly
6	**Public visibility of industry**		
	Largely ignored	☐☐☐☐☐☐☐	Closely watched by media or special-interest groups
7	**Dependence on government funding and political access**		
	Low: operates largely independent of government	☐☐☐☐☐☐☐	High: sensitive to politics and the funding climate
8	**Dependence on global economy**		
	Low: affected principally by domestic conditions	☐☐☐☐☐☐☐	High: affected by global conditions

IV	VOLATILITY OF YOUR ENVIRONMENT			
1	**Number of surprises by high-impact events in the past three years**			
		None	□□□□□□□	Three or more
2	**Accuracy of past forecasts**			
		High: small deviations from actual forecasts	□□□□□□□	Low: results differs greatly from forecasts
3	**Market growth**			
		Slow and stable	□□□□□□□	Rapid and unstable
4	**Growth opportunities**			
		Have decreased dramatically in the past three years	□□□□□□□	Have increased dramatically in the past three years
5	**Speed and direction of technological change**			
		Very predictable	□□□□□□□	Highly unpredictable
6	**Behavior of key competitors, suppliers, and partners**			
		Very predictable	□□□□□□□	Highly unpredictable
7	**Posture of key rivals**			
		Live-and-let-live mentality	□□□□□□□	Hostile (aggressive)
8	**Susceptibility to macroeconomic forces**			
		Low sensitivity to price changes, currencies, business cycle, tariffs, etc	□□□□□□□	High sensitivity to price changes, currencies, business cycles, tariffs, etc.
9	**Dependence on financial markets**			
		Low	□□□□□□□	High
10	**Customer and channel power**			
		Low	□□□□□□□	High
11	**Sensitivity to social changes (fashion and values)**			
		Low: mostly gradual change from the past	□□□□□□□	High: good chance of major disruptions and changes in business models
12	**Potential for major disruptions in the next five years**			
		Low: few surprises expected, mostly things we can handle	□□□□□□□	High: several significant business shocks are expected, without knowing which in particular

7.3 Interview Templates

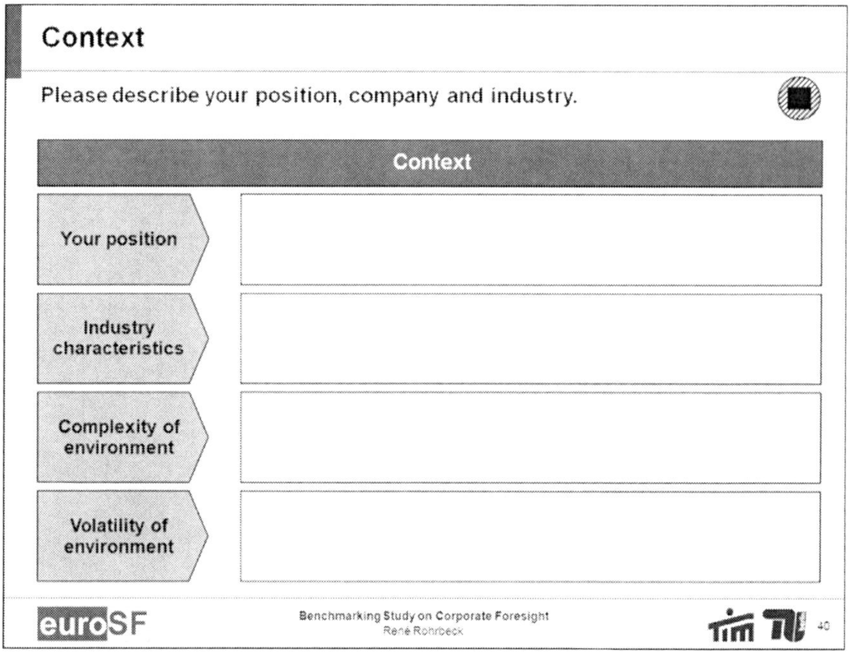

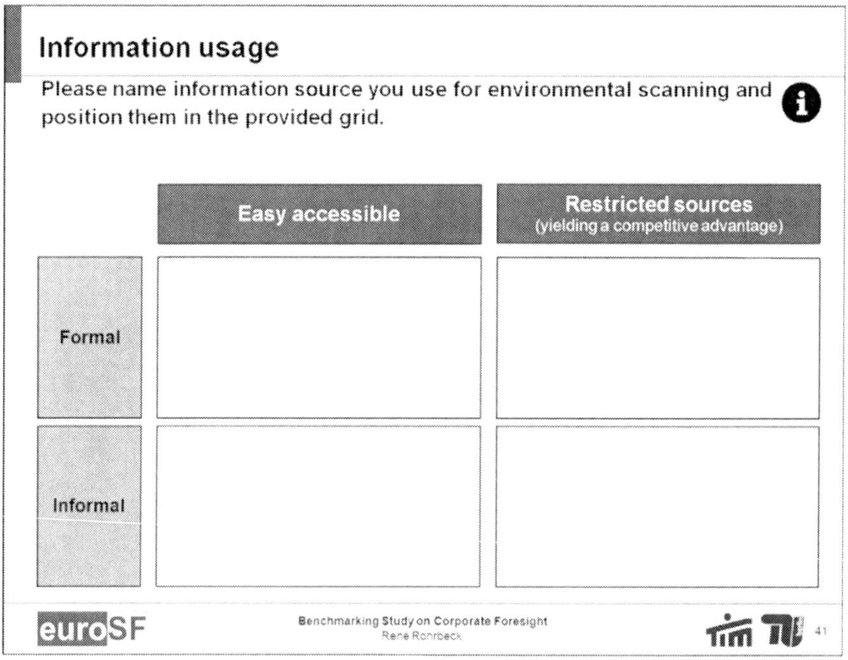

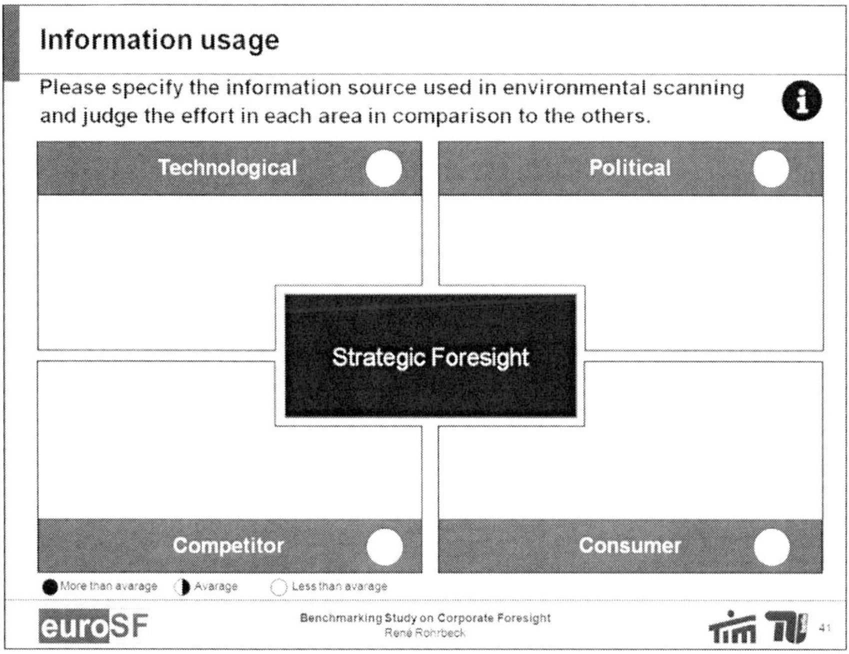
Information usage
Please specify the information source used in environmental scanning and judge the effort in each area in comparison to the others.
Technological
Political
Strategic Foresight
Competitor
Consumer
More than avarage
Avarage
Less than avarage
euroSF
Benchmarking Study on Corporate Foresight
René Rohrbeck
41

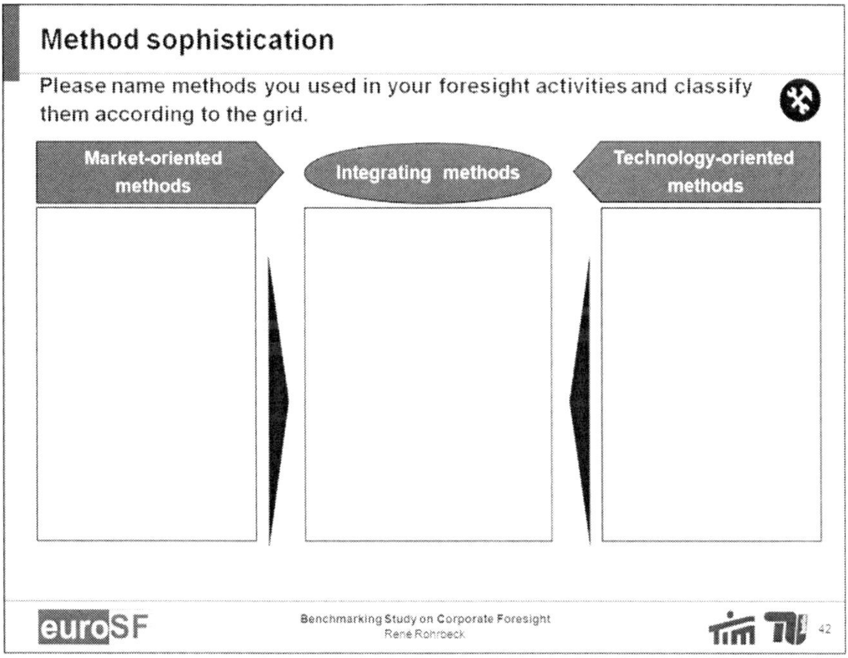
Method sophistication
Please name methods you used in your foresight activities and classify them according to the grid.
Market-oriented methods
Integrating methods
Technology-oriented methods
euroSF
Benchmarking Study on Corporate Foresight
René Rohrbeck
42

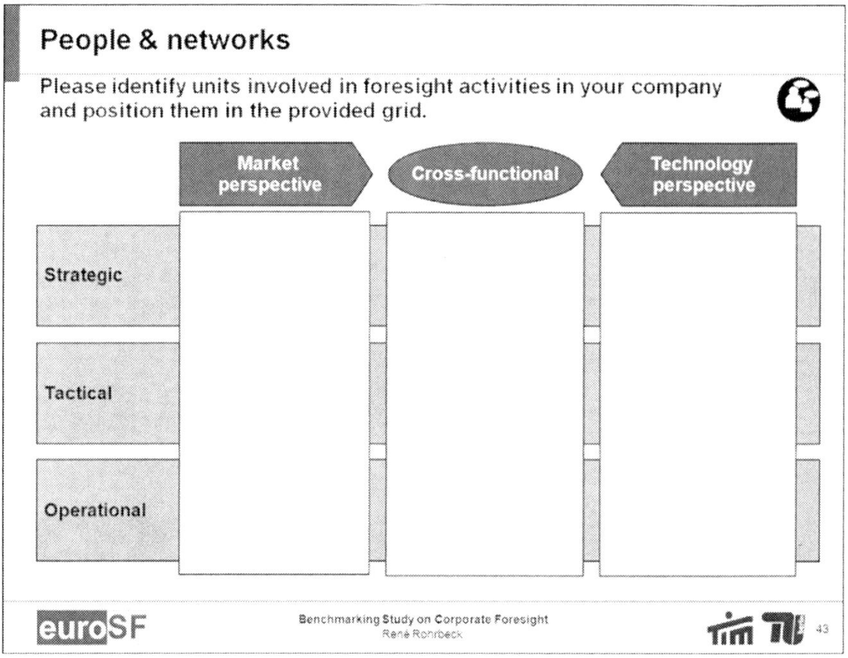
People & networks
Please identify units involved in foresight activities in your company and position them in the provided grid.
Market perspective
Cross-functional
Technology perspective
Strategic
Tactical
Operational
euroSF
Benchmarking Study on Corporate Foresight
René Rohrbeck
43

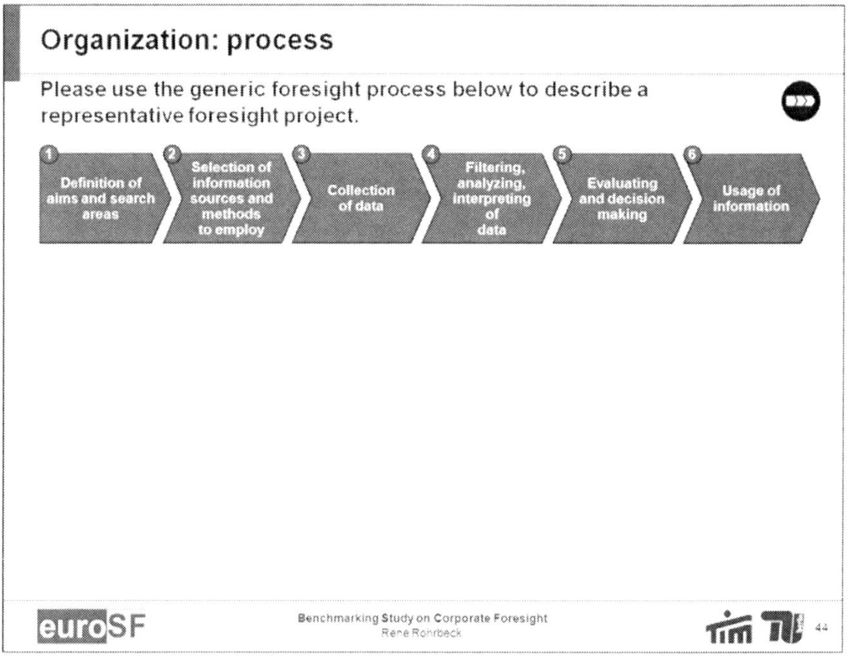
Organization: process
Please use the generic foresight process below to describe a representative foresight project.
1 Definition of aims and search areas
2 Selection of information sources and methods to employ
3 Collection of data
4 Filtering, analyzing, interpreting of data
5 Evaluating and decision making
6 Usage of information
euroSF
Benchmarking Study on Corporate Foresight
René Rohrbeck
44

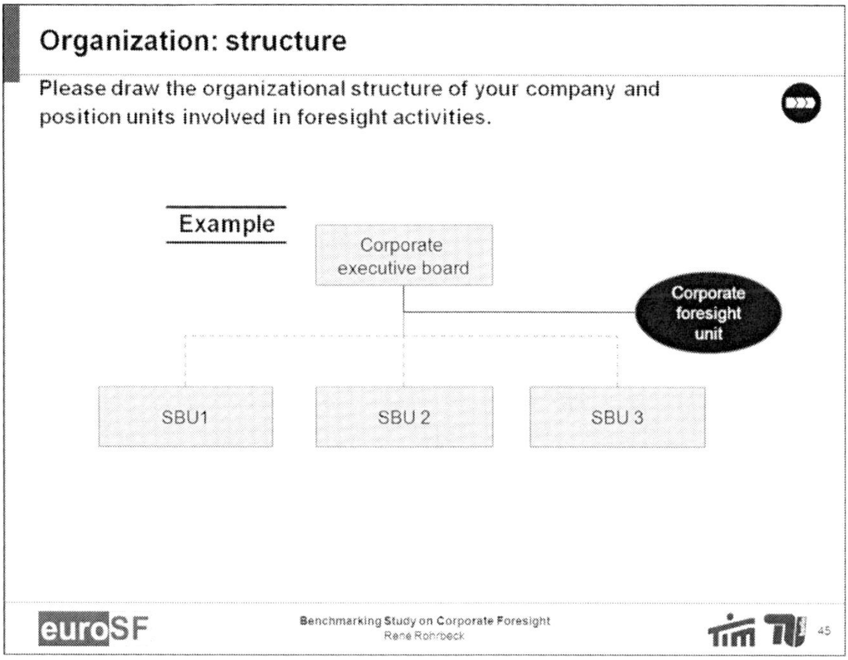
Organization: structure
Please draw the organizational structure of your company and position units involved in foresight activities.
Example
Corporate executive board
Corporate foresight unit
SBU1
SBU 2
SBU 3
euroSF
Benchmarking Study on Corporate Foresight
Rene Rohrbeck
45

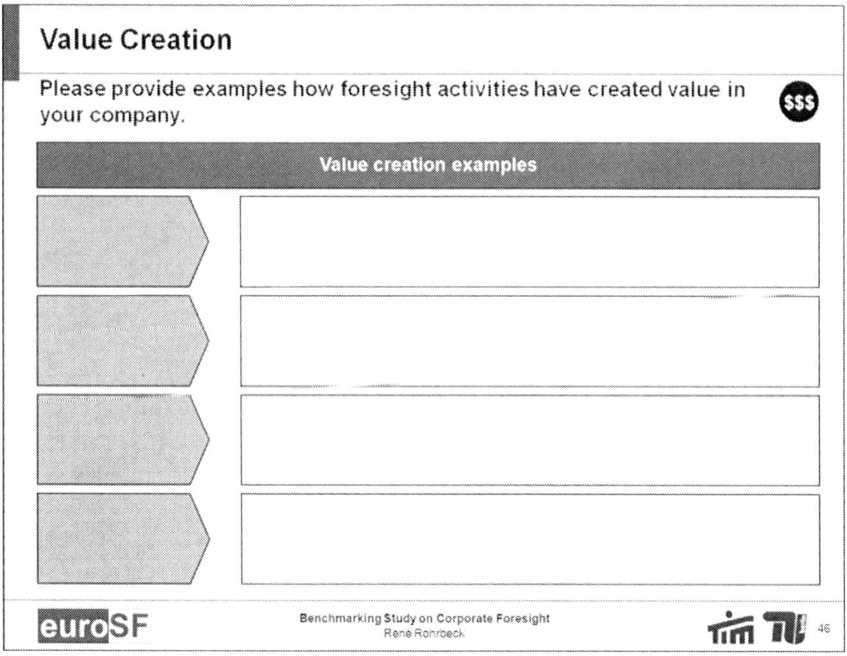
Value Creation
Please provide examples how foresight activities have created value in your company.
$$$
Value creation examples
euroSF
Benchmarking Study on Corporate Foresight
Rene Rohrbeck
46

7.4 Informants

Informants in case studies

Cases	Informant	Role		
		IC	AM	AT
Deutsche Telekom	Dr. Heinrich Arnold, T-Labs, Head of Innovation Management		✓	
	Mr. Peter Bockelmann, T-Com, Head of Strategic Product Planning	✓		
	Mrs. Marie Dowling, T-Venture, Investment Manager	✓		
	Mr. Jürgen Eder, T-Online, Technology Marketing	✓		
	Mr. Oliver Fietz, T-Venture, Investment Manager	✓		
	Mrs. Helga-Marion Foken, T-Labs, Consumer Foresight			✓
	Mr. Philipp Haberstock Group Strategy	✓		
	Mr. Christoph Hartmann, T-Venture, Controlling	✓		
	Mr. Matthias Heibert T-Online, Product House	✓		
	Mr. Jörg Heuer, T-Labs, Technology Exploration		✓	
	Dr. Sven Hischke, Group Product House	✓		
	Mr. Gregor F. Lex, T-Venture, Investment Manager	✓		
	Mr. Marc von Lillienskiold, T-Venture, CFO	✓		
	Mr. Klaus Milczewsky, T-Online, Product House	✓		
	Mr. T. Mueller-Kassner, T-Systems, Strategy & Portfolio M.	✓		
	Mr. Johannes Nünning, T-Systems, ZMD-4	✓		
	Mr. Norbert Schenkel, T-Venture, Controlling	✓		
	Mr. Ralph Schepp, Group Product House		✓	
	Mrs. Annika Schröder T-Labs, Customer Foresight			✓
	Dr. Fee Steinhoff, T-Labs, Head of User Driven Innovation		✓	
	Dr. Christoph Trump, Group Product House	✓		
	Mr. Ralf Ullmann, T-Systems, ZMD-4	✓		
	Dr. Stephan Verglas, T-Systems: Head of Innovation Management	✓		
	Mr. Heinrich Wenz, T-Online, Product House	✓		
	Mr. Martin Wilckens, Head of Group Strategy	✓		
Telekom Austria	Mr. Manfred Egger, Head of Strategic Controlling	✓		
	Mr. Andreas Engel, Head of Business and Market Intelligence		✓	
	Mr. Franz Fertl, Head of Service Development	✓		
	Mr. Gerald Glerckx, Head of Platform and Technology Planning		✓	
	Dr. Artan Halimi, Strategic Innovation and Portfolio Management			✓
	Mr. Robert Hofer, Head of Portfoliomanagement			✓
	Mr. Mario Huterer, Head of Marketing, Wholesale		✓	
	Mr. Harald Mayrböck, Innovation Manager	✓		
	Mrs. Simone Schalk, Head of Project Office			✓
	Mrs. Schiffbänker, Marketing Retail und Media			✓
	Mr. Martin Schlicksbier, Platform and Technology Management			✓
	Mr. Armin Sumesgutner, Head of Disruptive Innovations		✓	
British Telecom	Mr. Dave Brown, Head of Strategic Foresight		✓	
	Mr. Ian Neild, Futurologist & pervasive ICT			✓
	Mr. Ian Pearson, Futurologist			✓

Telefonica	Mr. José Montero Cebrian, Head Strategy and Portfolio M.	✓		
	Mr. Salvador Pérez Crespo, Head of Technology Foresight and Innovation Controlling		✓	
Volkswagen	Mr. Stefan Liske, formerly Head of Product Strategy, today: Partner PCH Berlin-Los Angeles GmbH		✓	
	Mr. Niclas Maier, Member in large foresight project			✓
	Mr. Lars-Alexander Mayer, Partner Trommsdorff + Drüner			✓
	Mr. Gantimur Meissner, Partner PCH Berlin-Los Angeles GmbH			✓
	Mr. Alexander Nolte, Partner PCH Berlin-Los Angeles GmbH			✓
	Dr. Olaf Pleuss, Future Research, Technology Foresight		✓	
	Dr. Kai-Christen Rose, European Scouting Platform			
	Mrs. Claudia Spindler, Consultant Trommsdorff + Drüner			✓
	Mr. Peter Walde, Future Research		✓	
Continental (formally Siemens VDO)	Mr. Roger Deckers, Head Technology Board	✓		
	Mr. Volkmar Döricht, Consultant Corporate Technologies, Siemens			✓
	Dr. H. Stuckenschneider, Head of Strategic Marketing CT, Siemens		✓	
ThyssenKrupp Automotive	Mr. Dirk Bartels, Technology Scout		✓	
	Dr. Peter Dahlmann, Chief Technology Officer	✓		
	Mr. Falk Nüßle, Head of Competence Center Automotive Solutions		✓	
	Mr. Wilfried Riemann, Head of Strategic Platform Management	✓		
	Mr. Ralf Sünkel, Manager Product Innovation Projects		✓	
Philips	Mr. Ruud Gal, Innovation Improvement Manager			✓
	Mr. Pieter Groenveld, former Senior Staff Officer	✓		
	Mr. Frans van Roemburg, Innovation Director Consumer Healthcare		✓	
Osram	Dr. Beate Schlageter, Senior Consultant CT, Siemens			✓
	Dr. H. Stuckenschneider, Head of Strategic Marketing CT, Siemens		✓	
	Dr. Reinhard Weitzel, Head Corporate Innovation Managagement	✓		
	Mr. Torsten Ziercke, Innovation Management	✓		
Bosch Siemens Hausgeräte (BSH)	Dr. Andreas Hanau, Head of Innovation Washer		✓	
	Mr. Andreas Iffländer, Innovation Management			✓
	Mr. Ulf Pillkahn, Senior Consultant CT, Siemens			✓
	Dr. Christoph Thim, Head of Innovation Management		✓	
	Prof. Werner Vogt, Executive Board	✓		
Infineon	Dr. Darko Piscevic, Head of Product Strategy	✓		
	Dr. Barbara Schaden, Head of Market Intelligence		✓	
Vattenfall Europe	Mr. Bekker, Head of Human Resources	✓		
	Mr. Georg Friedrichs, Head of Corporate Development	✓		
	Mr. Litwiakow, Communication and Policy		✓	
	Mr. Arwed Mallow, Corporate Development		✓	
	Dr. Klemens Millonig, Head of Strategic Planning		✓	
	Dr. Markus Sauthoff, Head of Strategy, Generation	✓		
	Dr. Jürgen Schmidberger, Head of Finance and Controlling	✓		
	Dr. Oliver Weinmann, Head of Innovation Management			✓
	Mr. Weißheit, Head of Strategy, Sales			✓
	Mr. Markus Witt, Head of Market Forecast		✓	

Endesa	Mrs. Maria Alvarez, Junior Analyst Technology & Innovation			✓
	Mr. David Fernandez, Intellectual Property Rights and Foresight			✓
	Dr. Jose Pardos Gotor, Deputy Head of Technology & Innovation	✓		
	Mr. Pablo Ruiz, Senior Analyst, Interligare			✓
	Mr. Miguel Scolfinni, Senior Analyst, Interligare			✓
Iberola	Mr. Carlos Gasco Traverso, Senior Manager Foresight			✓
	Mr. Carlos Lozano Herguedas, Head of Foresight & Markets		✓	
Energias de Portugal (EDP)	Mr. Antonio Coutinho, Senior Manager Strategic Planning	✓		
	Mr. Miguel Setas, Senior Manager Sales	✓		
	Mr. Antonio Vidigal, Director Innovation		✓	
GE Energy	Mr. Markus Becker, EU Energy Policy Executive		✓	
	Mr. Dietmar Gruidl, Head of GE Energy Germany	✓		
	Dr. Carlos Härtel, Managing Director Global Research Center		✓	
	Mrs. Heidi Janda, Director Business Development		✓	
	Mr. Bart Stoffer, Principal Power Investment Economics Europe		✓	
	Mr. T. Vlassopoulos, Strategic Marketing & Competitor Analysis		✓	
MAN Turbo	Dr. Rolf Habel, Head of Marketing, Strategy & Business Dev.		✓	
	Mr. Mathias Scherer, Head of Oil & Gas	✓		
Deutsche Bank Research	Dr. Jan Hofmann, DB Research			✓
	Dr. Ingo Rollwagen, DB Research			✓
	Mr. Stefan Schneider, DB Research		✓	
Hugo Boss	Mr. Bernd Hake, Brand Director BOSS Black und BOSS Selection	✓		
	Mrs. Katharina Köpernick, Brand Manager BOSS Black		✓	

IC internal customer, *AM* activity manager, *AT* activity team

7.5 Internal Documents

Internal documents

Cases	Informant	Documents
Deutsche Telekom	Dr. Heinrich Arnold	• R&D Strategy 2006
		• Presentation on Open Innovation
	Mr. Matthias Heibert	• T-Online's Innovation Process
	Mr. Jörg Heuer	• Technology Radar of Deutsche Telekom
	Mr. Ralph Schepp	• Product & Service Radar
		• Report: Concumer Foresight
		• Report: Changes in Consumer Spending

	Dr. Fee Steinhoff	• Presentation on User Clinics • Overview of User Driven Innovation Methods and Tools
Telekom Austria	Mr. Martin Schlicksbier	• Product-Life-Cycle process • Technology Strategy development
British Telecom	Mr. Dave Brown	• Presentation on Strategic Foresight Unit • Presentation on Innovation Management at BT • BT's Technology Timeline • BT's IT-Collaboration Tools
Telefonica	Mr. Salvador Pérez Crespo	• Presentation on the Technology Foresight Unit
Volkswagen	Mr. Stefan Liske	• Project presentation: Moonraker consumer scouting in the USA • Overview Methods and Tools of Scouting • Method profile "Learning from other industries"
	Dr. Kai-Christen Rose	• Project: Cross-Industry Radar Rings
Continental (formally Siemens VDO)	Mr. Roger Deckers	• Siemens VDO Organizational Structure • Project presentation: "Future of Automotive"
ThyssenKrupp Automotive	Mr. Dirk Bartels	• Internal Technology Magazine
	Mr. Wilfried Riemann	• Project presentation: INCAR
	Mr. Ralf Sünkel	• Overview Foresight at ThyssenKrupp, including future project with another company
Philips	Mr. Ruud Gal	• Strategic architecture planning process
	Mr. Pieter Groenveld	• "Blue Box Model" for roadmapping and innovation planning
Osram	Dr. Beate Schlageter	• "Picture of the Future"-methodology
	Mr. Torsten Ziercke	• Final presentation of the "Picture of the Lighting Future"
Bosch Siemens Hausgeräte (BSH)	Dr. Andreas Hanau	• Presentation, self-developed Idea Management Tools
	Prof. Werner Vogt	• Innovation Management and Planning Tools of BSH
Infineon	Dr. Barbara Schaden	• Presentation on Market forecast tool
Vattenfall Europe	Dr. Klemens Millonig	• Strategic planning process
Endesa	Mr. Miguel Scolfinni	• Data mining process and employed tools
Deutsche Bank Research	Dr. Ingo Rollwagen	• Project presentation on "Germany 2020: New challenges for a land on expedition" • Final report on "Germany 2020: New challenges for a land on expedition"

7.6 Public Information Sources

Public information sources

Document	Case	Documents
Annual report	Deutsche Telekom	Deutsche Telekom AG (2007)
	Telekom Austria	Telekom Austria Group (2007)
	British Telecom	British Telecom Group plc (2007)
	Telefonica	Telefonica (2007)
	Volkswagen	Volkswagen AG (2007)
	Continental	Continental (2007)
	TK Automotive	ThyssenKrupp (2008)
	Philips	Philips (2007)
	Osram	Siemens AG (2007:57)
	BSH	Bosch Siemens Hausgeräte (BSH) (2008)
	Infineon	Infineon (2007)
	Vattenfall Europe	Vattenfall Group (2007)
	Endesa	Endesa (2007)
	Iberdrola	Iberdrola (2007)
	EDP	EDP (2007)
	GE Energy	General Electric (2007)
	MAN Turbo	MAN Turbo AG (2008)
	Deutsche Bank Research	Deutsche Bank AG (2008)
	Hugo Boss	Hugo Boss AG (2008)
Company Web site	Deutsche Telekom	http://www.telekom.de
	Telekom Austria	http://www.telekomaustria.com
	British Telecom	http://www.bt.com
	Telefonica	http://www.telefonica.com
	Volkswagen	http://www.volkwagen.com
	Continental	http://www.conti-online.com
	TK Automotive	http://www.thyssenkrupp-automotive-systems.de/en
	Philips	http://www.philips.de
	Osram	http://www.osram.com/
	BSH	http://www.bsh-group.de/
	Infineon	http://www.infineon.com
	Vattenfall Europe	http://www.vattenfall.de/
	Endesa	http://www.endesa.com/Portal/en
	Iberdrola	http://www.iberdrola.es/
	EDP	http://www.edp.pt
	GE Energy	http://www.gepower.com
	MAN Turbo	http://www.manturbo.com/
	Deutsche Bank Research	http://www.dbresearch.de
	Hugo Boss	http://www.hugoboss.com/

7.7 Academic Publications by Informants

Academic publications

Cases	Informant	Documents
Deutsche Telekom	Dr. Heinrich Arnold	Arnold (2003), Arnold and Freese (2007), Arnold et al. (2006), Rohrbeck and Arnold (2006), Rohrbeck et al. (2006), Schläffer and Arnold (2007)
	Dr. Fee Steinhoff	Rohrbeck et al. (2008), Steinhoff (2006)
British Telecom	Mr. Dave Brown	Brown (2006), Monteiro (2006)
Volkswagen	Mr. Stefan Liske	Jasner (2006)
Philips	Mr. Pieter Groenveld	Groenveld (1997, 2007)
Osram	Dr. Heinrich Stuckenschneider	Stuckenschneider and Schwair (2005), Gruber et al. (2003), Gruber and Venter (2006), Schwair (2001), Theis (2006)
	Dr. Ulf Pillkahn	Pillkahn (2007)
Deutsche Bank Research	Dr. Ingo Rollwagen	Hofmann et al. (2007), Roehl and Rollwagen (2004), Rollwagen (2008), Rollwagen et al. (2008)

7.8 Coding Tree

Coding tree with number of references and coded sentences

Codes	Informants	Sentences
Context		
Size of the company	6	7
Nature of strategy	9	10
Corporate culture	5	5
Source of competitive advantage	4	4
Complexity of environment	8	9
Industry clockspeed	9	10
Capabilities		
Information usage		
Reach	22	77
Scope	33	149
Technology	27	88
Competitors	29	57
Customers	35	130
Political	24	65
Sources	38	148
Time horizon	28	62
Method sophistication		
Communication capacity	25	52
Integrative capacity	29	59
Match with context	8	15
Match with problem	10	17
People and networks		

Characteristics of foresighters	28	63
Broad knowledge	7	13
Deep knowledge	2	3
Curious, receptive	8	15
Open minded, passionate	7	11
Strong external network	6	13
Strong internal network	5	6
Internal communication	39	98
Network scope	39	136
Organization		
Mode	29	60
Integration with other processes	43	105
Formal diffusion of insights	14	31
Accountability	9	40
Incentives and rewards	8	17
Culture		
Organization's attitude toward periphery	3	8
Readiness to listen to external sources	7	10
Informal diffusion of insights	3	3
Willingness to share across functions	9	28
Willingness to challenge assumptions	6	16
Value creation		
Reduction of uncertainty	56	188
Early warning	19	27
Challenge basic assumptions and dominant business logic	31	70
Trend identification, interpretation, and prediction	28	66
Improve decision making	20	31
Triggering actions	63	315
Trigger R and D projects (innovation management)	36	109
Change current product portfolio (marketing)	38	77
Trigger new business development (corporate development)	30	81
Trigger strategic change (strategic management)	28	69
Influencing others to act	24	82
Influence other companies	7	13
Influence policy making	18	79
Secondary benefits	23	50
Marketing and sales	7	18
Organizational learning	18	34
Other codes		
Barriers to corporate foresight	12	25
Drivers of corporate foresight	7	12

References

Abernathy W, Townsend P (1975) Technology, productivity and Process change. Technol Forecast Soc Change 7(4):379–396

Adner R (2002) When are technologies disruptive? A demand-based view of the emergence of competition. Strateg Manage J 23(8):667–688

Adner R, Zemsky P (2005) Disruptive technologies and the emergence of competition. Rand J Econ 36(2):229–254

Afuah AN, Utterback JM (1997) Responding to structural industry changes: a technological evolution perspective. Ind Corp Change 6(1):183–202

Agar J (2003) Constant touch: a brief history of the mobile phone. Icon, Cambridge

Åhman M, Nilsson LJ (2008) Path dependency and the future of advanced vehicles and biofuels. Util Pol 16(2):80–89

Allen TJ, Piepmeier JM, Cooney S (1971) International Technological Gatekeeper. Technol Rev 73(5):36–43

Amanatidou E, Guy K (2008) Interpreting foresight process impacts: steps towards the development of a framework conceptualising the dynamics of foresight systems'. Technol Forecast Soc Change 75(4):539–557

Ambrosini V, Bowman C (2009) What are dynamic capabilities and are they a useful construct in strategic management? Int J Manage Rev 11(1):29–49

Ament RH (1970) Comparison of delphi forecasting studies in 1964 and 1969. Futures 2(1):35–44

Andersen PD et al (2004) Sensor foresight – technology and market. Technovation 24(4):311–320

Anderson J (1997) Technology foresight for competitive advantage. Long Range Plann 30 (5):665–677

Anderson P, Tushman ML (1990) Technological discontinuities and dominant design – a cyclical model of technological-change. Adm Sci Q 35(4):604–633

Andriopoulos C, Gotsi M (2006) Probing the future: mobilising foresight in multiple-product innovation firms. Futures 38(1):50–66

Andriopoulos C, Lewis MW (2009) Exploitation-exploration tensions and organizational ambidexterity: managing paradoxes of innovation. Organ Sci 20(4):696–717

Ansoff HI (1980) Strategic issue management. Strateg Manage J 1(2):131–148

Ansoff HI, Declerck RP, Hayes RL (1976) From strategic planning to strategic management. Wiley, London

Arendt LA, Priem RL, Ndofor HA (2005) A CEO-adviser model of strategic decision making. J Manage 31(5):680–699

Arnold HM (2003) Technology shocks: origins, management responses and firm performance. Physica Verlag Springer-Verlag GmbH & Co.KG, Heidelberg

Arnold HM, Freese B (2007) Deutsche Telekom Laboratories: Kombination von Universitäts- und Industrieforschung für Telekommunikations- und Medieninnovationen. Medienwirtschaft 2007(3):54–59

R. Rohrbeck, *Corporate Foresight*, Contributions to Management Science,
DOI 10.1007/978-3-7908-2626-5,

© Springer-Verlag Berlin Heidelberg 2011

Arnold HM, Linke D, Rohrbeck R (2006) Corporate Entrepreneurship – Diskussion verschiedener Konzepte zur Förderung von Unternehmertum in Multinationalen Unternehmen. FGF G-Forum für Gründungs-Forschung. Förderkreis Gründungs-Forschung e.V., Berlin

Ashton WB, Klavans RA (1997) Keeping abreast of science and technology: technical intelligence for business. Battelle Press, Columbus, OH

Audretsch DB (1995) Innovation, growth and survival. Int J Indust Organ 13(4):441–457

Ayres RU (2000) On forecasting discontinuities. Technol Forecast Soc Change 65(1):81–97

Bader MA (2008) Managing intellectual property in inter-firm R&D collaborations in knowledge-intensive industries. Int J Technol Manage 41(3–4):311–335

Bahrami H (1992) The emerging flexible organization – perspectives from Silicon Valley. Calif Manage Rev 34(4):33–52

Barker D, Smith DJH (1995) Technology foresight using roadmaps. Long Range Plann 28 (2):21–28

Barney J (1991) Firm resources and sustained competitive advantage. J Manage 17(1):99–120

Baum JR, Wally S (2003) Strategic decision speed and firm performance. Strateg Manage J 24 (11):1107–1129

Bayus BL, Kang W, Agarwal R (2007) Creating growth in new markets: a simultaneous model of firm entry and price. J Prod Innov Manage 24(2):139–155

Becker P (2002) Corporate foresight in Europe: a first overview working paper European Commission. European Commission, Brussels, p 31

Bellone F et al (2008) Market selection along the firm life cycle. Ind Corp Change 17(4):753–777

Bessant J et al (2005) Managing innovation beyond the steady state. Technovation 25 (12):1366–1376

BITCOM (2009) ITK-Standort Deutschland: Zur Zukunft von Forschung und Entwicklung in Deutschland. Berlin

Björk J, Magnusson M (2009) Where do good innovation ideas come from? Exploring the influence of network connectivity on innovation idea quality. J Prod Innov Manage 26 (6):662–670

Blackman DA, Henderson S (2004) How foresight creates unforeseen futures: the role of doubting. Futures 36(2):253–266

Blass E (2003) Researching the future: method or madness? Futures 35(10):1041–1054

Blind K, Cuhls K, Grupp H (1999) Current foresight activities in central Europe. Technol Forecast Soc Change 60(1):15–35

Bodelle J, Jablon C (1993) Science and technology scouting at Elf Aquitaine. Res Technol Manage 36(5):24–28

Bogner WC, Barr PS (2000) Making sense in hypercompetitive environments: a cognitive explanation for the persistence of high velocity competition. Organ Sci 11(2):212–226

Bondu J (2001) Benchmarking des Pratiques d'Intelligence Économique Intelligence Scientifique, Technique et Economique. ESIEE, Paris, p 126

Bortz J, Döring N (2006) Forschungsmethoden und Evaluation für Human-und Sozialwissenschaftler. Springer, Wiesbaden

Bosch Siemens Hausgeräte (BSH) (2008) Group annual report. Munich, Germany

Bourgeois LJ, Eisenhardt KM (1988) Strategic decision-processes in high-velocity environments – 4 cases in the microcomputer industry. Manage Sci 34(7):816–835

Breiner S, Cuhls K, Grupp H (1994) Technology foresight using a Delphi approach – a Japanese-German cooperation. R D Manage 24(2):141–153

Brenneman WB, Keys JB, Fulmer RM (1998) Learning across a living company: the Shell Companies' experiences. Organ Dyn 27(2):61–70

Bridges W (1986) Managing organizational transitions. Organ Dyn 15(1):24–33

British Telecom Group plc (2007) Annual report. London, UK

Brockhoff K (1993) Technologiemanagement – Das S-Kurven-Konzept. In: Hauschildt J, Grün O (eds) Ergebnisse empirischer betriebswirtschaftlicher Forschung: zu einer Realtheorie der Unternehmung: Festschrift für Eberhard Witte. Schäffer-Poeschel, Stuttgart, pp 328–353

Brockmann EN, Anthony WP (2002) Tacit knowledge and strategic decision making. Group Organ Manage 27(4):436–455

Brown D (2006) Embracing open innovation: a new approach to creating sustainable value BT white paper. British Telecom, London

Brown SL, Eisenhardt KM (1997) The art of continuous change: linking complexity theory and time-paced evolution in relentlessly shifting organizations. Adm Sci Q 42(1):1–34

Buganza T, Verganti R (2006) Life-cycle flexibility: how to measure and improve the innovative capability in turbulent environments. J Prod Innov Manage 23(5):393–407

Bulinge F (2006) Le cycle du renseignement: analyse critique d'un model empirique. In: Moinet N, Chirouze Y (eds) L'intelligence économique. Edicions ESK, Paris

Burmeister K et al (2002) Zukunftsforschung und Unternehmen – Praxis, Methoden, Perspektiven. Druck- und Verlagskooperative stattwerk e. G, Essen

Burmeister K, Neef A, Beyers B (2004a) Corporate foresight. Murmann Verlag GmbH, Hamburg

Burmeister K, Neef A, Meyers B (2004b) Corporate Foresight: Unternehmen gestalten Zukunft. Murmann Verlag, Hamburg

Burt G (2007) Why are we surprised at surprises? Integrating disruption theory and system analysis with the scenario methodology to help identify disruptions and discontinuities. Technol Forecast Soc Change 74(6):731–749

Cairns G et al (2006) Enhancing foresight between multiple agencies: issues in the use of scenario thinking to overcome fragmentation. Futures 38(8):1010–1025

Camerona J et al (2008) 'The Navigator Network': a new Zealand futurewatch case study. Technol Anal Strateg Manage 20(3):271–285

Camp RC (2003) Best practice benchmarking: the path to excellence. GBN Rev 2003/2004:12–17

Carlson LW (2004) Using technology foresight to create business value. Res Technol Manage 47 (5):51–60

Chandler AD (1962) Strategy and structure: chapters in the history of the industrial enterprise. MIT, Cambridge

Chandy RK, Tellis GJ (1998) Organizing for radical product innovation: the overlooked role of willingness to cannibalize. J Mark Res 35(4):474–487

Chandy RK, Tellis GJ (2000) The incumbent's curse? incumbency, size, and radical product innovation. J Mark 64(3):1–17

Chen CJ, Watanabe C (2006) Diffusion, substitution and competition dynamism inside the ICT market: the case of Japan. Technol Forecast Soc Change 73(6):731–759

Chermack TJ (2005) Studying scenario planning: theory, research suggestions, and hypotheses. Technol Forecast Soc Change 72(1):59–73

Chermack TJ, Lynham SA, Ruona WEA (2001) A review of scenario planning literature. Futures Res Q 17(2):7–31

Chermack TJ, Lynham SA, van der Merwe L (2006) Exploring the relationship between scenario planning and perceptions of learning organization characteristics. Futures 38(7):767–777

Chermack TJ, van der Merwe L, Lynham SA (2007) Exploring the relationship between scenario planning and perceptions of strategic conversation quality. Technol Forecast Soc Change 74 (3):379–390

Chesbrough HW (2003) The era of open innovation. MIT Sloan Manage Rev 44(3):35–41

Child J (1972) Organizational structure, environment and performance – role of strategic choice. Sociol – J Br Sociol Assoc 6(1):1–22

Child J (1997) Strategic choice in the analysis of action, structure, organizations and environment: retrospect and prospect. Organ Stud 18(1):43–76

Choo CW (1996) The knowing organization: how organizations use information to construct meaning, create knowledge and make decisions. Int J Inf Manage 16(5):329–340

Christensen CM (1997) The innovator's dilemma: when new technologies cause great firms to fail. Harvard Business School Press, Boston, MA

Christensen CM, Overdorf M (2000) Meeting the challenge of disruptive change. Harv Bus Rev 78 (2):66–76

Coates JF (1985) Foresight in federal government policy making. Futures Res Q 1:29–53
Cohen WM, Levinthal DA (1990) Absorptive-capacity – a new perspective on learning and innovation. Adm Sci Q 35(1):128–152
Collis D, Montgomery C (1995) Competing on resources: strategy in the 1990s. Harv Bus Rev 73 (4):118–128
Continental (2007) Annual report. Hanover, Germany
Coombs R, Hull R (1998) Knowledge management practices and path-dependency in innovation. Res Policy 27(3):237–253
Cooper RG (1983) Process model for industrial new product development. IEEE Trans Eng Manage 30(1):2–11
Corner PD, Kinicki AJ, Keats BW (1994) Integrating organizational and individual information-processing perspectives on choice. Organ Sci 5(3):294–308
Costanzo LA (2004) Strategic foresight in a high-speed environment. Futures 36(2):219–235
Cuhls K (2001) Foresight with Delphi surveys in Japan. Technol Anal Strateg Manage 13 (4):555–569
Cuhls K (2003) From forecasting to foresight processes – new participative foresight activities in Germany. J Forecast 22(2–3):93–111
Cunha MP, Palma P, da Costa NG (2006) Fear of foresight: knowledge and ignorance in organizational foresight. Futures 38(8):942–955
Cunningham SW, Porter AL, Newman NC (2006) Special issue on tech mining. Technol Forecast Soc Change 73(8):915–922
Daft RL, Weick KE (1984) Toward a model of organizations as interpretation systems. Acad Manage Rev 9(2):284–295
Daft RL, Sormunen J, Parks D (1988) Chief executive scanning, environmental characteristics, and company performance – an empirical-study. Strateg Manage J 9(2):123–139
Daheim C, Uerz G (2006) Corporate foresight in Europe: ready for the next step? Second international seville seminar on future-oriented technology analysis: impact of FTA approaches on policy and decision-making. Seville, Spain, 16
Daheim C, Uerz G (2008) Corporate foresight in Europe: from trend based logics to open foresight. Technol Anal Strateg Manage 20(3):321–336
Daim TU et al (2006) Forecasting emerging technologies: use of bibliometrics and patent analysis. Technol Forecast Soc Change 73(8):981–1012
Danneels E (2004) Disruptive technology reconsidered: a critique and research agenda. J Prod Innov Manage 21(4):246–258
Danneels E (2008) Organizational antecedents of second-order competences. Strateg Manage J 29 (5):519–543
Darby MR, Zucker LG (2003) Growing by leaps and inches: creative destruction, real cost reduction, and inching up. Econ Inq 41(1):1–19
Davis A (2008) Barrieren bei der Implementierung von Corporate Foresight im Unternehmen und im Strategischen Management Fakultät für Wirtschaftswissenschaften, Institut für Wirtschaftspolitik und Wirtschaftsforschung (IWW). University of Karlsruhe, Karlsruhe, p 245
Day DL (1994) Raising radicals – different processes for championing innovative corporate ventures. Organ Sci 5(2):148–172
Day GS, Schoemaker P (2004a) Peripheral vision: sensing and acting on weak signals. Long Range Plann 37(2):117–121
Day GS, Schoemaker PJH (2004b) Driving through the fog: managing at the edge. Long Range Plann 37(2):127–142
Day GS, Schoemaker PJH (2005) Scanning the periphery. Harv Bus Rev 83(11):135–148
Day GS, Schoemaker PJH (2006) Peripheral vision: detecting the weak signals that will make or break your company. Harvard Business School, Boston, MA
de Geus AP (1988) Planning as learning. Harv Bus Rev 66(2):70–74
De Geus A (1997a) The living company. Harvard Business School Press, Boston, MA
De Geus A (1997b) The living company. Harv Bus Rev 75(2):51–59

De Toni A, Tonchia S (2005) Definitions and linkages between operational and strategic flexibilities. Omega 33(6):525–540

Dean JW, Sharfman MP (1996) Does decision process matter? A study of strategic decisionmaking effectiveness. Acad Manage J 39(2):368–396

DenHond F, Groenewegen P (1996) Environmental technology foresight: new horizons for technology management. Technol Anal Strateg Manage 8(1):33–46

Department of Trade and Industry UK (DTI) (2006) The 2006 R&D scoreboard. DTI publications, London

Deutsch CH (2008) At Kodak, some old things are new again New York times. New York Times, New York

Deutsche Bank AG (2008) Annual report. Frankfurt, Germany

Deutsche Telekom AG (2007) Annual report. Bonn

Dew N, Goldfarb B, Sarasvathy S (2006) Optimal inertia: when organizations should fail ecology and strategy. Jai-Elsevier Ltd, Kidlington, pp 73–99

Dodgson M, Gann D, Salter A (2006) The role of technology in the shift towards open innovation: the case of Procter & Gamble. R D Manage 36(3):333–346

Donaldson L (1999) The normal science of structural contingency theory. In: Clegg S, Hardy C (eds) Studying organization: theory & method. Sage, London

Drew SAW (2006) Building technology foresight: using scenarios to embrace innovation. Eur J Innov Manage 9(3):241–257

Drucker PF (1969) The age of discontinuity; guidelines to our changing society. Harper & Row, New York

Drucker P (1992) The age of discontinuity: guidelines to our changing society. Transaction Publishing, New Jersey

Durand R (2003) Predicting a firm's forecasting ability: the roles of organizational illusion of control and organizational attention. Strateg Manage J 24(9):821–838

Dushnitsky G, Lenox MJ (2005a) When do firms undertake R&D by investing in new ventures? Strateg Manage J 26(10):947–965

Dushnitsky G, Lenox MJ (2005b) When do incumbents learn from entrepreneurial ventures? Corporate venture capital and investing firm innovation rates. Res Policy 34(5):615–639

Dutta S, Narasimhan O, Rajiv S (2005) Conceptualizing and measuring capabilities: methodology and empirical application. Strateg Manage J 26(3):277–285

Dutton JE, Jackson SE (1987) Categorizing strategic issues – links to organizational action. Acad Manage Rev 12(1):76–90

Dutton JE, Ottensmeyer E (1987) Strategic issue management-systems – forms, functions, and contexts. Acad Manage J 12(2):355–365

Dutton JE et al (1997) Reading the wind: how middle managers assess the context for selling issues to top managers. Strateg Manage J 18(5):407–423

EC (2007) European energy and transport: trends to 2030 – update 2007. European Commission, Brussels

EDP (2007) Annual report. Lisbon, Portugal

EIRMA (1998) Technological roadmapping. Delivering business vision working group reports. European Industrial Research Management Association, Paris

Eisenhardt KM (1989) Building theories from case-study research. Acad Manage Rev 14(4): 532–550

Eisenhardt KM, Graebner ME (2007) Theory building from cases: opportunities and challenges. Acad Manage J 50:25–32

Eisenhardt KM, Martin JA (2000) Dynamic capabilities: what are they? Strateg Manage J 21 (10–11):1105–1121

Elenkov DS (1997) Strategic uncertainty and environmental scanning: the case for institutional influences on scanning behavior. Strateg Manage J 18(4):287–302

Endesa (2007) Annual report. Madrid, Spain

Eppler MJ, Platts KW (2009) Visual strategizing: the systematic use of visualization in the strategic-planning process. Long Range Plann 42(1):42–74

Eto H (2003) The suitability of technology forecasting/foresight methods for decision systems and strategy – a Japanese view. Technol Forecast Soc Change 70(3):231–249

Ettlie JE, Bridges WP, Okeefe RD (1984) Organization strategy and structural differences for radical versus incremental innovation. Manage Sci 30(6):682–695

Faems D, Van Looy B, Debackere K (2005) Interorganizational collaboration and innovation: toward a portfolio approach. J Prod Innov Manage 22(3):238–250

Fine CH (1998) Clockspeed: winning industry control in the age of temporary advantage. Perseus Books, Reading, MA

Fink A et al (2005) The future scorecard: combining external and internal scenarios to create strategic foresight. Manage Decis 43(3):360–381

Flick U (2007) Triangulation: eine Einführung. VS Verlag für Sozialwissenschaften, Wiesbaden

Floyd SW, Wooldridge B (1997) Middle management's strategic influence and organizational performance. J Manage Stud 34(3):465–485

Franz O et al (2006) Potenziale der Informations-und Kommunikations-Technologien zur Optimierung der Energieversorgung und des Energieverbrauchs (eEnergy)-Studie für das Bundesministerium für Wirtschaft und Technologie (BMWi). Studie für das Bundesministerium für Wirtschaft und Technologie (BMWi). Bad Honnef: wik-Consult, Fraunhofer ISI, Fraunhofer ISE

Galbraith CS, Ehrlich SB, DeNoble AF (2006) Predicting technology success: identifying key predictors and assessing expert evaluation for advanced technologies. J Technol Transf 31 (6):673–684

Garcia-Morales VJ, Ruiz-Moreno A, Llorens-Montes FJ (2007) Effects of technology absorptive capacity and technology proactivity on organizational learning, innovation and performance an empirical examination. Technol Anal Strateg Manage 19(4):527–558

Gáspár T, Nováky E (2002) Dilemmas for renewal of futures methodology. Futures 34(5):365–379

Gassmann O, Gaso B (2005) Organisational frameworks for listening post activities. Int J Technol Intell Plann 1(3):241–265

Gemünden HG, Kock A (2009) Bei radikalen Innovationen gelten andere Spielregeln In: Harland PE, Schwarz-Geschka M (eds) Immer eine Idee voraus: Wie innovative Unternehmen Kreativität systematisch nutzen. Harland media

Gemünden HG, Heydebreck P, Herden R (1992) Technological interweavement: a means of achieving innovation success. R D Manage 22(4):359–376

Gemünden HG, Ritter T, Heydebreck P (1996) Network configuration and innovation success: an empirical analysis in German high-tech industries. Int J Res Mark 13(5):449–462

Gemünden HG, Salomo S, Hölzle K (2007) Role models for radical innovations in times of open innovation. Creativity Innov Manage 16(4):408–421

General Electric (2007) Annual report. Fairfield, CA

Georghiou L, Keenan M (2006) Evaluation of national foresight activities: assessing rationale, process and impact. Technol Forecast Soc Change 73(7):761–777

Gerbing DW, Hamilton JG, Freeman EB (1994) A large-scale 2nd-order structural equation model of the influence of management participation on organizational planning benefits. J Manage 20 (4):859–885

Gersick CJG (1991) Revolutionary change theories – a multilevel exploration of the punctuated equilibrium paradigm. Acad Manage Rev 16(1):10–36

Gerybadze A (1990) Technological forecasting. In: Tschirky H, Hess W, Lang P (eds) Technologie-Management: Erfolgsfaktor mit zunehmender Bedeutung. Verlag Industrielle Organisation, Zürich, pp 71–100

Gerybadze A (1994) Technology forecasting as a process of organisational intelligence. R D Manage 24(2):131–140

Ghemawat P (1991) Market incumbency and technological inertia. Mark Sci 10(2):161–171

Gillham B (2000) Case study research methods. Continuum Intl Pub Group, New York

Gladwell M (2001) The tipping point – how little things can make a big difference. Little, Brown and Company, New York

Godet M, Roubelat F (1996) Creating the future: the use and misuse of scenarios. Long Range Plann 29(2):164–171

Godet M, Monti R, Roubelat F (2004) Manuel de prospective stratégique – 1. Une indiscipline intellectuelle. Dunod, Paris

Goll I, Rasheed AMA (1997) Rational decision-making and firm performance: the moderating role of environment. Strateg Manage J 18(7):583–591

Gordon TJ, Glenn JC (2003) Futures research methodology. Millennium Project of the American Council of the United Nations University, New York

Gordon TJ, Hayward H (1968) Initial experiments with the cross impact matrix method of forecasting. Futures 1(2):100–116

Govindarajan V, Kopalle PK (2006) The usefulness of measuring disruptiveness of innovations ex post in making ex ante predictions. J Prod Innov Manage 23(1):12–18

Grant L (1998) Why Kodak still isn't fixed America's other famous troubled giants–IBM, GM, sears–got turned around. Not this one. Can CEO George Fisher's big new shakeup do the job? Fortune

Groenveld P (1997) Roadmapping integrates business and technology. Res Technol Manage 40 (5):48–55

Groenveld P (2007) Roadmapping integrates business and technology. Res Technol Manage 50 (6):49–58

Gruber M, Venter C (2006) "Die Kunst, die Zukunft zu erfinden" – Theoretische Erkenntnisse und empirische Befunde zum Einsatz des Corporate Foresight in deutschen Großunternehmen. Zeitschrift für betriebswirtschaftliche Forschung (zfbf) 2006(11):958–984

Gruber M et al (2003) Die Rolle des Corporate Foresight im Innovationsprozess: Ziele, Ausgestaltung und Erfahrungen am Beispiel der Siemens AG. Zeitschrift Führung + Organisation (zfo) 72(5):285–290

Grupp H, Linstone HA (1999) National technology foresight activities around the globe – resurrection and new paradigms. Technol Forecast Soc Change 60(1):85–94

GSM Association (2008) Brief history of the GSM and GSMA. http://www.gsmworld.com/about-us/history.htm last accessed 10 Oct 2010

Gunasekaran A, Lai KH, Cheng TCE (2008) Responsive supply chain: a competitive strategy in a networked economy. Omega Int J Manage Sci 36(4):549–564

Hambrick DC (1982) Environmental scanning and organizational strategy. Strateg Manage J 3 (2):159–174

Harroussi S (2004) Système de veille stratégique basé sur un réseau d'experts: méthodes et outils. Aix-en-Provence: Universität Paul Cézanne, Aix-Marseille III, 246

Harvey E (1968) Technology and the structure of organizations. Am Sociol Rev 33:247–259

He X, Probert DR, Phaal R (2008) Funnel or tunnel? A tough journey for breakthrough innovations. IEEE international conference on management of innovation and technology, IEEE, Bangkok, Thailand pp 368–373

Helfat CE (2007a) Dynamic capabilities: understanding strategic change in organizations. Blackwell, Malden, MA

Helfat CE (2007b) Stylized facts, empirical research and theory development in management. Strateg Organ 5(2):185–192

Helfat CE, Peteraf MA (2003) The dynamic resource-based view: capability lifecycles. Strateg Manage J 24(10):997–1010

Helmer O (1972) Cross-impact gaming. Futures 4(2):149–167

Henderson R (1993) Underinvestment and incompetence as responses to radical innovation – evidence from the photolithographic alignment equipment industry. Rand J Econ 24(2): 248–270

Henderson RM, Clark KB (1990) Architectural innovation – the reconfiguration of existing product technologies and the failure of established firms. Adm Sci Q 35(1):9–30

Heraud JA, Cuhls K (1999) Current foresight activities in France, Spain, and Italy. Technol Forecast Soc Change 60(1):55–70

Hergert R (2007) Strategische Früherkennung: Wahrnehmung relevanter Umweltanreize oder wie ticken Unternehmen? Metropolis Verlag, Marburg

Herrmann A, Gassmann O, Eisert U (2007) An empirical study of the antecedents for radical product innovations and capabilities for transformation. J Eng Technol Manage 24(1–2): 92–120

Herzhoff M (2004) Szenario-Technik in der chemischen Industrie: Untersuchung von Software-Tools am Beispiel einer Studie zum Markt für Flammschutzmittel im Jahr 2010 und der praktischen Bedeutung der Szenario-Technik Fakultät II – Mathematik und Naturwissenschaften. Technische Universität Berlin, Berlin, p 240

Hilbert M, Miles I, Othmer J (2009) Foresight tools for participative policy-making in inter-governmental processes in developing countries: lessons learned from the eLAC policy priorities Delphi. Technol Forecast Soc Change 76(7):880–896

Hines A (2002) A practitioner's view of the future of futures studies. Futures 34(3–4):337–347

Hitt MA, Tyler BB (1991) Strategic decision-models – integrating different perspectives. Strateg Manage J 12(5):327–351

Hitt M, Keats B, DeMarie S (1998) Navigating in the new competitive landscape: building strategic flexibility and competitive advantage in the 21st century. Acad Manage Exec 12(4): 22–42

Hofmann J, Rollwagen I, Schneider S (2007) Deutschland 2020 – new challenges for a land on expedition. In: Bergheim S (ed) Deutsche bank research. Deutsche Bank Research, Frankfurt am Main

Höjer M, Mattsson L-G (2000) Determinism and backcasting in future studies. Futures 32(7): 613–634

Horton A (1999) A simple guide to sucessful foresight. Foresight 1:5–9

Hough JR, Ogilvie DT (2005) An empirical test of cognitive style and strategic decision outcomes. J Manage Stud 42(2):417–448

Hough JR, White MA (2003) Environmental dynamism and strategic decision-making rationality: an examination at the decision-level. Strateg Manage J 24(5):481–489

Hugo Boss AG (2008) Annual report. Metzingen, Germany

Humphrey WS (1989) Managing the software process. Addison-Wesley, Reading, MA

Hurmelinna P et al (2005) Striving towards R&D collaboration performance: the effect of asymmetry, trust and contracting. Creativity Innov Manage 14(4):374–383

Huy QN, Mintzberg H (2003) The rhythm of change. MIT Sloan Manage Rev 44(4):79

Iberdrola (2007) Legal information. Madrid, Spain

IEA (2008) World energy outlook. International Energy Agency, Paris

Ilmola L, Kuusi O (2006) Filters of weak signals hinder foresight: monitoring weak signals efficiently in corporate decision-making. Futures 38(8):908–924

Infineon (2007) Annual report. Munich, Germany

Ireland RD et al (1987) Strategy formulation processes – differences in perceptions of strength and weaknesses indicators and environmental uncertainty by managerial level. Strateg Manage J 8(5):469–485

Jain SC (1984) Environmental scanning in United-States corporations. Long Range Plann 17(2): 117–128

Jasner C (2006) Walk of pain. McKinsey Wissen 17(1):44–49

Jemison DB (1984) The importance of boundary spanning roles in strategic decision-making. J Manage Stud 21(2):131–152

Jennings D, Lumpkin J (1992) Insights between environmental scanning activities and Porter's generic strategies: an empirical analysis. J Manage 18(4):791–803

Josse G (2004) Strategische Frühaufklärung in der Touristik: Aufbau eines zielgebietsorientierten Frühaufklärungssystems für Reiseveranstalter. Deutscher Universitäts-Verlag

Judge WQ, Douglas TJ (1998) Performance implications of incorporating natural environmental issues into the strategic planning process: an empirical assessment. J Manage Stud 35(2): 241–262

Kahn KB, Barczak G, Moss R (2006) Perspective: establishing an NPD best practices framework. J Prod Innov Manage 23(2):106–116

Kameoka A, Yokoo Y, Kuwahara T (2004) A challenge of integrating technology foresight and assessment in industrial strategy development and policymaking. Technol Forecast Soc Change 71(6):579–598

Kaplan RS, Norton DP (2006) How to implement a new strategy without disrupting your organization. Harv Bus Rev 84(3):100–109

Käslin B (2008) Systematische Früherkennung von Emerging Risks in der Versicherungswirtschaft. Hochschule St. Gallen, St. Gallen, p 277

Katz R, Allen TJ (1982) Investigating the not invented here (NIH) syndrome – a look at the performance, tenure, and communication patterns of 50 R-and-D project groups. R D Manage 12(1):7–19

Kelley D (2009) Adaptation and organizational connectedness in corporate radical innovation programs. J Prod Innov Manage 26(5):487–501

Kessler EH, Bierly PE (2002) Is faster really better? an empirical test of the implications of innovation speed. IEEE Trans Eng Manage 49(1):2–12

Kessler EH, Chakrabarti AK (1996) Innovation speed: a conceptual model of context, antecedents, and outcomes. Acad Manage Rev 21(4):1143–1191

Khandwalla PN (1977) The design of organizations. Harcourt Brace Jovanovich, New York

Kim WC, Mauborgne R (2005) Blue ocean strategy: how to create uncontested market space and make the competition irrelevant. Harvard Business School Press, Boston, MA

Kinra A, Kotzab H (2008) A macro-institutional perspective on supply chain environmental complexity. Int J Prod Econ 115(2):283–295

Kodama M (2007) Innovation and knowledge creation through leadership-based strategic community: case study on high-tech company in Japan. Technovation 27(3):115–132

Konnola T, Brummer V, Salo A (2007) Diversity in foresight: insights from the fostering of innovation ideas. Technol Forecast Soc Change 74(5):608–626

Krubasik EG (1982) Strategische Waffe. Wirtschaftswoche 26(25):28–33

Krystek U (2007) Strategische Frühaufklärung. Zeitschrift für Controlling & Management 2007 (Sonderheft 2):50–58

Krystek U, Müller-Stewens G (1993) Frühaufklärung für Unternehmen: Identifikation und Handhabung zukünftiger Chancen und Bedrohungen. Schäffer-Poeschel, Stuttgart

Krystek U, Müller-Stewens G (1999) Strategische Frühaufklärung. In: Hahn DT, Taylor B (eds) Strategische Unternehmungsplanung — Strategische Unternehmungsführung. Springer, Berlin, pp 497–517

Kuhn TS (1970) The structure of scientific revolutions. University of Chicago Press, Chicago, IL

Kumar R et al (2005) On the bursty evolution of blogspace. World Wide Web 8(2):159–178

Lackman CL, Saban K, Lanasa JM (2000) Organizing the competitive intelligence function: a benchmarking study. Competitive Intell Rev 11(1):17–27

Lambe CJ, Spekman RE (1997) Alliances, external technology acquisition, and discontinuous technological change. J Prod Innov Manage 14(2):102–116

Lamnek S (2005) Qualitative Sozialforschung: Lehrbuch. Beltz, PVU, Weinheim

Langerak F, Hultink EJ (2005) The impact of new product development acceleration approaches on speed and profitability: lessons for pioneers and fast followers. IEEE Trans Eng Manage 52(1):30–42

Langley A (1999) Strategies for theorizing from process data. Acad Manage Rev 24(4):691–710

Lawrence PR, Lorsch JW (1967) Organization and environment; managing differentiation and integration. Division of Research, Graduate School of Business Administration, Harvard University, Boston, MA

Lee T (1998) Using qualitative methods in organizational research. Sage, Thousand Oaks, CA

Lee H, Smith KG, Grimm CM (2003) The effect of new product radicality and scope on the extent and speed of innovation diffusion. J Manage 29(5):753–768
Leenders MA, Wierenga B (2002) The effectiveness of different mechanisms for integrating marketing and R&D. J Prod Innov Manage 19(4):305–317
Leifer RP (1997) Organizational and managerial correlates of radical technological innovation. Paper presented at the PICMET Conference 1997: Innov Technol Manage – The Key to Global Leadership, Portland, OR pp. 134–137
Lesca H, Caron M-L (1995) Veille stratégique : créer une intelligence collective au sein de l'entreprise. Revue francaise de Gestion, pp 10558–10568
Levinthal D (1992) Surviving Schumpeterian environments: an evolutionary perspective. Ind Corp Change 1(3):427–443
Lichtenthaler E (2002) Organisation der Technology Intelligence – Eine empirische Untersuchung der Technologiefrühaufklärung in technologieintensiven Grossunternehmen. Verlag Industrielle Organisation
Lichtenthaler E (2005) The choice of technology intelligence methods in multinationals: towards a contingency approach. Int J Technol Manage 32(3–4):388–407
Lichtenthaler U (2008a) Integrated roadmaps for open innovation. Res Technol Manage 51(3): 45–49
Lichtenthaler U (2008b) Open innovation in practice: an analysis of strategic approaches to technology transactions. IEEE Trans Eng Manage 55(1):148–157
Lichtenthaler U (2009) Absorptive capacity, environmental turbulence, and the complementarity of organizational learning processes. Acad Manage J 52(4):822–846
Liebl F (1996) Strategische Frühaufklärung: Trends – issues – stakeholders. Oldenbourg, München
Liebl F (2005) Technologie-Frühaufklärung: Bestandsaufnahme und Perspektiven. In: Albers S, Gassmann O (eds) Handbuch Technologie- und Innovationsmanagement: Strategie Umsetzung – Controlling. Gabler, Wiesbaden, pp 119–136
Lischka J-M, Gemünden HG (2008) Technology roadmapping in manufacturing – a case study at Siemens power generation. Int J Technol Intell Plann 4(2):201–214
Loveridge D (2001) Foresight – seven paradoxes. Int J Technol Manage 21(7–8):781–791
Lucas HC, Goh JM (2009) Disruptive technology: how Kodak missed the digital photography revolution. J Strateg Inf Syst 18(1):46–55
Macher JT, Richman BD (2004) Organizational reponses to discontinuous innovation: a case study approach. Int J Innov Manage 8(1):87–114
MAN Turbo AG (2008) Annual report. Oberhausen, Germany
Markides C (2006) Disruptive innovation: in need of better theory. J Prod Innov Manage 23(1): 19–25
Martin BR (1995) Foresight in science and technology. Technol Anal Strateg Manage 7(2): 139–168
Martinet B, Ribault J-M (1989) La veille technologique, concurrentielle et commerciale: Sources, méthodologie, organisation. Les Éditions D'Organisation, Paris
Matthyssens P, Pauwels P, Vandenbempt K (2005) Strategic flexibility, rigidity and barriers to the development of absorptive capacity in business markets: themes and research perspectives. Ind Mark Manage 34(6):547–554
May RC, Stewart WH, Sweo R (2000) Environmental scanning behavior in a transitional economy: evidence from Russia. Acad Manage J 43(3):403–427
Mayer H (2006) Interview und schriftliche Befragung: Entwicklung, Durchführung und Auswertung. Oldenbourg Wissenschaftsverlag
Mayring P (2002) Einführung in die qualitative Sozialforschung: eine Anleitung zu qualitativem Denken. Beltz, Weinheim
McDowall W, Eames M (2006) Forecasts, scenarios, visions, backcasts and roadmaps to the hydrogen economy: a review of the hydrogen futures literature. Energy Policy 34(11): 1236–1250

McMaster M (1996) Foresight: exploring the structure of the future. Long Range Plann 29(2):149–155
Mietzner D, Reger G (2005) Advantages and disadvantages of scenario approaches for strategic foresight. Int J Technol Intell Plann 1(2):220–230
Miles I (1999) Foresight and services: closing the gap? Serv Ind J 19(2):1–27
Miller D (1993) The architecture of simplicity. Acad Manage Rev 18(1):116–138
Miller S (1997) Implementing strategic decisions: four key success factors. Organ Stud 18(4): 577–602
Mintzberg H, Westley F (1992) Cycles of organizational-change. Strateg Manage J 13:39–59
Mittelstaedt RE (1992) Benchmarking: how to learn from best-in-class practices. Natl Prod Rev 11(3):301–315
Möhrle MG (2004) TRIZ-based technology-roadmapping. Int J Technol Intell Plann 1(1):87–90
Möhrle MG, Isenmann R (2005) Technologie-Roadmapping – Zukunftsstrategien für Technologieunternehmen. Springer-Verlag GmbH & Co. KG
Monteiro LF (2006) Sensing the globe for external knowledge: uncovering the technology scouting process. London Business School, Working Paper, London Business School, London, p 42
Monteiro LF, Sull D (2006) BT Group: bringing external innovation inside. ecch Case, Case 307-045-01(London Business School case CS-07-005), p 39
Moore JF (1993) Predators and prey – a new ecology of competition. Harv Bus Rev 71(3):75–86
Moore G (2006) Dealing with Darwin. Portfolio, New York
Müller A (2008) Strategic Foresight – Prozesse strategischer Trend- und Zukunftsforschung in Unternehmen. Universität St. Gallen, St. Gallen, Switzerland, p 425
Müller-Stewens G, Müller A (2009) Strategic Foresight – Trend- und Zukunftsforschung als Strategieinstrument. In: Reimer M, Fiege S (eds) Perspektiven des strategischen Controllings. Gabler, Wiesbaden
Nadkarni S, Narayanani VK (2007) Strategic schemas, strategic flexibility, and firm performance: the moderating role of industry clockspeed. Strateg Manage J 28(3):243–270
Neill S, McKee D, Rose GM (2007) Developing the organization's sensemaking capability: precursor to an adaptive strategic marketing response. Ind Mark Manage 36(6):731–744
Neugarten ML (2006) Foresight–are we looking in the right direction? Futures 38(8):894–907
Niazi M, Wilson D, Zowghi D (2005) A maturity model for the implementation of software process improvement: an empirical study. J Syst Softw 74(2):155–172
Nick A (2008) Wirksamkeit strategischer Frühaufklärung – Eine empirische Untersuchung Fakultät für Technologie und Management. Berlin, University of Technology, Berlin, p 232
Nieto M, Quevedo P (2005) Absorptive capacity, technological opportunity, knowledge spillovers, and innovative effort. Technovation 25(10):1141–1157
Nijssen EJ, Hillebrand B, Vermeulen PAM (2005) Unraveling willingness to cannibalize: a closer look at the barrier to radical innovation. Technovation 25(12):1400–1409
Nochur KS, Allen TJ (1992) Do nominated boundary spanners become effective technological gatekeepers? IEEE Trans Eng Manage 39(3):265–269
Noke H, Perrons RK, Hughes M (2008) Strategic dalliances as an enabler for discontinuous innovation in slow clockspeed industries; evidence from the oil and gas industry. R D Manage 38(2):129–139
Nutt PC (2007) Intelligence gathering for decision making. Omega 35(5):604–622
O'Connor GC, DeMartino R (2006) Organizing for radical innovation: an exploratory study of the structural aspects of RI management systems in large established firms. J Prod Innov Manage 23(6):475–497
O'Connor GC, Veryzer RW (2001) The nature of market visioning for technology-based radical innovation. J Prod Innov Manage 18(4):231–246
O'Reilly CA, Tushman ML (2004) The ambidextrous organisation. Harv Bus Rev 82(4):74–81
O'Reilly CA, Harreld JB, Tushman ML (2009) Organizational ambidexterity: IBM and emerging business opportunities. Calif Manage Rev 51:75–99
OECD (1996) Special issue on governmental technology foresight exercises. Science, Technology and Industry Review, 1995(2):1–195

Oner M, Gol S (2007) Pitfalls in and success factors of corporate foresight projects. Int J Foresight Innov Policy 3(4):447–471

Ono R, Wedemeyer DJ (1994) Assessing the validity of the Delphi technique. Futures 26(3): 289–304

Oriesek DF, Friedrich R (2003) Blick in die Zukunft. Harv Bus Manager May: 65–72

Osborn CS (1998) Systems for sustainable organizations: emergent strategies, interactive controls and semi-formal information. J Manage Stud 35(4):481–509

Paap J, Katz R (2004) Anticipating disruptive innovation. Res Technol Manage 47:13–22

Pagani M (2009) Roadmapping 3G mobile TV: strategic thinking and scenario planning through repeated cross-impact handling. Technol Forecast Soc Change 76(3):382–395

Paladino A (2009) Financial champions and masters of innovation: analyzing the effects of balancing strategic orientations. J Prod Innov Manage 26(6):616–626

Parry ME et al (2009) The impact of NPD strategy, product strategy, and NPD processes on perceived cycle time. J Prod Innov Manage 26(6):627–639

Paulk MC (1995) The capability maturity model: guidelines for improving the software process. Addison-Wesley, Reading, MA

Pennings JM (1975) Relevance of structural-contingency model for organizational-effectiveness. Adm Sci Q 20(3):393–410

Penrose ET (1959) The theory of the growth of the firm. Wiley, New York

Perks H, Kahn K, Zhang C (2009) An empirical evaluation of R&D–marketing NPD integration in Chinese firms: the Guanxi effect. J Prod Innov Manage 26(6):640–651

Perona M, Miragliotta G (2004) Complexity management and supply chain performance assessment. A field study and a conceptual framework. Int J Prod Econ 90(1):103–115

Peters L, O'Connor GC (2002) Building the capacity for change: radical innovation and new product development in the multinational firm IEMC – managing technology for the new economy. Cambridge, UK, pp 612–616

Peterson JW (2002) Leveraging technology foresight to create temporal advantage. Technol Forecast Soc Change 69(5):485–494

Petrick IJ, Echols AE (2004) Technology roadmapping in review: a tool for making sustainable new product development decisions. Technol Forecast Soc Change 71(1–2):81–100

Petrick IJ, Provance M (2005) Roadmapping as a mitigator of uncertainty in strategic technology choice. Int J Technol Intell Plann 1(2):171–184

Phaal R et al (2003) Technology roadmapping: starting-up roadmapping fast. Res Technol Manage 46(2):52–58

Phaal R, Farrukh CJP, Probert DR (2004a) Collaborative technology roadmapping: network development and research prioritisation. Int J Technol Intell Plann 1(1):39–54

Phaal R, Farrukh CJP, Probert DR (2004b) Technology roadmapping – a planning framework for evolution and revolution. Technol Forecast Soc Change 71(1–2):5–26

Philips (2007) Annual report. Eindhoven, The Netherlands

Phillips F (2007) On S-curves and tipping points. Technol Forecast Soc Change 74(6):715–730

Pillkahn U (2007) Trends und Szenarien als Werkzeuge zur Strategieentwicklung: wie Sie die unternehmerische und gesellschaftliche Zukunft planen und gestalten. Publicis Corporate Publ, Erlangen

Pina e Cunha M, Chia R (2007) Using teams to avoid peripheral blindness. Long Range Plann 40(6):559–573

Pittaway L et al (2004) Networking and innovation: a systematic review of the evidence. Int J Manage Rev 5–6(4–5):137–168

Pitterman B (2000) Telcordia technologies: the journey to high maturity. IEEE Softw 17(4):89–96

Porter ME (1980) Competitive strategy: techniques for analyzing industries and competitors. Free Press, New York

Porter AL, Cunningham SW (2005) Tech mining: exploiting new technologies for competitive advantage. Wiley, Hoboken, NJ

Porter AL et al (2004) Technology futures analysis: toward integration of the field and new methods. Technol Forecast Soc Change 71(3):287–303
Poskela J, Martinsuo M (2009) Management control and strategic renewal in the front end of innovation. J Prod Innov Manage 26(6):671–684
Pouillot D, Puissochet A (2002) R&D spending on ICT – overall evolution in the major industrial countries, and close-up on telecom operators' new organization. Commun Strateg 48(4):33–51
Pradayrol A, Cyrot J-L (2008) Telecom operators – in the eye of the telecom-media storm. Arthur d. Little, Paris, London, p 96
Prahalad CK (2004) The blinders of dominant logic. Long Range Plann 37(2):171–179
Probert DR, Farrukh CJP, Phaal R (2003) Technology roadmapping – developing a practical approach for linking resources to strategic goals. Proc Inst Mech Eng B – J Eng Manufact 217(9):1183–1195
Product Development Management Association (PDMA) (2006) Body of knowledge: Product Development Management Association (PDMA) http://bok.pdma.org/, last accessed 10 Oct 2010
Qualls W, Olshavsky RW, Michaels RE (1981) Shortening of the PIC – an empirical test. J Mark 45(4):76–80
Quist J, Vergragt P (2006) Past and future of backcasting: the shift to stakeholder participation and a proposal for a methodological framework. Futures 38(9):1027–1045
Radnor Z, Noke H (2006) Development of an audit tool for product innovation: the innovation compass. Int J Innov Manage 10(1):1–18
Raisch S (2008) Balanced structures: designing organizations for profitable growth. Long Range Plann 41(5):483–508
Raisch S et al (2009) Organizational ambidexterity: balancing exploitation and exploration for sustained performance. Organ Sci 20(4):685–695
Reger G (2001a) Technology foresight in companies: from an indicator to a network and process perspective. Technol Anal Strateg Manage 13(4):533–553
Reger G (2001b) Strategic management of technology in a global perspective: differences between European, Japanese and US Companies. In: Kocaoglu DF, Anderson TR (eds) Paper presented at the PICMET Conference 2001: Technology management in the knowledge era. Portland, OR
Reger G (2006) Technologie-Früherkennung: Organisation und Prozess. In: Gassmann O, Kobe C (eds) Management von Innovation und Risiko. Quantensprünge in der Entwicklung erfolgreich managen. Springer, Berlin, pp 303–330
Reid SE, de Brentani U (2004) The fuzzy front end of new product development for discontinuous innovations: a theoretical model. J Prod Innov Manage 21(3):170–184
Renfro WL (1987) Issues management: the evolving corporate role. Futures 19(5):545–554
Rice MP et al (2001) Radical innovation: triggering initiation of opportunity recognition and evaluation. R D Manage 31(4):409–420
Richards L (2005) Handling qualitative data: a practical guide. Sage, London Thousand Oaks, CA
Ritter T, Gemunden HG (2003) Network competence: its impact on innovation success and its antecedents. J Bus Res 56(9):745–755
Roehl H, Rollwagen I (2004) Club, Syndikat, Party – wie wird morgen kooperiert? OrganisationsEntwicklung 04(3):30–41
Rohrbeck R, Arnold HM (2006) Making university-industry collaboration work – a case study on the Deutsche Telekom Laboratories contrasted with findings in literature. In: Torkkeli M, Zutshi R, Conn S (eds) ISPIM 2006 conference: "Networks for Innovation". International Society for Professional Innovation Management (ISPIM), Athens, Greece, p 11
Rohrbeck R, Heuer J, Arnold HM (2006) The technology radar – an instrument of technology intelligence and innovation strategy. The 3rd IEEE international conference on management of innovation and technology, Singapore. IEEE Conference Publishing, Piscataway, NJ, pp 978–983
Rohrbeck R, Steinhoff F, Perder F (2008) Virtual customer integration in the innovation process: evaluation of the web-platforms of multinational enterprises (MNE). PICMET conference

2008, Portland International Center für Management of Engineering and Technology, Cape Town, South Africa, pp 469–479
Rohrbeck R, Döhler M, Arnold H (2009a) Creating growth with externalization of R&D results – the spin-along approach. Glob Bus organ Excell 28(4):44–51
Rohrbeck R, Hölzle K, Gemünden HG (2009b) Opening up for competitive advantage – How Deutsche Telekom creates an open innovation ecosystem. R D Manage 39(4):420–430
Rohrbeck R et al (2009c) Benchmarking Report: strategic foresight in multinational companies, p 38. http://ssrn.com/abstract=1470050. Accessed 12 Oct 2009
Roll M (2004) Strategische Frühaufklärung: Vorbereitung auf eine ungewisse Zukunft am Beispiel des Luftverkehrs. Dt. Univ.-Verl, Wiesbaden
Roll M, Weber J (2006) Gestaltung strategischer Frühaufklärungssystems im Lichte neuer empirischer Erkenntnisse. In: Hutzschenreuter T, Griess-Nega T (eds) Krisenmangement: Grundlagen – Strategien – Instrumente. Gabler, Wiesbaden, p 815
Rollwagen I (2008) Zeit und Innovation. Zur Synchronisation von Wirtschaft, Wissenschaft und Politik bei der Genese der Virtual-Reality-Technologien. Transcript Verlag, Bielefeld
Rollwagen I, Hofmann J, Schneider S (2008) Improving the business impact of foresight. Technol Anal Strateg Manage 20(3):335–347
Romanelli E, Tushman ML (1994) Organizational transformation as punctuated equilibrium – an empirical-test. Acad Manage J 37(5):1141–1166
Rothwell R (1992) Successful industrial-innovation – critical factors for the 1990s. R D Manage 22(3):221–239
Rothwell R (1994) Towards the fifth-generation innovation process. Int Mark Rev 11(1):7–31
Rowe G, Wright G (1999) The Delphi technique as a forecasting tool: issues and analysis. Int J Forecast 15(4):353–375
Rowe G, Wright G, McColl A (2005) Judgment change during Delphi-like procedures: the role of majority influence, expertise, and confidence. Technol Forecast Soc Change 72(3):377–399
Rubin H, Rubin I (2005) Qualitative interviewing: the art of hearing data. Sage, CA
Ruff F (2006) Corporate foresight: integrating the future business environment into innovation and strategy. Int J Technol Manage 34(3–4):278–295
Saffo P (2007) Six rules for effective forecasting. Harv Bus Rev 85(7–8):122–131
Salo AA (2001) Incentives in technology foresight. Int J Technol Manage 21(7–8):694–710
Salo A, Cuhls K (2003) Preface – technology foresight – past and future. J Forecast 22(2–3):79–82
Salo A, Gustafsson T, Ramanathan R (2003) Multicriteria methods for technology foresight. J Forecast 22(2–3):235–255
Sandström C, Magnusson M, Jörnmark J (2009) Exploring factors influencing incumbents' response to disruptive innovation. Creativity Innov Manage 18(1):8–15
Sanz-Menendez L, Cabello C, Garcia CE (2001) Understanding technology foresight: the relevance of its S & T policy context. Int J Technol Manage 21(7–8):661–679
Saritas O, Aylen J (2008) Using scenarios for roadmapping: the case of clean production. R&D management conference "Emerging Issues in R&D Management", R&D Management Association, Ottawa, Canada, pp 1–18
Saritas O, Oner MA (2004) Systemic analysis of UK foresight results: joint application of integrated management model and roadmapping. Technol Forecast Soc Change 71(1–2):27–65
Saunders M, Lewis P, Thornhill A (2007) Research methods for business students. Financial Times/Prentice Hall, Harlow, England
Savioz P (2002) Technology Intelligence in technology-based SMEs. ETH Zurich, Zurich
Sawyerr OO (1993) Environmental uncertainty and environmental scanning activities of Nigerian manufacturing executives – a comparative-analysis. Strateg Manage J 14(4):287–299
Scapolo F (2005) New horizons and challenges for future-oriented technology analysis—The 2004 EU–US seminar. Technol Forecast Soc Change 72(9):1059–1063
Schläffer C, Arnold HM (2007) Media and network innovation – technological paths, customer needs and business logic. Elektrotechnik & Informationstechnik 124(10):317–322

Schoemaker P (1993) Multiple scenario develoment: its conceptual and behavioral foundation. Strateg Manage J 14(3):193–213
Schoemaker PJH, Heijden CAJMvd (1992) Integrating scenarios into strategic planning at Royal Dutch/Shell. Plann Rev 20(3):41–46
Schofield JW (2002) Increasing the generalizability of qualitative research. In: Huberman AM, Miles MB (eds) The qualitative research companion. Sage, Thousand Oaks, CA
Schreyögg G (1978) Umwelt, Technologie und Organisationsstruktur: eine Analyse des kontingenztheoretischen Ansatzes. Haupt, Bern
Schulz W et al (2005) Die Entwicklung der Energiemärkte bis zum Jahr 2030 – Energiewirtschaftliche Referenzprognosen Study for the Federal Ministry of Economics and Labour (Bundesministerium für Wirtschaft und Arbeit – BMWA). Prognos AG, Institute of Energy Economics, University of Cologne, Essen
Schumpeter J, Opie R (1934) The theory of economic development. Springer, Berlin
Schwair TM (2001) Inventing the future, not only predicting the future – futures research at Siemens AG, corporate technology. Futures Res Q 17(3):35–41
Schwarz J (2005) Pitfalls in implementing a strategic early warning system. Foresight 7(4):22–30
Schwarz J-O (2007) Assessing future disorders in organizations: implications for diagnosing and treating schizophrenic, depressed or paranoid organizations. Foresight 9(2):15–26
Schwarz JO (2009) Business wargaming: developing foresight within a strategic simulation. Technol Anal Strateg Manage 21(3):291–305
Schwenk CR (1984) Cognitive simplification processes in strategic decision making. Strateg Manage J 5:111–128
Seefeldt F, Wünsch M, Schlesinger M (2007) The future role of coal in Europe final report. Prognos AG, Berlin
Shavelson R, Towne L (2002) Scientific research in education. Joseph Henry Press, Washington, DC
Shrivastava P, Grant JH (1985) Empirically derived models of strategic decision-making processes. Strateg Manage J 6(2):97–113
Siemens AG (2007) Annual report. Munich, Germany
Siggelkow N, Rivkin JW (2005) Speed and search: designing organizations for turbulence and complexity. Organ Sci 16(2):101–122
Slaughter RA (1997) Developing and applying strategic foresight. ABN Rep 5(10):13–27
Slaughter RA (1998) Futures studies as an intellectual and applied discipline. Am Behav Sci 42(3):372–385
Slaughter R (1999) Futures for the third millenium: enabling the forward view. Prospect, St. Leonards
Sood A, Tellis GJ (2005) Technological evolution and radical innovation. J Mark 69(3):152–168
Sorenson O, Rivkin JW, Fleming L (2006) Complexity, networks and knowledge flow. Res Policy 35(7):994–1017
Sorescu AB, Chandy RK, Prabhu JC (2003) Sources and financial consequences of radical innovation: insights from pharmaceuticals. J Mark 67(4):82–102
Specht D, Mieke C, Behrens S (2003) Methoden der Technologiefrühaufklärung. Industriemanagement 19(3):71–74
Stadler C, Hinterhuber HH (2005) Shell, Siemens and DaimlerChrysler: leading change in companies with strong values. Long Range Plann 38(5):467–484
Steensma HK, Fairbank JF (1999) Internalizing external technology: a model of governance mode choice and an empirical assessment. J High Technol Manage Res 10(1):1–35
Steinhoff F (2006) Kundenorientierung bei hochgradigen Innovationen – Konzeptualisierung, Empirische Bestandsaufnahme und Erfolgsbetrachtung. Deutscher Universitätsverlag, Wiesbaden
Stevens GA, Burley J (2003) Piloting the rocket of radical innovation. Res Technol Manage 46(2):16–25
Stillman HM (1997) How ABB decides on the right technology investments. Res Technol Manage 40(6):14–22

Strauss JD, Radnor M (2004) Roadmapping for dynamic and uncertain environments. Res Technol Manage 47(2):51–57

Stubbart CI, Knight MB (2006) The case of the disappearing firms: empirical evidence and implications. J Organ Behav 27(1):79–100

Stuckenschneider H, Schwair T (2005) Strategisches Innovations-Management bei Siemens. In: Albers S, Gassmann O (eds) Handbuch Technologie- und Innovationsmanagement – Strategie – Umsetzung – Controlling. Gabler, Wiesbaden, pp 763–780

Szulanski G, Amin K (2001) Learning to make strategy: balancing discipline and imagination. Long Range Plann 34(5):537–556

Talke K (2007) Corporate mindset of innovating firms: influences on new product performance. J Eng Technol Manage 24(1–2):76–91

Taylor A, Helfat CE (2009) Organizational linkages for surviving technological change: complementary assets, middle management, and ambidexterity. Organ Sci 20(4):718–739

Teece DJ, Pisano G, Shuen A (1997) Dynamic capabilities and strategic management. Strateg Manage J 18(7):509–533

Telefonica (2007) Annual report. Madrid, Spain

Telekom Austria Group (2007) Annual report. Vienna, Austria

Tellis GJ (2006) Disruptive technology or visionary leadership? J Prod Innov Manage 23(1):34–38

Theis D (2006) Pictures of the future: an industrial foresight and innovation source PICMET 2006. Technol Manage Glob Future 2:837–869

Thomas JB, McDaniel RR (1990) Interpreting strategic issues – effects of strategy and the information-processing structure of top management teams. Acad Manage J 33(2):286–306

Thomas JB, Clark SM, Gioia DA (1993) Strategic sensemaking and organizational performance – linkages among scanning, interpretation, action, and outcomes. Acad Manage J 36(2):239–270

ThyssenKrupp (2008) Annual report 2007–2008. Düsseldorf, Germany

Trinczek R (2005) Wie befrage ich Manager? Methodische und methodologische Aspekte des Experteninterviews als qualitativer Methode empirischer sozialforschung. In: Bogner A, Häder M, Littig B, Menz W (eds) Das Experteninterview: Theorie, Methode, Anwendung. VS Verlag für Sozialwissenschaften, Wiesbaden

Tripsas M, Gavetti G (2000) Capabilities, cognition, and inertia: evidence from digital imaging. Strateg Manage J 21(10–11):1147–1161

Tsoukas H, Shepherd J (2004a) Coping with the future: developing organizational foresightfulness – introduction. Futures 36(2):137–144

Tsoukas H, Shepherd J (2004b) Managing the future: foresight in the knowledge economy. Blackwell, Malden, MA

Tushman ML, Anderson P (1986) Technological discontinuities and organizational environments. Adm Sci Q 31(3):439–465

Tushman ML, Oreilly CA (1996) Ambidextrous organizations: managing evolutionary and revolutionary change. Calif Manage Rev 38(4):8–30

Tushman ML, Virany B, Romanelli E (1985) Executive succession, strategic reorientations, and organization evolution – the Minicomputer industry as a case in point. Technol Soc 7(2–3): 297–313

Tushman ML, Newman WH, Romanelli E (1986) Convergence and upheaval – managing the unsteady pace of organizational evolution. Calif Manage Rev 29(1):29–44

Union E (2008) Climat change: commission elcomes final adoption of Europe's climate and energy package. European Union, Brussels

Upbin B (2000) Kodak's digital moment. http://www.Forbes.com

van de Vrande V, Lemmens C, Vanhaverbeke W (2006) Choosing governance modes for external technology sourcing. R D Manage 36(3):347–363

Van Den Bosch F, Volberda H, de Boer M (1999) Coevolution of firm absorptive capactiy and knowledge environment: organizational forms and combinative capabilities. Organ Sci 10(5): 551–568

Van der Duin PA, den Hartigh E (2007) Linking futures research with management science: improving innovation and strategy processes within companies. From Oracles to Dialogue; exploring new ways to explore the future, COST A22 conference, Athens, Greece
Van der Heijden K (2005) Scenarios: the art of strategic conversation. Wiley, Chichester, West Sussex
Van der Helm R (2007) Ten insolvable dilemmas of participation and why foresight has to deal with them. Foresight 9(3):3–17
Van der Meulen B, Lohnberg A (2001) The use of foresight: institutional constraints and conditions. Int J Technol Manage 21(7–8):680–693
van der Meulen B, de Wilt J, Rutten H (2003) Developing futures for agriculture in the Netherlands: a systematic exploration of the strategic value of foresight. J Forecast 22(2–3): 219–233
Van Nottena WF, Sleegersb AM, Van Asselt MBA (2005) The future shocks: on discontinuity and scenario development. Technol Forecast Soc Change 72(2):175–194
Vandermerwe S, Birley S (1997) The corporate entrepreneur: leading organizational transformation. Long Range Plann 30(3):345–352
Vanhaverbeke W, Peeters N (2005) Embracing innovation as strategy: corporate venturing, competence building and corporate strategy making. Creativity Innov Manage 14(3):246–257
Vanhaverbeke W, Duysters G, Noorderhaven N (2002) External technology sourcing through alliances or acquisitions: an analysis of the application-specific integrated circuits industry. Organ Sci 13(6):714–733
Vattenfall Group (2007) Annual report. Stockholm, Sweden
Vickery G, Wunsch-Vincent S (2007) Participative web and user-created content: Web 2.0, wikis and social networking. OECD Publishing, Paris
Visser MP, Chermack TJ (2009) Perceptions of the relationship between scenario planning and firm performance: a qualitative study. Futures 41(9):581–592
Volberda HW, Lewin AY (2003) Guest editors' introduction – co-evolutionary dynamics within and between firms: from evolution to co-evolution. J Manage Stud 40(8):2111–2136
Volkswagen AG (2007) Annual report. Wolfsburg, Germany
von Zedtwitz M, Gassmann O (2002) Market versus technology drive in R&D internationalization: four different patterns of managing research and development. Res Policy 31(4):569–588
Voss C, Tsikriktsis N, Frohlich M (2002) Case research in operations management. Int J Oper Prod Manage 22(2):195–219
Vroom V, Jago A (1988) Managing participation: a critical dimension of leadership. Development 7(5):32–42
Vroom VH, Yetton PW (1973) Leadership and decision-making. University of Pittsburgh Press, Pittsburgh, PA
Wack P (1985) Scenarios: uncharted waters ahead. Harv Bus Review (Sept–Oct): 73–89
Walter A (1999) Relationship promoters: driving forces for successful customer relationships. Ind Mark Manage 28(5):537–551
Watman K (2003) War gaming and its role in examining the future. Brown J World Aff 2003(10): 51–61
Weick KE (1988) Enacted sensemaking in crisis situations. J Manage Stud 25(4):305–317
Weimer-Jehle W (2006) Cross-impact balances: a system-theoretical approach to cross-impact analysis. Technol Forecast Soc Change 73(4):334–361
Wells R et al (2004) Technology roadmapping for a service organization. Res Technol Manage 47 (2):46–51
Wernerfelt B (1984) A resource-based view of the firm. Strateg Manage J 5(2):171–180
Wilson IH (1973) Futures forecasting for strategic planning at general electric. Long Range Plann 6(2):39–42
Wiltbank R et al (2006) What to do next? The case for non-predictive strategy. Strateg Manage J 27(10):981–998

Winter SG (2004) Specialised perception, selection, and strategic surprise: learning from the Moths and Bees. Long Range Plann 37(2):163–169
Wirtz BW, Mathieu A, Schilke O (2007) Strategy in high-velocity environments. Long Range Plann 40(3):295–313
Wissema JG (1981) Futures research – is it useful? Long Range Plann 14(2):29–32
Wolff MF (1992) Scouting for technology. Res Technol Manage 35(2):10–12
Woodward J (1958) Management and technology. H. M. Stationery Off, London
Yamamura G (1999) Process improvement satisfies employees. IEEE Softw 16(5):83–85
Yasai-Ardekani M, Nystrom PC (1996) Designs for environmental scanning systems: tests of a contingency theory. Manage Sci 42(2):187–204
Yin RK (2003) Case study research: design and methods. Sage, Thousand Oaks, CA
Yoon B, Phaal R, Probert D (2008) Morphology analysis for technology roadmapping: application of text mining. R D Manage 38(1):51–68
Zahra SA, George G (2002) Absorptive capacity: a review, reconceptualization, and extension. Acad Manage Rev 27(2):185–203
Zehir C, Ozsahin M (2008) A field research on the relationship between strategic decision-making speed and innovation performance in the case of Turkish large-scale firms. Manage Decis 46(5–6):709–724

Breinigsville, PA USA
31 January 2011
254132BV00002BA/2/P

DISCARDED
CONCORDIA UNIV. LIBRARY
CONCORDIA UNIVERSITY LIBRARIES
MONTREAL